Writing place

Investigations in Architecture and Literature

Edited by:

Klaske Havik

Jorge Mejía Hernández

Susana Oliveira

Mark Proosten

Mike Schäfer

nai010publishers

CONTENT

Writingplace

PREFACE 5

INTRODUCTION

Writingplace - Investigations in Architecture and Literature 9

Klaske Havik, Jorge Mejía Hernández, Susana Oliveira, Mark Proosten and Mike Schäfer

1 IMAGINATION

Literature, Architecture and Urban Life

Learning from Stories. Narrative Imagination in Urbanism and Architectural Design *Bart Keunen* 18

Reality without Colours. Imagining Architecture through Calvino's Eyes *Daria Ricchi* 34

The Critical Relevance of Fictional Buildings *Deborah Levy* 44

2 MEMORY

Narrative and Poetics in Architectural History

Language, Literary Approaches and Architectural Meaning *Alberto Pérez-Gómez* 54

The Semiotics of Timelessness. Reading 'Mythic' Architecture *Nadia Sels* 66

Writing The Renaissance Villa *Yvonne Elet* 74

Fox / River / House : a Translation *Nora Wendl* 88

3 OPENNESS

Narrative Experiments in Architecture

Narrative as an Educational Approach. Literary Methods in Architectural Education *Wim van den Bergh and Mark Proosten* 110

Archives, Narratives and Bricolage. More Themes from the Manhattan Transcripts *Ioanna Angelidou* 132

Exhausting the Narration / Exhausting the Architecture *Esteban Restrepo Restrepo* 146

4 COMPLEXITY

Writing as a Mode of Architectural Investigation

Between Sites and Stories, Between Texts and Times. A Dialogue *Katja Grillner and Klaske Havik* 158

Practical Ambivalence: a Dialogical Approach to Design and Public Space *Thomas-Bernard Kenniff* 174

A Marvellous Real: Configuring Beiruts Vague Urbain *Carole Levesque* 184

5 INCLUSIVITY

Towards an 'Architextural' Praxis

The Westward Moving House and Other Stories J.B. Jackson Reading and Telling the Landscape *Bruno Notteboom* 194

Textual Cities / Working Drawings. Re-Reading the Space of Drawing *Sophia-Konstantina Banou* 206

Moments and Spaces *Wim Cuyvers* 216

BIBLIOGRAPHY 230

BIOGRAPHIES 246

CREDITS 254

PREFACE

The contributions collected in this volume are the outcome of the international conference *Writingplace, Literary Methods in Architectural Research and Design,* held in 2013 at the Faculty of Architecture of Delft University of Technology as a follow-up to the first conference on architecture and fiction *Once Upon a Place: Haunted Houses Imaginary Cities*, held at the Lisbon Faculty of Architecture in 2010.[1] Both events are part of a host of like-minded initiatives that, over the past decade, addressed the links between disciplines.

In 2006, the Dutch-Belgian architecture journal *OASE* presented an issue specifically devoted to the connections between architecture and literature. The editors observed that the interest in literary sources in architecture, present in the 1970s and 1980s in the work of, for instance, Bernard Tschumi and John Hejduk, had been overshadowed by the global, image-oriented tendencies in architecture around the turn of the millennium. *OASE* intended 'to reconsider the relation between architecture and literature, now that literary references in architectural discourse and practice seem to have slowly moved out of sight'.[2] Indeed, a new interest in 'the potential, and possibly even the necessity, of a more literary approach',[3] in search of more reflection and imagination in the field of architecture, became apparent through a number of initiatives across Europe.

In the same year, the Munich Architekturmuseum held an exhibition exploring the way architecture is represented in literary books. The exhibition included both archive material of literary projects such as sketches and models of literary spaces, and the work of students of architecture, who had drawn and built the spaces they read in novels.[4] In 2007, the Bartlett School of Architecture and the Slade School of Fine Arts hosted the conference, workshops and exhibition *Telling Places: Narrative and Identity in Art and Architecture*. Following a seminar at the University of Strathclyde, Glasgow, the book *Writing the Modern City*, focusing on narrative and urban space, was published in 2011.[5] The exhibition and accompanying publication *Arquitectura Escrita* in 2010-2011 was a result of the collaboration of the architecture schools in Munich and Granada.[6] The exhibition set holy texts, stories, utopias and dystopias, poems, plays and novels against scale models, props and other graphic material developed by architecture students from both universities, after an in-depth study of all literary works on display. In 2012, the conference *Spatial Perspectives: Literature and Architecture* was carried out in Oxford; while in 2013 the symposium *Architecture & Literature: Forms of Memory*, was organized by the University of Nottingham. Similar events include *Espaços Narrados*, organized by the Faculdade de Arquitectura da Universidade de São Paulo in 2012; the international conference *Arch&Lit: Inter-*

Arts Dialogue(s), organized in 2014 by the Faculdade de Ciências Sociais e Humanas da Universidade Nova de Lisboa; and the *Reading Architecture* conference held in Athens, Greece, in 2015.[7]

Pedagogical ventures have also emerged in this field of research. Initiatives include, for instance, the interdisciplinary workshop *Laboratory of Literary Architecture*, in which architecture students try to design literary – yet not literal – visions based on a series of writings. Meanwhile, the curriculums at Delft University of Technology, RWTH Aachen, KTH Stockholm, FA.U Lisbon and other architecture schools have introduced courses that bring literary tools and literary sources into the realm of architectural design. In fact, most of the contributors and editors of this volume are actively exploring the connections between architecture and literature with their students.

Acknowledging the work of many colleagues (architects, theorists and writers alike) who have addressed this theme before us and with us, it is our ambition to mark a step forward in the emerging debate on architecture and literature by means of this book, entitled *Writingplace. Investigations in Architecture and Literature.* From the many excellent papers of the *Writingplace* conference, we chose to select the contributions that specifically reflect on the operative potential of literary methods for architecture, landscape architecture and urban planning. With our choice of papers and the structure of the book in rather open, inviting chapters, we hope to fuel new reflections and imaginations in this emerging field of research and design.

For their support to make this book more than a fiction, we have to thank, first of all, the Faculty of Architecture in Delft and specifically Prof. Tom Avermaete, chair of Methods & Analysis, for supporting the *Writingplace* conference in 2013. Negar Sanaan Bensi and Ivan Thung have helped to organize the conference and assisted in the early phases of this book. Further, our gratitude goes to Marcel Witvoet of Nai010 publishers for supporting the idea and making it happen, to D'Laine Camp for the English copy editing, and to Sanne Dijkstra for the graphic design of the entire project, from conference to book. We have received generous support from the Dutch Creative Industries Fund. In different ways, the following academic institutes have supported our initiative: Faculty of Architecture of Delft University of Technology, Ghent University, RWTH Aachen, Corporeal Artez Arnhem, and the CIAUD/FA.UL research centre of the Faculty of Architecture, Lisbon University. Finally, we express our sincere thanks to the academic committee for its critical reflections, to all of the participants of the *Writingplace* conference in 2013, and to the authors who contributed to this book.

1 This conference resulted in the following book: Pedro Gadanho, and Susana Oliveira (eds.), *Once Upon a Place. Architecture and Fiction* (Lisbon: Caleidoscopio, 2013).

2 Christoph Grafe, Klaske Havik and Madeleine Maaskant (eds.), *OASE* 70, *Architecture & Literature, Reflections / Imaginations* (Rotterdam: NAi Publishers, 2006), 4.

3 Ibid.

4 Winfried Nerdinger (ed.), *Architektur wie sie im Buche steht, Fiktive Bauten und Städte in der Literatur* (Munich: Architekturmuseum der Technische Universität/Verlag Anton Pustet, 2007).

5 Sarah Edwards and Jonathan Charley, *Writing the Modern City. Literature, Architecture, Modernity* (London: Routledge, 2012).

6 The exhibition, held from February to March 2010 in Madrid and from November 2010 to March 2011 in Granada, was co-produced by the Parque de las Ciencias de Granada, the Facultad de Bellas Artes de Madrid, the Munich Architekturmuseum and the Sociedad Estatal de Comemoraciones Culturales, in collaboration with the Escuela Técnica Superior de Arquitectura de Granada. Juan Calatrava and Winfried Nerdinger (eds.), *Arquitectura escrita* (Madrid: Círculo de Bellas Artes, 2010).

7 *Reading Architecture* was organized by the History and Theory Program of the School of Architecture of McGill University, and held in June 2015 at the Benaki Museum of Athens, Greece, under the auspices of the Hellenic Institute of Architecture.

INTRODUCTION

Writing place

Investigations in Architecture and Literature

Klaske Havik, Jorge Mejía Hernández, Susana Oliveira, Mark Proosten and Mike Schäfer

Exploring the interrelations between architecture and literature, this book brings together a series of reflections on written language as a key element of architectural culture and, more particularly, on the potential of using literary methods in architectural research and design. Writing and building are elemental human acts, intertwined at the roots of culture. Historical relations between architecture and literature can be traced back to Gilgamesh,[1] and evince a remarkable sense of continuity through the work of authors as disparate as Francesc Eiximenis, Rogelio Salmona, Federico García Lorca, Aldo Rossi and William Gibson. Testing the relationship between both disciplines, these and many other authors have not only built a collective *imaginaire*, which both mirrors and feeds the built environment; they have also contributed specific discursive and formal knowledge to the architectural discipline.

In literature, writers create places, and thus play a leading role in urban histories that transcend the built and tangible. From the field of architecture, every project delineates a fiction, and raises the fundamental literary question: 'What if . . . ?' Both disciplines empathize with those they expect to engage with. With this book we not only aim to explore these parallels, but moreover hope to find out how they could be operative in the analysis and design of spatial imaginations. Indeed, as we mentioned earlier: 'By studying the tools that writers employ in constructing their spatial imaginations, we can learn new ways to imagine architecture.' (Havik 2014: 24)

Literature offers evocative descriptions of architecture, and is inextricably linked to the urban question, perceived through the eyes, ears and memories of others. Writers constantly find ingenious ways to deal with abstract questions such as character, perception and memory, which are intrinsically connected to architectural experience. 'Literary' ways of dealing with architectural questions can be found in the work of architects who write, who research spaces and places described in literary fiction, or engage in a 'literary exploration' of a particular environment. Research methods based on literary techniques recur in the work of well-known designers like Bernard Tschumi, John Hejduk and Rem Koolhaas, to name a few. Since Vitruvius (and later Alberti), texts explain ideas and intentions that simply cannot be expressed through sketches or scale models, and enable the definition of non-specific agendas in manifestos, journals and other descriptive documents. In turn, writers have often played a central role in popular architectural debates. Jacques Derrida, for example, used architectural metaphors to describe textual structures, while he advised architects on the Parc de la Villette design competition. The writings of Thomas Hardy, Arundhaty Roy, Max Frisch, John Dos Passos and Orhan Pamuk are obviously conditioned by their architectural training.

According to Gaston Bachelard, narrative is incorporated in the spaces we live in; we are able to 'read' or 'write' a room or a house as if they were a story. Writers attempt to hold a reader's attention and, at the same time, intend to open doors for the reader to escape into his or her own thoughts, memories and fantasies. In the reader's interpretation, the narrated space multiplies and amplifies itself, past all the information given by the text. In *Stoner* (Williams 2012), for instance, John Williams shows how architecture is both a stage and a mirror for literary fiction, and for the questions that most deeply inhabit and haunt it, sometimes in reciprocal ways.

> *As he worked on the room and as it began slowly to take a shape, he realised that for many years, unknown to himself, he had had an image locked somewhere within him like a shamed secret, an image that was ostensively of a place but which was actually of himself. So it was himself that he was attempting to define as he worked on his study. . . . as he repaired his furniture and arrange it in the room, it was himself that he was slowly shaping, it was himself that he was putting into a kind of order, it was himself that he was making possible.* (Williams 2012: 100)

As in *Stoner*, architecture and literature establish a sort of common ground to explore our architectural imagination – an idea that is maintained throughout the *Writingplace* project, and that has led us to pose a set of crucial questions regarding the potential of literary methods for architectural and urban research and design. If literature can offer an alternative perspective to the experience, use and imagination of place, how can a literary gaze generate alternative methods for site research and architectural design? How can the reading of sites allow for new interpretations of historical traces, for new writings of place? How can we re-read eminent literary works and learn from these for contemporary architectural and urban practice? What can literary methods, such as narrative, character, scenario and poetry writing mean in regard to architectural and urban analysis and design? From the reconsideration of urban landscapes based on literary texts to the advancement of pedagogic strategies supported on writing techniques, and from inquiries into architecture's representational demands to exercises in the appropriation of the elusive notion of place, the contributions to this book aim to explore alternative ways of understanding and designing architecture, urban places and landscapes through literary means. The contributions to this book are organized around the following themes: Imagination, Memory, Openness, Complexity and Inclusivity – themes that each imply some sort of ambiguity. This ambiguity is intentional. The very virtue of a literary approach in architecture is that it allows us to open new directions, rather than to order ideas into strict categories, to explore the boundaries of the disciplines, rather than to try to give definitions, to bring together memory and imagination, using various temporalities simultaneously, to construct a narrative, but to allow the reader to explore it in multiple ways and to find connections between the different parts.

In the opening chapter, 'Imagination: Literature, Architecture and Urban Life', Bart Keunen reveals a few strategies employed by storytellers, and hints at their architectural value. Drawing away from the more obvious notions of visual and perceptual imagination, Keunen elaborates on the question of narrative imagination and the implied disciplining process that enables the imaginary construct to function both as a tool and as the realm of emotional and theoretical judgment. In turn, Daria Ricchi considers the dichotomy between 'black and white' and colour as a tool to revaluate the assumed distinction between the 'real' and the 'imagined' in Italo Calvino's turn from neorealism to the fantastic. Calvino's *Invisible Cities* of 1972 conflates fantasy and reason, and parallels a shift from interiors to urban spaces. Deborah Levy uses a short story by Jorge Luis Borges to discuss how a fictional building inside a fictive text may yield relevant architectural knowledge, and prompt fresh theoretical reflections. While Bart Keunen provides a substantiated case regarding narrative imagination as a relevant mechanism for architectural design, both Ricchi and Levy disclose and examine some lesser-known pieces by Calvino and Borges. Jointly, the three provide fresh insights on the intimate associations, tangible forms and sociospatial processes fostered by narrative imagination.

In the following chapter, 'Memory: Narrative and Poetics in the History of Architecture', the phenomenological strain of contemporary architectural theory is presented as a valid contender to the overwhelming prevalence of images in the transmission and production or architectural knowledge. Beyond contesting visual paradigms – these authors suggest – architectural discourse can be the source of ingenious solutions to confront the shortcomings of those visual paradigms.
An erudite reconstruction of the historical timeline leading to the form/function gridlock that feeds most postmodern theory and practice, allows Alberto Pérez-Gómez to uphold language as an agent of progress. His argument follows a short but consistent list of researchers who have explored language as a source of new ideas for architecture. Among these researchers, a considerable faction claims that studies in the production of meaning hold valuable information in the face of the crises of modern architecture. This semiotic tradition is followed by Nadia Sels, who exemplifies the workings of a theory of symbols by attempting a phenomenology of myths. Her syncretic strategy situates her arguments beyond dichotomous simplification.
In the same vein, Yvonne Elet introduces elements of openness into the architectural discussion, by valuing the nuances and revealing the multilayeredness of architectural design. Finally, Nora Wendl proposes to replace linear history by the much heftier notion of translation. As a proposition, Wendl's move towards interpretation as a value in its own right establishing strong ties with Alberto Pérez-Gómez, who – we should have mentioned – assumes that the pertinence of language in contemporary architectural thought lies in its phenomenological capacity, but also in its hermeneutic potential. Interpretative thought – these authors appear to coincide – remains a powerful hypothesis, able to account for both allegory and analysis, to simultaneously attempt criticism and demonstration.

Turning towards experience and phenomenological approaches within both disciplines, the third chapter 'Openness: Narrative Experiments in Architecture', explores openness in both formal and performative terms, as a necessity, the *mother* of invention. Acknowledging the fertile ground that experiments within architectural education and institutes such as the Cooper Union in New York and the AA-school in London have provided, Wim van den Bergh and Mark Proosten reflect on the open relations that can be generated when literary methods inform architectural pedagogy.

By bringing together experiments at Cooper Union with more recent projects in architectural education in Aachen, the article forms a reflection upon the literary methodologies applied while, at the same time, it gives insight into the pedagogy via concrete examples of student work. While Ioanna Angelidou also ponders on education, she offers a theoretical reflection upon Tschumi's *Manhattan Transcripts*, as well as a historical analysis upon its development, discussing his use of narrative. Finally, Esteban Restrepo Restrepo draws attention to the work of Samuel Beckett and the way his narrative techniques invoke spatiality while questioning basic habits and customs such as geometry and the function of objects. Together, these three approaches call for more attention to sensory experience of the built environment, and to the processes implied in architectural design. They propose a transcultural understanding of architecture and suggest an underlying narrative origin for the art of building, seeing architecture as the transformation and communication of narratives.

The fourth chapter, 'Complexity: Writing as a Mode of Architectural Investigation', challenges the antiquated division of theory and practice. Investigation is seen as a clue-finding process, meant to reconstruct processes and connections, unravelling latent complexities. Even though architectural research is generally expressed in writing, the active use of literary modes of writing as a form of research is less common. In dialogue, Katja Grillner and Klaske Havik discuss how fictional and semi-fictional worlds open up alternative modes of inquiry in academic research. By presenting a number of research projects that use fictional writing as a critical mode of investigation, Havik and Grillner offer several directions for the use of 'productive imagination' and foreground fiction as a mode of investigation that could have serious scientific value, offering other kinds of knowledge production than those offered by conventional research methods. The dialogical approach of Bakthin plays a central role in Thomas-Bernard Kenniff's contribution 'Practical Ambivalence', as a point of departure for investigation into public space. Kenniff suggests that the range of concepts Bakhtin develops from literature, linguistics and creative acts like writing, are particularly relevant when it comes to understanding design as a collective and ultimately unfinalizable process. Following that of Kenniff, Carole Leveque's contribution constructs a double dialogue. At a theoretical level, she stages an encounter between Carpentier's literature of the marvellous real, and Ricoeur's acts of configuration. At a methodological level, she investigates the potential of combining narrative and drawing in site-specific research.

Towards the end of the book, the chapter 'Inclusivity: Towards an "Architextural" Praxis' blurs the limits between academia and practice, literature and architecture, writing and acting. First, Bruno Notteboom ponders on the work of J.B. Jackson, through his contributions to the journal *Landscapes*. Jackson described landscapes and architecture in short stories, narrated through the everyday practices of inhabitants. This approach, seeing landscape and architecture through the dynamics of practices, is taken to a more urban level by Sophia-Konstantina Banou, who explores the problem of transcription. Banou argues that the working drawing is a form of writing, which is always in process, like the city. By different means, both contributions value incompleteness and ambiguity as tools with which to address existential questions that can be found in either the city or in landscape. Confronting existential questions that do not follow categorical boundaries is exactly what a literary approach to architecture has to offer, argues Wim Cuyvers in the closing article of the book. This also implies a different role of the architect, who at times may need to silently analyse, listen and explore, and at other times become present, speak and interfere. Cuyvers makes a plea for the merging of research, education and practice, in a 'praxis' that transcends fixed schemes and limited interpretations.

With the present collection, we aim to encourage readers, creators, authors, architects, educators and students to think and enrich a place with their own interpretations of the spatial conditions they experience, share and design. As some of the authors in this book argue, we can see the whole conception process in architecture and urban planning as the shared narrations of life scenarios, through individual and collective spatial stories, continuously and endlessly retold and reinvented. Acknowledging the possibilities of literature as a field of research, able to explore architectural imaginations, *Writingplace* hopes to establish a common ground for international scholars, writers and architects, a common ground to further investigate the productive connections between architecture and literature, or a place to engage in writing.

1 *The Epic of Gilgamesh* is an earlier Sumerian poem that is considered the first great work of literature. In the epic, Gilgamesh is a demigod of superhuman strength who builds the city walls of *Uruk* to defend his people and travels to meet the sage Utnapishtim, who survived the Great Flood. See: http://www.britannica.com/topic/Epic-of-Gilgamesh.

1 IMAGINATION

Literature, Architecture and Urban Life

Learning from Stories

Narrative Imagination in Urbanism and Architectural Design

Bart Keunen

Imagination is of great importance in the design and the assessment of buildings and urban space. Few people working within architectural theory and urban studies will deny this. Is it not true that architects and urbanists always dream of projects that stimulate the imagination of the users? Do they not imagine in the same manner that they envisioned it? Whether they are outspoken about it or not, do they not wish the spaces they conceived to be experienced with an enthusiastic application of imaginative power? This is more than likely the reason why Edward Soja's concept of 'thirdspace' has become so widely accepted among architects and urbanists. His thesis that space should be perceived as a social given in which reality and imagination meet has found general consensus. In sum, the concept of imagination holds a high position among urbanists and architects. This is explained by the fact that their artistic practice shows many affinities with that of the visual arts, at least on the surface.

There is perhaps less consensus about the claim that the type of imagination engaged in architectural and urbanistic design is in many cases nothing more than narrative imagination. Nevertheless, this is precisely what I would like to argue here. Drawing on literary theory, I'll attempt to show that there are good reasons to take narrative imagination seriously in discussions about architecture and urbanism. I will define narrative imagination as the 'disciplinization' of imagination and argue that, in a fictional world, associations of the imagination are brought into line, disciplined and turned into a coherent whole with one purpose: to make it possible to experience these associations, and comment on them, in the same way as real situations. This process of disciplinization profoundly deviates from the visual systematics that can characterize objects from the visual arts. It has greater affinity with the way in which we attempt to get a hold over complex and seemingly unpredictable situations that pose a problem.

Distinguishing Perception, Imagination and Narrative Imagination

By way of introduction, I will first throw some light on the concept of imagination that occupies the centre stage in my argument. Next, I will distinguish between narrative imagination and spontaneous, visual imagination. In its common sense meaning, imagination refers to the mental activity by which a subject simulates perceptions in the brain. Undoubtedly, this connotation is fostered by the etymological kinship between image and imagination. Psychologists and philosophers generally subscribe to a more nuanced definition of imagination by pointing out that it involves much more than 'pictures in the head'. After all, these pictures in our heads also refer to complex mental operations that are applied to such 'perceptions'.[1] In *The Concept of Mind,* English philosopher Gilbert Ryle makes short work of the common sense definition. While trying to explain the distinction between images of perception and images of imagination, Ryle refers to the recollected (and therefore imagined) perception of the mountain Helvellyn in Lake District:

> *Seeing Helvellyn in one's mind's eye does not entail, what seeing Helvellyn and seeing snapshots of Helvellyn entail, the having of visual sensations. It does involve the thought of having a view of Helvellyn and it is therefore a more sophisticated operation than that of having a view of Helvellyn.*
> (Ryle 1990: 255)

Ryle's perspective implies a difference between imagining and perceiving, because imagining a 'possible world' involves cognitive operations that can also be applied in actual worlds: connections are made, ratios are estimated, hierarchies are established and classifications are set up that lend a certain systematics or logic to the images.[2] Thus, imagination is certainly much more than the creation of visual simulations. It can even play a role in very abstract mental operations, for instance conceiving relations between abstract numbers or figures in 'mathematical imagination'. (see Efland 2003: 29) Because it is a mental activity that involves as much reflection as it does perception, the philosopher Alquié claimed that imagination is probably one of the most complex of all mental processes, an amalgam of various operations.

> *The power of invention that resides in us relates not only to combinations of images but also to ideas, judgments. Consequently, 'imagination' should be understood as every operational thought that contemplates or combines representative materials. Indeed, imagination is nothing other than thought itself.* (Alquié 1939: 266)

The sort of thought that Alquié has in mind is something different from the logico-mathematical thought we commonly associate with the faculty of reasoning. The successes of modern technological and scientific practices led to a semantical overlap between the faculty or act of 'thinking' and what is called 'deductive-nomological reasoning'. Nomological explanation involves 'seeing particular events as instances of general laws which always hold regardless of the time and place of their occurrence'. (Stephenson 2000: 113) Typical of the inventive thought that we call imagination, however, is that it unfolds based on possible matters of fact and possible worlds.[3] The representation of possible (non-actualized) facts can even be considered as the 'differentia specifica' of imagination; it is the property that distinguishes 'imagining' from other states of consciousness such as perceiving, remembering, believing, desiring, anticipating, conceiving and supposing. (Gendler 2011) Hence, an efficient definition of imagination necessarily makes use of the concept of 'fiction'. This concept, for that matter, will enable us to strike a bridge towards 'narrative imagination'.

Fiction is a term that refers to knowledge that only arises in a specific context of communication. Whenever a receiver is asked to 'imagine' an object of knowledge according to certain rules of the game, knowledge is called up that withdraws from empirical verification. (Walton 1990; Currie 1990) Even if there is no empirical evidence whatsoever for the existence of horses that have horns, we are willing to picture a unicorn within the fairy tale's rules of the game, and even, if desired, to accept that this creature is gifted with the faculty of speech. Many forms of imagination make use of fictional objects and situations (for example in: 'imagine a world without war'). Narrative imagination, however, is most consistently based on the principle of fictionality. In narrative fiction, we consciously withdraw from empirical verification and live according to Samuel Coleridge's dictum of the 'willful suspension of disbelief'. Whoever confuses the fictional world of a novel with a series of false matters of fact – as, for example, Amsterdam coffee broker Droogstoppel does in Multatuli's *Max Havelaar* (1860) – foils the proper functioning of fictional communication from the start. When the logic behind the fictional 'facts' is not taken seriously, the imagined world becomes a kind of Fata Morgana, devoid of any relation to empirical reality. In other words, we must realize that the operation of imagining is situated in a broader framework, in order to see the message behind the specific reality of imagination. (Ronen 1988) The facts are relevant only in their interconnection. Fiction has meaning only within a semantical whole that must be reconstructed through processes of thought, and that gathers (imaginary and/or empirically verifiable) facts in a closed narrative. In this sense, Coleridge does not push the defence of the fictional to its logical boundary. Simply demanding respect for the value of making up and inventing things, of feigning and lying – in short for the importance of disbelief – is not enough. When only this minimalist view of fictionality is considered, only the spontaneous representations of visual imagination are taken into account. In order to arrive at a definition of imagination that captures its complexity, it is crucial to emphasize that the knowledge obtained through a fictional world gives a more intensive and systematic insight into the experiences we have in the real world. Such a rather maximalist perspective of fictionality must do justice to Alquié's view, considering a fictional world as a world of imagination in which ideas and judgments also play an elementary role. This more extensive perspective finds a laconic expression in an ironic remark by Mark Twain: 'The only difference between reality and fiction is that fiction needs to be credible.' With this observation, Twain unwillingly gives the perfect definition of what we should understand by narrative imagination (and by a maximalist concept of fictionality). Stories are products of the imagination. In the same way as many other constructs of imagination in the everyday world, they make use of fictional objects, situations and events. In contrast with the everyday fictions, however, these objects, situations and events are included in a broader construction that derives its credibility from the fact that it is set up in a systematic way – because it originates from a 'disciplined' imagination.

Studying Narrative Imagination

The work of literary theorists, cognitivist psychologists and philosophers such as David Herman, Jerome Bruner and Paul Ricoeur, respectively, provides sufficient elements for a primary description of what exactly lends systematics and credibility to narrative imagination, as well as for a clear demarcation of narrative imagination from spontaneous, visual operations of imagination. I believe there are three conditions that need to be met before we can rightfully speak of narrative imagination. First, the mimetic simulations, typical of narratives, must be constructed as a significant whole. Secondly, the imaginary construction must possess enough details to be able to provoke a 'lived experience' (it must lead to the phenomenon of 'immersion' and especially to an emotional involvement that goes along with it).[4] Thirdly, symbolic and conceptual associations must be induced by the imaginary world. These three conditions represent a framework that connects imagination and empirically acquired knowledge in such a way that imagination becomes a way of thinking and starts to react with the empirical world. In a sense, these are the preconditions that enable the imaginary construct to function, both as a tool within problem-solving strategies and as a laboratory for emotional and theoretical judgments.

The first of these three preconditions, and the only one I'm able to discuss in this paper,[5] is in some way the most fundamental. Narrative imagination that is worthy of the name will assume the form of a mimetic construction, a simulation of the every-day world of experience. But, by designating 'mimesis' as a fundamental property of stories, there is a risk of getting caught in a dated and heavily contested debate on mimesis and imitation. I have no intention whatsoever to reduce the simulation of the experiential world brought up in stories to the simulation of visual similarities or formal correspondences. As I have already pointed out in the previous section, imagination, in my view, is first a cognitive operation that discovers relations and patterns in the simulated 'material'. Consequently, whenever I speak of 'mimesis', it is in a very strict sense, such as is found, for example, in the work of Paul Ricoeur. In *Temps et récit* (*Time and Narrative*), he states that fictional narratives only become narratives when they focus on creating a 'mimesis of action'. (1984: 290) Following Aristotle, he believes that narrative art is not dependent on the use of aesthetically relevant language. Even stylistically premature narratives constitute narratives as soon as they depict actions and processes. Indeed, Aristotle claims that the poet 'should be the maker of plots rather than of verses; since he is a poet because he imitates, and what he imitates are actions'. (1929: 51b27) Therefore, the motor behind constructions of narrative imagination is human action. This fundamental insight is elaborated in more recent studies. In a paper bearing the significant title 'How Stories Make Us Smarter' (2003a), David Herman discusses five problem-solving strategies that are 'exercised' by means of fiction. He believes that stories 'can be viewed a source of structure in humans' (shared) attempts to make sense of experience'. In addition, Herman views literature as a cultural activity that buckles down to operations of imagination relevant to all cultural activities. By studying fictional texts, a deeper insight is gained into the phenomenon that above was called 'narrative imagination'. Of the five strategies distinguished by Herman, four have a connection with mimesis: 'chunking experience into workable segments, imputing causal relations between events, managing problems with the "typification" of phenomena, (and) sequencing behaviors'.[6] (Herman 2003a: 172; see also Herman 2013: 298) By way of the four 'mimetic' processes of thought advanced by Herman, I want to demonstrate exactly how narrative imagination operates and to what extent the narrative imagination employed by storytellers can serve as a model for other cultural practices. In the following sections, I will browse through these processes and apply them to the narrative imagination as it can be found in architectural and urbanist design.

Chunking Experience into Temporal Units

The chunking strategy concerns the fact that narrative imagination isolates a chunk of reality. A story cuts out a 'slice of life' from experience and ascribes a beginning, a middle and an end to it. For example, experiences about the mental condition of depression are resumed in a series of (meticulously selected) images that together picture the life of Anna Karenina. At the end of a story a complete world is created, to which, in contrast with the real world, a definitive meaning can be attributed.[7] In this fundamental property of a story, David Herman detects a sign of creative intelligence:

> *Narrative affords ways of addressing the problem of how to chunk the ongoing stream of experience into (more or less sharply) bounded and thus manipulate structures. Stories allow experiences to be subdivided into (as Aristotle put it) a beginning, middle, and end, with those temporally structured segments in turn affording a basis for further operations of mind. (Herman 2013: 233)*

Evidently, a designer will not encode the spatial environment by means of a narrative structure with a beginning and an end. A design of a city, for example, does not have a point at which you enter the city, nor a closing event that lends a definitive meaning to the urban experience. That being said, narrative imagination can be detected in urbanist and architectural designs. The marginal conditions of a project (that have been put forward by the commissioning party), for example, can be viewed as a form of 'chunking'. The amalgam of possible experiences that exist or will exist on a particular location cannot be controlled without imposing limitations. This is why marginal conditions will function as a sort of confinement, as narrative preconditions. Sometimes the formulation of these marginal conditions is accompanied by an evocation of the location's history and of the social and/or psychological problems experienced by the inhabitants. In addition, a possible end point will be indicated – a set of objectives that must be realized by the project. Because of the importance of these marginal conditions in the designing process, the designer's narrative imagination will constitute something strange from the very start. The designers are not in a full sense the creators of the stories that they tell. This, however, does not mean that they will not attempt to enter the narrative world.

Chunking Experience into Spatiotemporal Units

Besides the temporal 'slice of life', a story also creates one or more worlds with a fixed spatiotemporal structure. Herman does not mention such worlds as a form of 'chunking of experience'. Nonetheless, the demarcation of a setting, and the demarcation of the events that take place in it, can certainly also be viewed as a form of problem-solving behaviour. In any case, this constitutes an important element in the type of narrative imagination that designers employ.

When narrative imagination simulates human activity, a beginning and an ending will be established in this mimetic construction. Spatial borders will also be imposed to the world. Out of all possible spaces, storytellers select a location that matches the specific experiences they want to address. In this way, a traditional adventure story invariably starts from a situation and an experience of equilibrium that is spatially anchored (the example that readily comes to mind is the idyllic setting of the village present on every album's first page in the comic series *Asterix & Obelix*). It then goes over to a situation of disequilibrium (the adventurous peripeteias with the Britons, the Helvetians or the Belgians). The transition from equilibrium to disequilibrium involves the crossing of a boundary, the abandoning of a secure, closed space and the entering of an open, unpredictable space. In other words, adventure stories operate within a universe split into an inner and an outer world. In this sense, the creation of the spatial setting of a story can be called a form of 'chunking of experience'.

Designers work in an analogous fashion. To illustrate this, I call to mind the projects developed within the New Urbanism movement. Cooper, Robertson & Partners' project of the Val d'Europe, for instance, is based on the idea that modernization and innovation merely resulted in the degradation of an original state of equilibrium ('un seul et unique challenge pour l'avenir de notre société et de son habitat' / 'a one and only challenge for the future of our society and its habitat', 'la dégradation des centres-villes' / 'the degradation of the inner-cities', 'la ségrégation croissante' / 'the growing segregation', 'l'oubli de notre héritage culturel' / 'the negation of our cultural heritage'). The objective, therefore, is to return to a more original way of life ('articulant avec bonheur et dans l'harmonie la même tétralogie fonctionnelle : "habiter, travailler, se détendre, se déplacer" dans une ville "proche de tout [et à la] croisée des réseaux"' / 'articulating with joy and in harmony the same functional tetralogy: "to live, to work, to relax, to move" in a city "close to everything [and at the] intersection of networks"').[8] In other words, the relevance of the urbanist intervention is explained via the depiction of an (authentic) inside world and an (alienating) outside world. The urbanist project is situated in opposition to a deviating and menacing chaotic world. This splitting into an internal and an external world is a clear demonstration of the extent to which designers mobilize narrative imagination with the aim of ordering their experiential reality.

The duality of inside and outside is a tried and tested recipe in fictional stories, where it can be observed to function in its most elementary form. Furthermore, the inside-outside duality can be best observed in cultures that mobilize narrative imagination in a radical manner for organizing everyday life. More particularly, archaic cultures that are governed by religion use the pattern of the adventure story to lend structure to their everyday experience. In *Mythical Thought*, Cassirer identifies cultures in which the narrative occupies centre stage as mythical cultures. In such cultures, a strange mix of fictionalization and empiricism arises that gives cause to distinctions between a spiritual and a profane world order, respectively. Of great importance are the special sacral places where the spiritual and the profane enter into conflict with each other. These are the places where the workings of narrative imagination are at their strongest.[9] According to Cassirer, a sacral place originates because of two preconditions: first, the fact that the spatial setting is partly closed; secondly, that the closed place starts to communicate in a peculiar way with the space that lies on the outside. The difference mainly resides in the fact that the individual behaves in a deviating manner inside the created 'inner space'. A different temporal regime (called heterochrony) operates, and certain conditions need to be met in order to be able to participate in the activities within the space (as such, it is a semi-public space that mildly restricts the private sphere).[10]

Even though designers are not continuously occupied in a quest for sacral spaces, they will split up the experiential world in 'chunks' in such a way that a boundary is created between a controlled inside world and an unordered, disorganized outside world. Designers invariably picture a delimited space, asking questions on how inner and outer space relate to each other. This is why the threshold-experience has grown into an important element in Peter Zumthor's work, and why he pays attention to the 'almost imperceptible transition between the inside and the outside'. He imagines how the end users of his designs 'suddenly become aware of being enclosed, of something enveloping [them]'. (cf. Havik 2014: 59) Zumthor, for that matter, is an architect who conceives his imaginative work explicitly as the staging of a fictional world. He likes to formulate his task as a designer in terms of staging. Designing, he says, is 'rather akin to designing a stage setting, directing a play'. He emphasizes that 'architecture is also a temporal art'. (2006: 43) Other examples can be found in the sphere of urban design. The already mentioned spatial imagination of New Urbanism offers plenty. The persuasive imagery of the future Paris depicted by the urbanist teams contributing to the Grand Paris consultation can certainly be seen as fine examples of this chunking strategy. (Keunen & Verraest 2012)

Attributing Causality to Virtual Events

A second problem-solving strategy that characterizes narrative imagination builds on the property of chunking. Typical of stories is that they systematically question the relevance and meaning of the created world. Stories continually revolve around the why of the depicted human actions. In the view of some literary theorists, it is impossible to tell a story without making some appeal to a minimally causal relation. In a famous formula (from *Aspects of the Novel*), novelist E.M. Forster laconically stated that a genuine story differs from a plotless story because of the fact that a causal relation overshadows the consecutive order of events: '"The king died and then the queen died" is a story. But "the king died and then the queen died of grief" is a plot.' (Forster 1927: 86) Therefore, one could claim that the element of plot forms the skeleton of a story, carrying largely the mimetic construction.[11] (See also Schank 1995 on the 'gist' of stories, and Ricoeur 1983: 72)

Just as storytellers, designers must thematically address 'reasons for action' whenever they imagine a project via mental simulation. They must possess the ability to view the space as a setting for a plot, as a social space that provides room for different causally connected chains of action. Kaplan and Kaplan rightly point out that underlying the aesthetic reactions 'is an assessment of the environment in terms of its compatibility with human needs and purposes'.

In their imaginative work, designers must take into account potential conflicts between the intentions of their protagonists and the obstacles that might present themselves in their fictional world. A good example is found in Shaftoe's book about the design of public spaces, when he discusses a promenade in Bristol:

> *For reasons presumably of visual aesthetics, a faux cobbled surface has been incorporated into the vehicular highway. As a result, traffic tire noise is higher than usual, to the detriment of those trying to have conversations on the adjacent seating areas. The fountains lining the center of the promenade, although*

visually intriguing, can hardly be heard because of the traffic noise and people are not encouraged to splash about or paddle in them. (Shaftoe 2008: 60)

This example clearly explains that designers need to be more than simple engineers. They also need to master thoroughly that other form of knowledge based on association and imagination. After all, designers will only be successful when they have found a way of efficiently programming the desired plot turns and ruling out the unwanted.

Typification and Sequencing Actions

In his study of narrative thought, David Herman emphasizes that the importance of 'unplanned events' in stories plays a large part in their ability to stimulate and train problem-solving thought. This does not only involve the fact that a story simulates and investigates causal patterns between events, but a phenomenon that he calls 'typification'. A story, he writes, helps us 'to balance expectations against outcomes, general patterns against particular instance – in short, the typical against the actual'. (2003b: 179) In narrative imagination, a double dynamics is active. On the one hand, it operates by way of 'typification', the result of our use of expectation patterns that are based on our everyday experience. (Think of the 'typifications' of 'commonsense constructs of the reality of daily life' that are discussed by phenomenological sociologist Alfred Schütz, see Schütz 1962: 6-7.) On the other hand, it will continuously adjust expectations by reacting to deviations.[12] From Shaftoe's example of the Bristol promenade, it becomes evident that designers, as if they are storytellers, must be able to picture the potential deviations and obstacles within their world of imagination. They must be able to imagine a space that meets the needs of its future users, and they must be prepared for deviations and elements of chance that potentially discredit their spatial solutions. At this point, too, it becomes obvious to what extent the imagination of designers should be viewed as narrative imagination. Even more, designers should also be able to reveal themselves as extremely accomplished narrators. They will only achieve a successful project if they are able to run through different narrative scenarios during the designing process. These scenarios must enable them to weigh the end users' expectations against the undesired causal patterns. Here, narrative imagination does not only mean that the designers imagine a story and that they subsequently realize this story. It also implies that they imagine narrative patterns that they, and all those involved, sincerely hope will not be realized.

Lucid storytellers know that unexpected occurrences and unfortunate elements of chance constitute an inalienable part of narrative imagination. They also know that these often coincide with what is vaguely called 'inspiration'. Honoré de Balzac wrote in his famous foreword to *La Comédie Humaine*: 'Chance is the greatest novelist of the world; to be productive, we only have to study it'. David Herman says something similar in terms of narratology when he argues that stories without conflicts inevitably score very low on 'tellability' (or 'noteworthiness'). (Herman 2002: 84) Of essential importance to a 'tellable' story is 'the thwarting of intended actions by *unplanned* events, which may or may not be the effect of other characters' intended actions'. (Herman 2005: 83; my italics) Interesting stories show how events elude the expectations and plans of individuals.

A special case of the typification strategy can be found in the way in which stories play with common sense constructions about human behaviour. According to Herman: 'Narratives support the sequencing of behaviours by modelling, in the storyworlds they encode, what, how, where, and when a particular course of action can or should be pursued.' (2013: 245) It is true that narrative imagination is an important tool for ordering, and commenting on, types of behaviour. Storytellers are admired because they are able to identify human behaviour in a striking way, and because they intelligently submit differences in behaviour to comparative examination. This is why novels function as touchstones in everyday life, or are used as tools for providing insight into experiences. In our daily lives, we often employ terms that are borrowed from novels. It is no coincidence that in our discursive practices regarding adultery, insatiable and overly romantic partners who deceive their other halves are accused of 'Bovarysm'. Nor is it a matter of chance that we ascribe the epithet 'quixotic' to idealists. It is only, and exactly, because Flaubert and Cervantes actually examined the logic of action present in adultery and unworldly naiveté in their fundamental structures, and because they did this with great lucidity, that we do this.

The 'sequencing of behaviours' also functions as an important problem-solving strategy in the practice of designers. The imaginative construction that accompanies the designing process also contains numerous action models. Sometimes a city is designed starting from the consumer patterns of the expected end users; sometimes it is designed with a view to activities within the family circle. The weighing of action models against each other and their integration constitutes one of the most important processes of thought needed to arrive at a successful architectural or urbanist project. It is simply impossible to be a creative designer without an implicit mimetic reconstruction of human action, without narrative imagination.

Concluding Remark: Metaphors versus Narratives

The preceding observations about the problem-solving power of narrative imagination attempted to show that architectural theory and urban studies can benefit from the concept of narrativity. By way of conclusion, I would like to use the concept of narrative imagination to point at a problematic tendency in today's discourse about literature and architecture. In many texts, the 'literary' aspect of architecture is reduced to a designing strategy that consists of inserting a visually perceptible entity (a building, a spatial structure) into a broader network of meaning guided by operations of imagination. Symptomatic of this type of theory is the one-sided use of the concept of metaphor. Technically speaking, a metaphor shows many correspondences to the concept of narrative. Yet in most cases, architectural theory confines itself to a narrow application of the metaphor concept, mainly focusing on metaphorical figures of speech.

Barie Fez-Barringten, one of the propagators of a more 'literary' approach to architecture, reports to have discovered 'that metaphor is also a disciplined system of thinking. Some would even say it is synonymous with thinking.' (Fez-Barringten 2012: 6) Such statements prove that the metaphor concept offers opportunities to focus on aspects that are also essential to my argument. Metaphors are forms of symbolic transfer that find a basis in mental operations of imagination to strike a bridge between different fields of experience. Cognitive linguistics is very much aware of this: 'From the experientialist perspective, metaphor is a matter of imaginative rationality. . . . New metaphors are capable of creating new understanding and, therefore, new realities.' (Lakoff & Johnson 2003: 235) Architecture theorists that concentrate on metaphors certainly make an important point. Nevertheless, their approach lacks the core of imagination's capabilities. Because of their one-sided focus on metaphorical figures of speech, the emphasis is put on what was called above 'visual' imagination. It is perhaps true that by doing so they learn a lot about the workings of aesthetic experience in architecture. Still, they remain blind to the wealth of processes of thought made possible by human imagination. It is exactly the narrative way of thinking that allows us to understand more complex forms of metaphorical thought.[13] Narratives are complex forms of metaphorical thought that involve the simulation of entire fields of reality, as well as their transfer on each other. Narrative imagination is not singularly concerned with visual information. Instead, it involves a complex series of mental operations. Following the definition used by Marie-Laure Ryan (2001: 4), I can safely state that a story does not only imply the making of choices about characters and setting, but also the formulation of a problem cluster and the steps to carry this problem cluster forward towards an end point. The transfer of meaning that is addressed here transcends the transfer of meaning that takes place with metaphorical figures of speech. It is a transfer of known situations, problems and outcomes to potential situations, problems and outcomes. The effect produced by this transfer is that the known, everyday situation can be viewed in a novel way.

The most fundamental question to be asked, especially for any interdisciplinary study of the relation between architecture and literature, is the question of how our reality is permeated in practice by experiences that are both empirical and imaginary.[14] The concept of narrative imagination can be helpful in addressing this issue. It is in narrative imagination that the mix of empirics and imagination manifests itself most clearly. By studying this specific imagination, we can learn to what extent 'the fictional competency' underlies experiences in which imagination plays the leading part – experiences, for example, that are called 'inspiration' or 'creativity'. Via the study of narrative imagination we can come to learn that the game with reality constitutes an important aspect of human knowledge, that it occurs in the most diverse practices (cinema, games), and that it plays a part in every stage of personal development (child, adolescent, adult).

Instead of exclusively focusing attention on the aesthetic added value of fictional constructs such as architectural metaphors, theorists working in architecture and urbanism would benefit from investigating two things. The first is the extent to which the fictional competency is present in daily life. The second is the degree in which creative processes are determined through and through by the systematics and the leniency of narrative imagination. It is high time that these theorists start taking the narrative turn in the humanities seriously. Because of the fixation on procedures that are mainly related to the visual arts (metaphorization being the most important), these disciplines seem to have missed the train of narrative studies. Consequently, they do not fully realize that, of all forms of imagination, narrative imagination is the most crucial and relevant to the creative design pursued by architects and urbanists. Since the 1970s, the humanities have seen scholars making a plea for 'the narrative turn'. This is because these scholars had understood that the knowledge that was essential to them is rife with reasoning and procedures that *are not* stories, but most certainly *possess* narrativity.[15] Thus, history as a science experienced a revolution when the insight was brought home that narrative imagination plays an important part in the argumentations developed by historians. Equally, in psychology, psychiatry, educational science, law studies and even theories of economic management, academics understood the benefits of this insight. (Hyvärinen 2006) An important point of reference was provided by very persuasive and frequently cited philosophical theories, such as those proposed by Martha Nussbaum in philosophical ethics, by Alistair McIntyre and Charles Taylor in philosophical anthropology, insisting on abandoning the nomological paradigm (see above) and on embracing concepts related to fictionality and imagination.

I argued that narrativity plays an important part in the spatial imagination that lends colour to the work of architects and urbanists. By applying narrative imagination, architects and urbanists are able to withdraw from the purely factual, and from the overkill of empirical information. By making use of the 'possible world' of fiction, facts are turned into more abstract schemes, which become more manageable. 'Fictions,' as Wayne Booth rightly puts it, are 'the most powerful of all the architects of ours souls and societies.' (Booth 1988: 39)

1 Cognitive psychologist J.R. Anderson points out that, even in the case of representations of empirical objects, we cannot assert that the mental image unambiguously reflects them. An imagined object always implies a coloured view of that object. It is never identical to a visual perception of the object, because the brain tends to represent things schematically: 'Although many people report experiences of visualizing objects in imagery tasks, an image does not seem to be a mental picture in the head. It differs from a picture in that it is not tied to the visual modality, it is not precise and can be distorted, and it is segmented into meaningful pieces.' (Anderson 1980: 63)

2 This position is nicely summarized in linguist Mark Johnson's remarks on Kant's view of imagination: 'Imagination is a pervasive structuring activity by means of which we achieve coherent, patterned, and unified representations. The conclusion ought to be, therefore, that imagination is absolutely essential to rationality, that is, to our rational capacity to find significant connections, to draw inferences, and to solve problems.' (Johnson 1987: 168)

3 The term 'possible world', as it is employed here, originates from recent narratology, referring to the 'secondary' universes that are constructed in the imaginative worlds of novels and other narrating texts. These make use of the primary universes of daily experience (empirical objects and objectifiable processes) and add new entities to them, subsequently transforming them with a view to exploring new possibilities or innovating modes of thought. (See Pavel 1986)

4 For the study of the 'lived experience' involved in narrative imagination, I refer to the work of Marie-Laure Ryan (1991, 2001) and David Herman (2009: 143-147), to Juhani Pallasma (2006) and to Yi-Fu Tuan (1977) for the link with architecture and landscape.

5 An analysis of the emotional and conceptual properties of narrative imagination in urbanist designs can be found in Keunen & Verraest 2012.

6 The fifth strategy ('distributing intelligence across social groups') rather belongs to the conceptual dimension of narrative imagination. A lack of space precludes any discussion in the current paper.

7 In *The Structure of the Artistic Text*, Lotman writes that a narrative is characterized by

its closed nature. (Lotman 1977: 216, 217) The closed nature of a work turns the story into a fenced fictional world, a closed off universe. The crosscut spaces reunite in the closed whole as one single image.

8 The citations were obtained from www.newurbanism.org and www.valdeurope.com. Keunen, Uyttenhove & Van Nuijs 2014 offers a case study on Val d'Europe.

9 Foucault's concept of heterotopian space comes close to the sacral places that Cassirer described in the 1920s as typical of cultures governed by mythical thought.

10 In literary theory, the relevant word is chronotope. (See Keunen 2011, Keunen & Verraest 2012) This should not come as a surprise. In his 1937 essay, Bachtin actually presents Cassirer's ideas as if they were his own. Within the closed space, material things and human practices acquire a different meaning that holds a powerful affective charge. Like religious, sacral spaces, heterotopian places are fascinating and enchanting. They constitute places in which the individual is able to rise temporarily above the empirical world through practices, beliefs and emotions that are experienced as singular or exceptional.

11 'L'imitation ou la représentation est une activité mimétique en tant qu'elle produit quelque chose, à savoir précisément l'agencement des faits par la mise en intrigue.' / 'Imitation or representation is a mimetic activity in its capacity of producing something, to wit, precisely the ordering of facts by inserting them into a plot.' Ricoeur's narrative philosophy has the great advantage of viewing stories as forms of thought, as instantiations of the human faculty of fictional communication (it is his aim to 'donner à l'intrigue une définition la plus englobante possible au sein de la communication fictionnelle' / 'to grant the plot the most encompassing definition possible in the lap of fictional communication', Ricoeur 1984: 19-30). It is this view that allows us to call him the pioneer of the theory of narrative imagination.

12 In this context, I would like to refer to the spatiotemporal typification discussed by Michael Bakhtin (1981) in his inquiries on the concept of the chronotope and in my study *Time and Imagination* (2011). These chronotopes involve more or less stable spatial constellations that appear together with stereotypical activities. Chronotopes are durable connections or associations that arise in a particular culture and connect space with time (in which the temporal aspect coincides with the agency). Examples from the literary world are 'the gothic castles', 'the salon conversations', 'the boring rural setting', or 'the idyllic situation'. In these cases, the spatial capitalizes on the interchange between the inside space and the outside space. In Bakhtin's view, this results in the threshold becoming one of the most significant literary chronotopes.

13 Mark Johnson's view is actually much richer. Johnson, who is the theorist most frequently cited by architecture theorists, asserts that metaphors must be seen as a kind of 'disciplined' form of imagination: 'Metaphorical projection is one fundamental means by which we project structure, make new connections, and remold our experience.' (1987: 168) In addition, the narrative element has acquired an essential place in his thought: 'There must be a central place for the notion of narrative unity. Not only are we born into complex and communal narratives, we also experience, understand, and order our lives as stories we are living out.' (1987: 171-172) Nonetheless, Johnson fails to consistently think through the role of narrativity and neglects to elaborate the relation between narrative and metaphor.

14 In a fairly recent writing, French aesthetician Schaeffer points out that literary studies should urgently change their tack: 'La question primordiale n'est pas celle des relations que la fiction entretient avec la réalité ; il s'agit plutôt de voir comment elle opère dans la réalité, c'est-à-dire dans nos vies.' / 'The essential issue is not that of the relations that

fiction maintains with reality; it is rather a matter of looking into how fiction operates in reality, that is to say, in our lives.' (Schaeffer 1999: 212)

15 Ryan makes a distinction between 'being a narrative' and 'possessing narrativity'. (2001: 6) A text *is* a narrative when it is 'produced with the intent to evoke a narrative script in the mind of the audience,' and when this intent is recognized by the receiver. (2001: 6-7) A text *has* narrativity, in contrast, when it evokes such a script, even though the author – if there is one – did not intend to write a narrative. (2001: 7)

Reality Without Colours

Imagining Architecture through Calvino's Eyes

Daria Ricchi

Although mostly remembered as a fantastical storyteller, Calvino's neorealist past was rooted in a time when black and white characterized cinema, politics and building construction. When an English translator rendered the title of Italo Calvino's short story *Senza Colori* (Without Colours) as 'In Black and White', Calvino rejected it by pointing out that black and white are indeed colours. We can consider 'black and white' as a heuristic tool to revaluate the assumed distinction between the 'real' as non-coloured versus the 'imagined' as coloured. I will question such implicit visual dichotomy by reinterpreting 'black and white' precisely as the colours of a neorealist post-war Italy, as a palette for the imagination. Calvino's evolution as a writer is multifaceted and reflects the historical evolution that simultaneously happened in literature, history and architecture theory. In fact, from his first novel written and published in 1947 to his last works, Calvino changed from a true-to-life style to a fantastic turn, a shift and evolution that happened in the late 1940s into the 1950s. Up until 1956 or 1957, in Italy, intellectual production could not be detached from political engagement. With little distinction between political propaganda and literature, there was no room for fictive construction, only for realist chronicles.

In both debates, 1957 is a seminal year of rupture. At the end of 1956, the Hungarian Revolution and the Soviet invasion led to widespread disapproval of the Communist

Party. Before then, intellectuals considered news revealed by the Party as truthful and part of History. But then it became clear that the Communist Party and 'Uncle Stalin' could and did in fact lie. From this point on, fiction and fantasy were again accepted as high forms of literature. Writers rediscovered that literature could entertain too and Calvino, among them, turned to his best inclination: fantasy.

Calvino experimented with every kind of literary genre: fiction – although favouring short stories over novels – journalist texts, critical essays and political papers, thus mixing styles and colours. His friend and fellow writer Elio Vittorini described his work eloquently as 'realism with a fantasy trust or fantasy with a realistic trust'.[1] Yet Calvino was convinced that politics and economy require documental research and not 'literary approximations'.[2] He believed *fabula fictia* to be something that could not engage with specialized problems. Novels as accounts had a limited life. These were more apt to 'inform how the world works', thus narrative should instead express 'new existential situations'.[3] Yet, to inform is a task more proper to journalism or sociological inquiries. Nevertheless, even if he had claimed to be against the report/novel as a genre, in 'The Cat and the Policemen', Calvino's prose is kin to the report genre.[4]

Within this mixture of realism and fantasy, the city and its architecture pervade Calvino's oeuvre. In his writings, architectural characters are of two types: interiors (places) and cities (spaces). I'll argue that the progress from interiors to urban spaces coincides precisely with the evolution from a more realistic approach to the colourful and fantastic later one. We can go so far as to eventually consider the paths to the places and spaces as a third typology, a blend within them and a blend within real and fantastic.

From Calvino's early period we can recall several of his books. Italo Calvino started his career in 1947 with the novel *The Path to the Nest of Spiders*,[5] a grey account of his life in the *resistenza*, whose title, though, is already turning realism into fairy tale. *The Crow Comes Last*, a collection of short stories published in 1949, followed it.[6] One other short novel, *A Plunge into Real Estate*,[7] a fictive, even if truthful, story about building construction, was conceived in 1955 as part of the 'The Chronicles of the Fifties', a series that remained unfinished. Although the depicting of the actual was never Calvino's forte, and even in his most realistic novel inspired by his partisan experience, the young hero undergoes rites of passage perhaps more proper to the realm of the fairy tale, it is nevertheless true that, disguised as fiction, the description of the city is not far from being a tangible one.

The Crow Comes Last[8] consists of 30 stories inspired by the novelist's own experiences fighting along with the Communist Garibaldi Brigades in the Maritime Alps, during the final phases of the Second World War. Although written largely in the neorealist style, many scenes are infused with visionary fable-like elements characteristic of Calvino's later fantasy period. In this collection of stories, architecture plays a crucial and overlooked role. In it, architecture becomes the protagonist, as buildings or landscapes are characters in the plot. Similarly, their descriptions in the story are never moments of suspension within the narrative, they are not just mere and static *ekphrasis*, not just passive descriptions, but depictions of rooms and detailed landscapes that offer impressions, optic illusions, changes in perspectives. The interiority of the protagonists gradually reveals itself through the interiors they inhabit.[9]

In 'Lazy Sons' one gains the understanding of a family unfolding through different rooms of their house. The father heavily steps from one room to the other. The mother, on the other hand, belongs to the kitchen, cleans glasses and tables, she does the dishes or the laundry.

'Sell it, the house, and let's eat the money, I say . . . in the meantime longer cracks open in the ceiling, rows of ants run along walls, grass and bushes climb from the untamed garden. In a little while, maybe we won't have anything but ruins covered with creepers,'[10] the main character says. The father's anger towards his lazy sons unfolds through the interiors of the house: he shouts walking down the stairs, he runs around the house, slams the doors, closes the gate. The boys keep sleeping, and then eventually wake up. The main character has breakfast, rearranges his books; his brother oversleeps then walks to the city to play pool. They all eat together in the kitchen, the brother goes out again, and our protagonist reads in his bedroom waiting for his brother to return, longing to hear about the city. Smoking at the window, they comment on the hill and the bright road that leads to it.

'Leaving Again Shortly' also has two brothers as protagonists. Here one of the two rarely comes back home. But the house represents stability while everything else changes. It dominates from the top of the hill, with its strange red colour hiding among olive trees. It is an ancient house, with arches like vaults. The second brother never moves, he is always at home. They could not be more different from each other but they can relate by returning back home.

> *But at home it's different, at home we've always behaved like this. Then we enter the house, both with our hands in our pockets, silent, a little embar-*

rassed, and all of a sudden my brother begins to talk as if we had just that moment interrupted a conversation.[11]

A third story, 'The House of the Beehives', focuses on an isolated house, hidden among bushes, where a man hides, and hides himself from a murder he committed. The house hides him and hides his crime. The only evidence of it is another home, the victim's home, as she never returns. The story's beginning leads to the house on top of the hill:

> *It is difficult to see from far away and even if someone had already been here once they could not remember the way back; there was a path here at one time, but I made brambles grow over it and wiped out every trace. It's well chosen, this home of mine, lost in this bank of broom, on a single floor that can't be seen from the valley, and covered in a chalky whitewash with windows picked out in red.*[12]

This start implies the importance of the route leading towards it. The house of the beehives is on top of the hill. In 'The Same Thing as Blood', the house of the communist is midway to the top of the hill, a small construction with only one ground room; from the outside, and overnight, it looks like a pile of stones.

'Fear on the Footpath' or 'Going to the Headquarters' all insist on the movement towards a place. The house is in general a secure place, one to go back to in search of comfort, safety and family. And when one does not have a house, one is lost. Indeed, in 'Men without a Roof', the house is lost, denied, it becomes a removed imperative, a secret reason of perennial dissatisfaction.

However, like typologies other than the house, this can also represent constrictions, in a similar way to the surrealist short story 'Seven Floors' by Dino Buzzati[13] in which each floor of a hospital coincides with the gravity of a patient's illness. The lower you go, the closer you are to the end of your life. In Buzzati's story, the protagonist Giuseppe Corte is continuously moving towards the basement of the Sanitarium, a symbol for death. Because he is unable to accept the severity of his illness, he is in denial until the very end. Does he get sicker due to moving towards the bottom, or is he getting sicker and consequently he gets moved towards the bottom? In other words, is architecture making him sick or contributing to his death? The same happens to be true in some of Calvino's stories. In 'Angst in the Barracks', distress and darkness are to be found in the walls of architecture.

To think about it, his illness started while in jail, the night after being caught: the noise of the sea, outside, like an airplane buzz, hope and fear of an air raid that would have freed or buried them.... Prison's cells, squalid offices, nervous faces of the German fascists and officials, the solemn but devastated hotels full of fearful hostages, finally the barracks with its distressing geometry of stairs, corridors and desert dormitories, its obtuse and pale inhabitants, all parts of a network of desperate people that grips the world.[14]

These barracks are imprisoning its visitors amid the geometry of corridors, staircases and balconies. It becomes a monument to injustice. Injustice is housed in the barracks that have become law. Here the construction is the main character of the story, it embodies the change of settings, the characters' anxieties and thoughts, but similarly it signifies bigger concerns with society and the state. 'The barracks, massive monument to injustice become law, looming over him with its stone staircases, scraped off doors, dreary offices.'[15]

In all early writings, the majority of events happen inside. Stories and events unfold indoors, while an ideology – a political fear towards urbanity – distances these buildings from the city, which is typically far away and down the hill. 'The House of the Beehives' is on top of the hill, the house of the communist half way up. Repeatedly, the city unfolds under the main protagonist. It is often forbidden to him and holds the smell of death. Nature underlines the geographical and conceptual remoteness from the city:

May everything go to similar ruin in the cities of the human race; may I, as I walk along one day, see the tops of chimneys emerging from the earth, meet parts of streets falling off into ravines, and stumble on strips of railway lines in the middle of the forest.[16]

There is a gradual progression from the interior of the house to the exterior of the cityscape. But the path cannot be walked twice, and the city only hosts ruins and destruction. However, Calvino's gloomy vision of cities, a complex symbol according to him, does not remain gloomy for too long, as for instance in his 1957 *A Plunge into Real Estate*, which evokes the construction boom and building speculation of the 1950s. His 1963 fictitious *Marcovaldo or the Seasons in the City* also recounts the effects of this wild expansion and the resulting sequential problems of urban life.
A Plunge into Real Estate[17] depicts a realistic setting and realistic characters, including a protagonist, the young intellectual Quinto Anfossi, who decides to invest money in

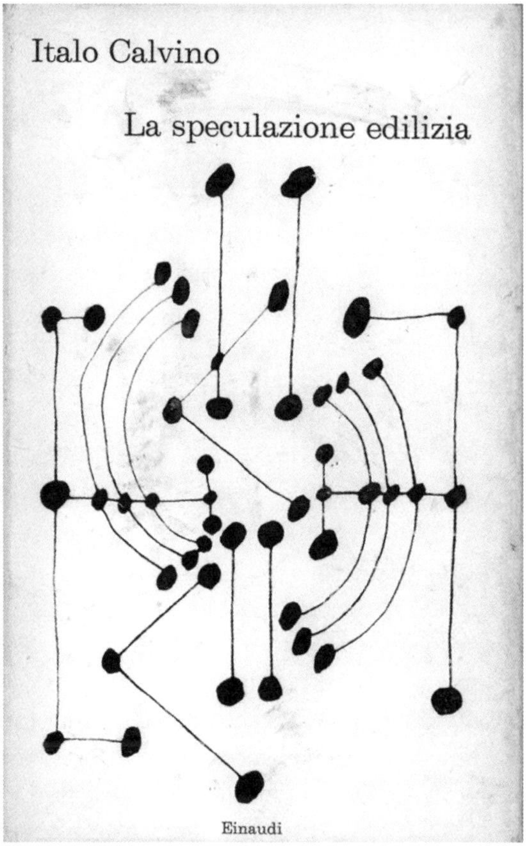

Figure 1. Italo Calvino, *La speculazione edilizia*, [A Plunge into Real Estate], Turin: Einaudi 1963. Copyright Giulio Einaudi Publishing House.

the Italian Riviera. In this book, Calvino sums up the fever of building construction at that time. A passage reads as follows:

> *The Riviera was gripped by a fever of cement. An apartment building here, the identical window boxes of geraniums on every balcony; there a building that had just gone up, the windows still marked with white, waiting for the Milanese families who wanted a place by the sea; a little farther on, some scaffolding, and below, the cement mixer in action and a sign advertising the local real estate office. . . . The town where Quinto lived had once been surrounded by shady gardens of eucalyptus trees and magnolias, where retired English colonels and elderly spinsters leaned over hedges and exchanged Tauchnitz editions and watering cans.*[18]

Although it sounds like a warning, this passage hardly differs from articles published in *Domus* and *Casabella* in the immediate post-war period, which denounce real estate speculation and the horrors of massive building construction on the coast. After an early and urgent debate on providing housing for millions of people, this overwhelming necessity led to uncontrolled development and wild expansion that architects and politicians were not able to manage. Calvino bluntly describes the mood during those years. And it is quite telling that he picked building construction as a major theme for, perhaps, his most realist novel. Though the book has an artistic flair, hardly the tone of a chronicle, as the title 'The Chronicles of the Fifties' would have suggested, he blended the realist with a fictitious account on the one hand, and the fairy tale on the other, quite well. He waved the colours of imaginations, and the greyness of contemporary building chronicles. The protagonist Quinto Anfossi represents the young intellectual, torn between his cerebral interests – that do not pay off – and the appeal of easy money through property investment. The quasi-autobiographic intellectual bourgeois, born and raised in a small town in Liguria, was once a communist partisan and moved to a big city in Piedmont to work. But Quinto cannot stand the motionless world of the Riviera compared to the excitement and fast development of the city. Quinto asks: 'If everybody's building, why don't we build too? . . . With the result that Quinto was now coming home to try his hand at real estate.'[19]

A more colourful and ironic book, *Marcovaldo or the Seasons in the City,* was published in 1963.[20] It is a collection of short stories, some of them written as early as 1953, in which a melancholic Marcovaldo cannot adapt himself to city life. Although many of the stories in the collection depict fantastical events, the description of the city in this book is highly realistic. Marcovaldo, his wife Domitilla and their six children are presented almost as caricatures yet they struggle with familiar urban problems in a city that could easily be Milan or Turin. With no money of their own, they watch others go shopping for entertainment. 'For the more money circulates, the more those without any can hope, sooner or later a bit of it will come into my pocket,'[21] Marcovaldo hopes, while getting lost in a labyrinthine supermarket. And while the urban spaces he depicts often lack names and proper locations, these works of the imagination represented precisely what was happening within the fields of urbanism and building construction. In fact, stories about property speculation filled the pages of every newspaper.

Calvino's stories were written in the early 1950s and thus are set in a very poor Italy, the Italy of neorealist movies. The last stories date from the mid-1960s, when the illusions of prosperity flourished thanks to the economic boom. During this period, Calvino evolved from an uncomfortable realist into the most sophisticated and suggestive postmodern fabulist. In one passage from *Marcovaldo*, realism and fantasy mix together to imaginatively describe a city governed by building regulations:

> *But in the vertical city, in this compressed city where all voids tend to fill up and every block of cement tends to mingle with other blocks of cement a kind of counter-city opens, a negative city that consists of empty slices between wall and wall of the minimal distances ordained by the building regulations between two constructions, between the rear of one construction and the rear of the next; it is a city of cavities, wells, air conduits, driveways, inner yards, accesses to basements, like a network of dry canals on a planet of stucco, and walls, that the ancient cat population still scurries.*[22]

And the structure of his narrative is important to consider. The composition structure of most of Calvino's books is based on a combinatory solution. Our knowledge of the real is always partial and uncertain; our ambition to grasp totality can be expressed only via circumscribed representations.

The example to end all examples is the seminal *Invisible Cities,* published in 1972, that embodies both a highly fantastic and imaginative dimension together with a highly rational component. The book is based on a complex mathematical construction. As Alberto Asor Rosa well described in the *Breve storia della letteratura italiana*: 'The cities can become too credible to be true . . . the possible true ceases to seem to be true and ends up becoming false.'[23] Here Calvino intertwined the characters' interiority and their dreams about fantastic spaces. He offered new visions and new versions of them, whose interpretation lies in the mind of the reader. It is as if Calvino added a new colour, a new layer of transparency, that of dreamlike imagination. We can go so far as to question if those visions are in fact real, if the external versions of the cities are not just a creation of our interior imagination.

1 'Realismo a carica fiabesca or fiaba a carica realistica', in: Italo Calvino, *Hermit in Paris* (New York: Vintage books 2004), 163.

2 Italo Calvino, 'Levels of Reality in Literature', in: *The Uses of Literature* (New York: Harcourt Brace Jovanovich, 1986), 102.

3 Ibid.

4 'He saw the gun lying between the faded lace-bordered velvet sofas, its muddy wheels on the carpet and the gun-carriage touching the chandelier; huge, filling the whole room, and scratching the polish off the piano.

'One evening the police made a raid on the working-class quarter and cordoned off an entire tenement. It was a large block with a tired, shabby air about it, as if supporting so much hedged-in humanity had deformed the walls and floors, turned them into porous, calloused flesh.

'The courtyard was cluttered with barrels of refuse, and round each floor ran railings and landings of twisted rusty iron, the railings with clothes and rags draped all over them, the landings with windows covered in bits of wood through which stuck the blackened pipes of stoves; at the end of each landing, one above the other like turrets in a ruined castle, were lavatory huts, interspersed from floor to floor by little windows clattering with sewing-machines and smoky with cooking, right on up to the battered skylights, the crooked gutters and the filthy attics.

'Criss-crossing up from the basement to the roof of the old building ran a labyrinth of foul stairs, like black veins, along which were scattered apparently haphazard the entrance door to mezzanine floors and flats.

'The police climbed up, their steps echoing lugubriously, trying to make out the names written on the doors; round and round the reverberating landings they went in single file, amid the peering heads of children and tousled women.' Italo Calvino, 'The Cat and the Policeman', in: *Adam, One Afternoon* (London: Secker & Warburg, 1957), 142-143.

5 *Il sentiero dei nidi di ragno* (Turin: Einaudi, 1947).

6 *Ultimo viene il Corvo* (Turin: Einaudi, 1949). Some of these stories have been translated in *Adam, One Afternoon* (London: Secker & Warburg, 1957). Some of them have never been translated.

7 Originally published as *La speculazione edilizia,* it was first published in the magazine *Botteghe Oscure* in 1957 and later by Einaudi in 1963.

8 Italo Calvino, *Ultimo viene il Corvo* (1949), *Racconti*, Vol. I (Turin: Mondadori, 1991).

9 Other examples are the description of landscapes in *A Plunge into Real Estate* and the description of internal spaces in *The Watcher*, which are never suspended moments in the story.

10 Italo Calvino, 'I figli poltroni', in: *Ultimo viene il corvo* (1949), *Racconti*, Vol. I (Turin: Mondadori, 1991), 198, translation by the author.

11 Italo Calvino, 'Leaving Again Shortly' (1949), in: *Adam, One Afternoon* (London: Secker & Warburg, 1957), 37.
12 Italo Calvino, 'The House of the Beehives' (1949), in: *Adam, One Afternoon* (London: Secker & Warburg, 1957), 43.
13 Dino Buzzati, 'Seven Floors' (1965), originally 'Sette Piani', in: *La Lettura* (1937).
14 Italo Calvino, 'Angoscia in caserma', In: *Romanzi e Racconti*, Vol. I (Milan: Mondadori, 1991), 237, translation by the author.
15 Idem, 242.
16 Italo Calvino, 'The House of the Beehives' (1949), in: *Adam, One Afternoon* (London: Secker & Warburg, 1957), 45.
17 'A Plunge into Real Estate', in: *Difficult Loves* (London: Secker & Warburg, 1983), originally 'La Speculazione Edilizia' (1957), in: *Botteghe Oscure*, no. 20 (1957).
18 Italo Calvino, 'A Plunge into Real Estate', in: *Difficult Loves* (London: Secker & Warburg, 1983), 163-164.
19 Idem, 166.
20 Italo Calvino, *Marcovaldo or the Seasons in the City* (San Diego, CA: Harcourt Brace Jovanovich, 1983), originally *Marcovaldo, ovvero le stagioni in città* (Turin: Einaudi, 1963).
21 Idem, 84.
22 Idem, 102.
23 Alberto Asor Rosa, *Breve storia della letteratura italiana* (Turin: Einaudi, 2013), 365.

The Critical Relevance of Fictional Projects
About Buildings That Do Not (Yet) Exist

Deborah Levy

> *It is a laborious madness and an impoverishing one, the madness of designing vast buildings – drawing plans and sections of an idea that can be perfectly set out orally in five minutes. The better way to go about it is to pretend that those buildings already exist, and offer a summary, a commentary on them.*[1]

The House of Doors and Windows

'The Flowering of an Art' is a short story taken from the *Chronicles of Bustos Domecq,* written by Jorge Luis Borges and Adolfo Bioy Casares and published in 1967.[2] In this collection, the fictional reporter Honorio Bustos Domecq dedicates himself to the critique of equally fictional books, sculptures, paintings and so on. 'The Flowering of an Art' thus appears to be a 'serious' review of what seems to be a fictional building, 'The House of Doors and Windows':

> *The building . . . covers a rectangular plot with a frontage of six yards and a depth of something slightly under eighteen. Each of the six doors that go to*

> *make up the facade of the ground floor, communicates, at a distance of some thirty-six inches, with a similar door, and so on in succession, until at the rear of the building we arrive at the eighteenth door. Severe panelling on each side divides the six parallel systems, which all together add up to the imposing sum of one hundred and eight doors. From the windows of houses across the street, the careful observer may make out that the second floor abounds in staircases of six steps that go up and down in zigzag form; that the third floor is made up entirely of windows; the fourth, of thresholds; and the fifth and last, of floors and ceilings.* (Borges and Bioy Casarès 1979: 80-81)

How can a short story taken from a work of fiction written by a fiction writer disguised as a fictional character discussing a fictional building enlighten us on anything? If, put like this, the text does not seem able to teach us anything, it is for two related reasons. On the one hand, unlike texts we usually read for broadening our knowledge of architecture, this one discusses a building that has no existence apart from the text. On the other, as soon as we consider the text as fiction, we instinctively assign it the essential task of pleasing us rather than of instructing us.[3]

Fictional Work

In the text, the unveiling of the 'House of Doors and Windows' is preceded by the descriptions of two other buildings: the 'Great Chaotic' and the 'Shrine of the Many Muses'. Like the 'House of Doors and Windows', these two monuments are created by the text. However, unlike the first, they refer directly to elements that exist apart from the text: architecture as represented in Piranesi's etchings. As it is the pure invention of Bustos Domecq, the 'House of Doors and Windows' requires a more in-depth description for the reader to picture it. Nevertheless, although details about the number and size of some of its elements partially overcome its lack of referent, the 'House of Doors and Windows' maintains a low degree of completeness if we, for instance, compare it to countless buildings that can be found in novels. Without thickness, colours or any imperfection, it is provided with a 'defective' existence. Not related to any lived human experience, it is disembodied, abstract. However, it possesses something that many literary descriptions of buildings lack. First, it is related to earlier buildings on which it makes a stand (the Great Chaotic and the Shrine of Many Muses), the school of thought within which it falls (Functionalism), the personalities who took part in its achievement (Verdussen, Prince Bernhard) and even the theory underlying it: 'Walls, windows, doors, floor, and ceiling constitute beyond all discussion the basic elements of modern man's habitat.' (Borges and Bioy Casarès 1979: 80) Then, inside the text itself, it receives an interpretation, a critique, a refutation and it is linked to a building that follows it. In short, unlike the excerpt from the novel, the text includes the finished object as much as the circumstances in which it was produced and its critical reception. Certainly, as a fictional object or, in other words, as the scene of lived experience, the 'House of Doors and Windows' is insubstantial. However, as the product of a cultural context and the subject of a critical discussion, that is to say as a 'fictional work', it is much more tangible.

Serious Review

Although the text is part of a collection of short stories, 'The Flowering of an Art' resembles an essay more than a piece of literary fiction. Straightaway, the chronicler presents the purpose of the text as being more argumentative than narrative. He then alludes to familiar names (Le Corbusier, Gropius, Wright, Ruskin and Piranesi), places (Rome, Utrecht), actual architectural movements (functionalism), known concepts (the machine for living), familiar books (*Toward an Uncompromising Architecture*, *The Seven Lamps of Architecture*), styles we can easily imagine (the Chaotic style) and plausible dates. Even more confusing, a well-known aphorism is credited to its legitimate author: 'Emerson, whose memory was usually inventive, attributes to Goethe the concept of architecture as frozen music.' (Borges and Bioy Casarès 1979: 78)

Certainly Bustos Domecq takes advantage of us being familiar with these references to strengthen our impression that we're dealing with a referential account and accredit the existence of the buildings he describes. But it is not the authors' ultimate purpose. The proof is that they partly fail due to the chronicler's inclusion of fully fictional referents. Also, the text is filled with irony. It is, after all, dedicated to 'Picasso, Joyce and Le Corbusier, those three forgotten greats.' (Borges and Bioy Casarès 1979: 7) Actually, more than a 'serious review' of a fictional building, 'The Flowering of an Art' is an 'imitation of a serious review', namely a *pastiche*.[4] As an article dedicated to the glory of contemporary architects and mimicking a half-critical, half-anecdotal apology, the text highlights the features of an authorized avant-garde and those of the discourse that legitimizes it. The role of the fictional buildings presented – the main feature of which is to be glorified, even though they are unusable as we dismantle them straight after their official opening – is to embody the dangers of such an alliance. In the end, the role of actual referents is to push the reader to establish analogies between fictional buildings and actual ones, with the aim of transferring the features of the first ones to the second ones. In other words, by establishing similarities with the actual dynamic of the twentieth-century architecture, the text gives fictional buildings the power to shed light on architectural issues of that period. Besides being, of course, a wonderful commentary about literature itself.

From True to Likely

Besides the issue of the object itself, fictional buildings raise the question of the way we discuss them. Is every commentary on fictional building bound to insert references to existing things, like Bustos Domecq does? If he does, it is because he aims at taking a stand on them: a commentary that would use fictional buildings to investigate a theoretical question, a spatial hypothesis or a design process would not be bound to insert references to actual elements. However, the simulation should conform to the laws of the world it aims to explore. Otherwise, it would not teach us anything about it. Consequently, as it is one of the laws of the real world, it has to comply with the principle of consistency. This means the commentary has to establish likely causal links between the object and the interactions simulated. If the commentary is likely, that is to say if it is consistent with the object, then it will – like any other form of criticism – be able to deliver knowledge that goes beyond the particular case of the fictional building described. Why, indeed, talk nonsense about something that does not exist?

From Fictional Object to Actual Work

Based on the analysis of this short story, a 'fictional work' could be defined when compared to an actual work and a fictional object. On the one hand, the fictional work would be a little more than the fictional object (those we find in most novels) since, unlike it, it would be displayed as a 'work', that is, as the product of a context and the subject of a critical discussion. This second difference mainly results in a heuristic benefit: the author or the reader of the work can therefore grasp every aspect of it, not only its final form. In fact, a 'comprehensive' fictional work would be as much an artefact stemming from an artistic, cultural, social, political and economic context and a subject for critical discussion, as it would be the result of a creative process, a trigger for perceptions, interpretations or social interactions, a precedent of future work and so on. Its inexhaustible commentary would then simulate all these aspects and all their interactions with society. Admittedly, such a text would be nearly impossible to write. Nonetheless, from the most elementary fictional object to the more exhaustive fictional work, there is an infinity of conditions under which fictional works can, for as many reasons, prove to be relevant. Depending on whether one is interested in the way buildings are created, produced, built, perceived, interpreted or lived, one will not produce the same object and will not discuss it in the same way. The way we discuss fictional buildings is, inseparable of what they can provide us, but it is also and above all symptomatic of what we expect from them, and hence from architecture.

On the other hand, a fictional work would be a little less than an actual work since it would not have been created, strictly speaking. A fictional book is a book that has not been written. A fictional painting is a painting that has not been painted. Likewise, a fictional building is not a building that has not been built but a building that, like the 'House of Doors and Windows', has not been designed. It exists somewhere 'below form' as a 'fictional project'. As such, it lacks many of the dimensions that characterize an actual project from the moment it is being designed. First of all, the fictional project is 'low style'. It is less shaped by the set of rules and habits available to architects at a precise time in history, making their project specific to that era. It is less defined by the combination of distinctive features of expression that originate from the deep individuality of an architect, making the project specific to him or the school he is part of. Both factors tend towards making the work more specific, though neither of them belongs to architecture as such. Rather, they define the limits of what is possible and what is not. Secondly, a fictional project is less subjected to the successive choices made by an architect who, retaining some possibilities while dismissing others, makes the completed project more and more contingent. Finally, fictional projects certainly escape influences of the parameters of reality that shape an architectural project.

Perfectly responding to Borges, who considers 'a laborious madness and an impoverishing one, the madness of composing vast books' (Borges 2000: 67), Oscar Wilde claims: 'I never read a book I must review; it prejudices you so.' (Wilde 1905: 152) He expresses the idea shared by other critics that he is less concerned about the work itself than about the 'idea of the work'.[5] Writers who do not write are interested in fictional works in the same way as critics who do not read: a work that did not take shape is essentially less 'specific' than a completed one. Such a notional object is relevant to them for two related reasons. First because they are less keen to unveil the work in its singularity than to position it in relation to other works, and anchor it within the totality of culture. Secondly, because they are in fact primarily searching for the essence of literature hidden behind specificities of real works. Unless maybe form is precisely the topic addressed by the fictional work . . .

From the Reception to the Creation of Fictional Projects

The figure of Honorio Bustos Domecq is far from being an insignificant prank. In fact, he enjoyed an actual existence as an art critic until the two Argentineans revealed the fraud.[6] Through its references, he moreover demonstrates the erudition granting him this legitimacy.[7] Fictional character, admittedly, but very actual critic and legitimate author of the text, he embodies the ideal activity of a creation-criticism through which works and knowledge would generate each other. As Bustos Domecq is a critic, the 'The Flowering of an Art' naturally simulates the reception of a fictional work.

Requiring less writing skills, references and culture than the articles of Bustos Domecq, Edouard Levé's *Œuvres* rather simulates the creation of fictional photographs, movies, installations, buildings and so on. Originally a painter and a photographer, Levé became a writer when his first book was published. The first sentence of *Œuvres* perfectly summarizes its content: '1. A book describes works of art the author had the idea of, but never produced.' (Levé 2002: 7) Indeed, 533 fictional works are described in a concise way, with straightforward sentences made of an everyday vocabulary. For the most part, the 533 commentaries focus less on the final aspect of the object or on its critical reception than on its creation process:

> *11. The friend of an artist picks descriptions of works of art in journals. The picture of the work is cut off and the article is sent to the artist for him to draw the work based on this description. The final work is a triptych composed of the drawing, the text and the picture . . .*[8] (Levé 2002: 9)

> *17. One litre of molten lead is poured in space without gravity. Being returned to earth, it is displayed as it solidified.*[9] (Levé 2002: 11)

> *476. Statements are engraved on the walls of a building. Only the ones facing east are true.*[10] (Levé 2002: 176)

The penultimate fragment clearly stresses the idea that the works are not designed yet: '532. After he published a book in which he describes fictional works, the author draws them and publishes a second book, made of as many drawings.' (Levé 2002: 192)

Four years later, and one before committing suicide, Edouard Levé produced one of the works he described in *Œuvres*[11]. Similarly, some of the experimental books described by Borges in *The Chronicles of Bustos Domecq* or in *An Examination of the Work of Herbert Quain*[12] turned out to be an incredible foresight of what literature in the second half of the twentieth century was to become.[13] Incidentally so, fictional works sometimes end up existing. So even if 'a book does not exist (or does not yet exist) it is not a reason to ignore it.' (Manguel 1996: 172) Could we then not imagine architecture critics who take an interest in projects that could exist and architects who imagine a possible architecture? Or should they cooperate? Literary theory has shown that, although they do not take action, theoreticians are able to describe possible books, to imagine their structure. Conversely, history is ripe with examples of writers who have found inspirations for their work in critic's speculations.

If fictional projects can explore many facets of architecture, they most importantly underpin an independent critic and a reflexive practice. In the end, they prove value because they (re)conciliate creation and criticism. For what would criticism be worth if it did not contribute to invent practice,[14] and what would architecture be worth if it were not endlessly in search of architecture?

In a way, the postscript of the 'The Flowering of an Art' expresses an 'empty box', inviting contemporary architects to take up the challenge.[15]

> *P.S.: Galley proofs of the foregoing survey already corrected, word reaches us by cable from Tasmania itself of a new offshoot. . . . With widespread and dazzling publicity, he announces a new uninhabitable that does away with such relics while at the same time it avoids the all-too-easy expedient of mere bulk and shapelessness. With unflagging interest, we look forward to the models, plans, and photographs of this latest expression of the Modern.* (Borges and Bioy Casarès 1979: 81)

1 This sentence is an adaptation of a statement written by Borges in his 'Introduction' for *The Gardens of Forking Paths*, first published in 1941. The original sentence is: 'Desvarío laborioso y empobrecedor el de componer vastos libros; el de explayar en quinientas páginas una idea. cuya perfecta exposición oral cabe en pocos minutos. Mejor procedimiento es simular que esos libros ya existen y ofrecer un resumen, un comentario.'

2 Original title: 'Eclosiona un arte', in: Jorge Luis Borges and Adolfo Bioy Casarès, *Crónicas de Bustos Domecq* (1967).

3 See the notion of 'immanent function' of fiction in Jean-Marie Schaeffer, *Pourquoi la fiction?*

4 See the analysis of André Lamontagne in 'Métatextualité postmoderne: de la fiction à la critique'.

5 In *Comment parler des livres que l'on a pas lus?*, Pierre Bayard gathers cases of critics who do not read, such as Oscar Wilde or Paul Valéry.

6 Between 1942 and 1955, Bustos Domecq published five stories under his own name. Later, the *Chronicles* and the *New Tales of Bustos Domecq*, although they remain fictionally attributed to him, also mentioned the names of Borges and Casares.

7 The character's erudition has moreover led to him being published in an architecture journal. See Adolfo Bioy Casarès and Jorge Luis Borges, 'Een kunst ontluikt, Kronieken van Bustus Domecq', in: *OASE*, no. 12 (1986).

8 Translated by the author. The original text is: 'L'ami d'un artiste choisit des descriptifs d'oeuvres dans des comptes rendus d'expositions publiés dans la presse. La photographie qui accompagne l'article est découpée et le texte lui est envoyé pour qu'il dessine l'oeuvre d'après sa seule description. L'oeuvre finale est un tryptique compose du dessin, du descriptive de l'oeuvre et de la photographie qui accompagnait l'article. Il y a quatre auteurs, directs ou indirects, volontaires ou non: l'artiste qui a réalisé l'oeuvre de rérence,

le rédacteur de l'article, l'ami qui a choisit et l'artiste qui a dessiné.'

9 Translated by the author. The original text is: 'Un litre de plomb en fusion est verse en apesanteur dans le vide. Rapporté sur terre, il est exposé tel qu'il a durcit.'

10 Translated by the author. The original text is: 'Des propositions sont gravées sur les murs d'un bâtiment. Seules celles des parois orientées à l'est sont vraies. »

11 Work no. 20 of *Œuvres* foreshadows *Amérique,* a series of photographs made by Edouard Levé in 2006.

12 Original title: 'Examen de la obra de Herbert Quain'. This short story was first published in *The Gardens of Forking Paths*. Similar to the *Chronicles of Bustos Domecq*, this short story surveys four fictional books written by fictional Irish author Herbert Quain. *The God of Labyrinth* is a detective story of which the solution is incorrect, *April March* is an story narrating nine versions of the same two days, *The Secret Mirror* is a play in which the first act is the work of a character who enters the scene from the second act, *Statements* proposes eight arguments deliberately ruined by the author.

13 Among others, one inevitably thinks of the experiments of OuLiPo or Nouveau Roman.

14 As wonderfully put by Gérard Genette about literature and criticism in *Nouveau discours du récit.*

15 Well-known figure to literary theory, the 'empty box' and the anecdote that illustrates the concept perfectly exemplify the way theory can foster the flowering of practice. In the double-entry tables he uses to define autobiography, literary critic Philippe Lejeune comes across an empty box that indicates a fact he has not observed yet: a main character of a novel who bears the same name as the author. In 1977, writer Serge Doubrovsky took up the challenge of writing a novel that meets such a criterion, paving the way to a prolific 'literary genre' that would later be called 'autofiction'.

2 MEMORY

Narrative and Poetics in Architectural History

Language, Literary Approaches and Architectural Meaning

54

Alberto Pérez-Gómez

Theoretical Premise

Architecture's primary function may well be to provide a communicative setting for cultures, one that speaks both intellectually and emotionally, creating attuned settings for significant human action. (Pérez-Gómez 2016) While engineers may be better equipped to solve building design problems in view of pragmatic use, structural efficiency and energy sustainability, we as architects like to think we can contribute something of specific significance beyond those issues. We are often told that regardless of our intentions architecture expresses political and economic power, we know that it can function as a sign like publicity and often becomes a commodity; and if we have a modicum of ethics, we worry that it doesn't merely express our own self-indulgence. But regardless of the representational intentions of our designs, which must be driven by a quest for both beauty and justice, it is evident that communication of some sort, evidently multi-layered, is the primary social and cultural function of our discipline. And yet, while we usually tend to think a lot about the role of pictures, drawings, forms or even spaces as geometric volumes, we generally disregard language, the languages we speak and write, and assume they have little to do with design and architectural meaning.

It is nevertheless obvious that living, natural languages, such as English, Spanish, Greek or French, constitute our primary mediation between pre-reflective embodied consciousness (with its motor skills) and intellectual articulation. The languages we speak (primarily oral) give us our cultural roots and are our primary medium to communicate. I want to address the importance of language and its relationship with a significant architecture, identifying the different aspects of this relationship and some specific strategies for its involvement in design.

I take to heart the linguistic nature of human reality, particularly Martin Heidegger's observation that there is no Being before man speaks. I take my cues from philosophical hermeneutics and the concept of emerging language as part of the flesh of the world, in continuity with habits and gestures. This position espoused by philosophers such as Maurice Merleau-Ponty, Paul Ricoeur and George Steiner is at odds with a constructivist concept of language as a more or less arbitrary code; a vastly complex and hotly debated issue. I will say a few more words about this philosophical position towards the end of this essay.

My concern with language is not as an auxiliary inspiration or as the unambiguous prose of technical specifications. Poetic – original, polysemic – language is central to the very possibility of retrieving cultural roots for architectural expression that may result in appropriate atmospheric qualities, responsive to pre-existing *places*. This concern is not current in architectural theory and practice. The contemporary world is generally suspicious of natural language, deemed fuzzy and deceitful, particularly when compared to so-called mathematical languages, such as those that our computers understand and that 'get things done'. In North America, some years ago, writers declared 'the end of theory' in architecture. Taking as a mantra certain observations by Foucault, they have retained a profound suspicion of language, construing it as an irredeemable instrument of power and manipulation. In recent years, this has resulted in the current obsessions with algorithms and parametric design; a strategy of form generation that deliberately bypasses language while it legitimizes itself with the prospect of infinite formal novelty and its presumed ethical neutrality.

The disregard of language by architects in the process of designing is not as recent as it may appear. In the wake of nineteenth-century positivism and its increasing acceptance of specialization in all areas of knowledge as the only way 'forward', professional disciplines such as architecture became driven by instrumental efficiency. Taking their cues from the theories of Jean-Nicolas-Louis Durand (1802-1805), who argued for rational self-referentiality, architects focused on pragmatic, functionalist concerns, believing that efficiently solving space-planning and structural problems would be sufficient for forms to communicate their function. Nothing else was needed. Intentional expression in analogy to poetic language, as had been theorized during the previous century, was deemed unnecessary and even an aberration. Trying to protect the discipline from the consequences of such a position, effectively becoming a subset of engineering, later architects subsequently reacted by associating architecture to the Fine Arts, stressing the importance of formal issues in building composition, mostly seeking a visual, stylistic coherence, whether motivated by political, religious or aesthetic ideologies, or by the egocentric concerns of an architect's self-expression. Although the result was in line with aesthetic concerns, the architectural mainstream generally assumed theory (discourse) could be nothing other than applied science or formal methodologies, and thus ignored a rich set of traditional discursive options rooted in mythical and poetic language that had been crucial to generate culturally significant work in the early stages of the history of architecture in Europe.

Narrative Language in Architectural Theory

To put my point across, I would like to highlight a few crucial historical moments that are particularly illuminating. Writing in the first century BCE, Vitruvius fully understood the primary communicative function of architecture. Respecting the divisions of knowledge first put forward by Aristotle, his theory – a form of narrative that is totally unlike what we generally take for theory today – included properly theoretical knowledge, *theoria* leading to *sophia*; practical knowledge leading to *phronesis*, narrative wisdom; and technical knowledge, *techne*. These were autonomous forms of knowing that contributed to the success of architecture as a communicative setting. Repeating the Ancient Greeks' conviction that architecture must imitate the perfect articulation of the superlunary cosmos, Vitruvius insisted on *dispositio* or order on the basis of proportions, stressing the importance of concepts such as commensurability: *symmetria* and *eurythmia*, significantly terms imported from both the plastic arts or *techne*, and the performing arts associated with the theatre – music, poetry and dance. (Vitruvius 1931: I) This articulation architecture afforded was the most cherished property of culture, it was the aim of Greek *theoria*, the contemplation of order in Nature associated by Plato with *mathemata,* and mostly present to the senses in the celestial realm. This theory was expressed in discursive texts (like philosophy), and Vitruvius tells us, is the same for a doctor or an architect. The actual practice of architecture, however, was never understood as the 'application' of such theory. It involved both practical knowledge, conveyed through stories in the language of everyday life to make wise and prudent decisions, and *techne-poiesis,* an irreducible knowledge of the body manifested in skills, induced at times by external forces and taught orally in relation to specific tasks while also acknowledging inborn talent. Indeed, Vitruvius's famous section where he describes how architectural forms should be disposed following mathematical proportions emulating the order of the cosmos, includes, *in continuity*, the importance of storytelling in relation to a category he named *decor* (decorum, correctness – associated also with ornament) that accounted for crucial issues of meaning and appropriateness of form to cultural situations – we would say programmes – and natural sites. We easily grasp today the formal issues involved in proportion, but often miss the importance of the stories: such as those that illuminate the presence of the famous caryatids in the Athenian Erechtheion. The languages of *mathesis* and everyday speech – or mythos – were complementary in Antiquity and remained so until the Renaissance. Thus architecture could open a clearing for dwelling in a menacing, mortal sublunary world, communicate articulated order creating harmonious and tempered atmospheres, mimetic of the heavenly star-dance, yet also dressed appropriately for specific tasks, situations or programmes, framing all-important cultural habits.

The nature of architectural theory started to change after the inception of Cartesian dualism in the seventeenth century, moving away from philosophical and rhetorical discourse and closer to technical knowledge. Nicolas Malebranche, a disciple of Descartes, affirmed that only God is a *true cause* of all things, because only He knows *how* He makes things happen, including the perceived relationship between our minds and our bodies. Even if we move our arm, we don't really know *how* we move it, we are only witnessing an *occasional* cause, and ultimately it is God that moves my arm. Conversely, we could infer that whenever we *know* mathematically – clearly and distinctly – *how* something happens, for example *how* a lever operates in terms of the proportions between distances to the fulcrum and applied forces, or *how* an architectural plan or elevation is generated from strict geometrical operations, as is often the case in Baroque design, then we are not only ethically and effectively creative, but our mind is in fact operating through the very same ideas that are 'in God'. Thus 'know-how', the expected aim of instrumental theories, previously *techné*, Aristotle's irreducible technical knowledge, acquired the status previously held by contemplative *theoria*, eventually becoming 'applied science'. In the short term, this assumption produced Baroque instrumental, yet transcendental theories of architect polymaths like the Theatine father Guarino Guarini (posth. 1737), and eventually the first truly proto-positivistic architectural theory in the Western tradition in the writings of Claude Perrault (1683).

Perrault questioned the fundamental assumption of architecture being capable of representing the order of the cosmos. In doing so, he opened up a modern awareness to the question of architecture's meaning. He believed that architecture, like human languages and civil law, changed in time and was the result of human conventions. The fact that the meanings of architecture may depend upon 'custom' rather than 'nature', however, did not make it any less important or culturally significant in his opinion. Like the French language itself, at that point perceived to have attained its summit and proper codification at the *Académie Française*, architecture could and should be open to further refinement and 'progress', thus eventually suggesting the possibility of architectural expression in the form of linguistic analogies.

In the Preface to his treatise, the *Ordonnance* (1683), Perrault questioned the analogy of architectural and musical harmony on the basis of the diversity of the two phenomena, addressed to independent senses conceived as autonomous mechanical receptors of sensory information. Thus he was the first writer ever to reject the usefulness of optical corrections to reconcile traditional theory's proportional prescriptions with the execution of buildings that should be expressive for an embodied synesthetic consciousness. For him, the only purpose of mathematical rules in architecture was to facilitate practice and systematize all dimensions in classical architecture, so that buildings, now understood as aesthetic objects rather than primarily as settings for events, could be built exactly following the designs of the architect: ideal – mathematical – perfection externalized into built form. Once this was understood, it became the task of the architect to innovate 'aesthetically' within the 'tradition', now perceived as a sort of ornamental syntax, making works increasingly more refined and magnificent, capable of reflecting the glory and accomplishments of France during this period.

During the Enlightenment, many architects questioned the instrumental intentions of Perrault's theories (which were easy to disbelieve given the conditions of pre-Industrial Revolution practice) and took his insights as a challenge to understand architectural meaning in relation to natural language rather than to mathematics, foregrounding the issue of *decor* from Vitruvius. Thus the problem of *expression* became primary.

The architectural theories of character and expression that developed during the eighteenth century are very diverse. They try to understand the potential significance of architecture both discursively and emotionally, and I shall not attempt in this summary to do justice to their intricate subtleties. Seeking harmony with a Divine nature could not be given up easily, particularly in view of the apparently definitive successes of Newtonian cosmology and its God/geometrician. A central concern, however, was to adequately *express* the uses for which a building was destined so that it could provide a harmonious setting to actions, as well as representing the status of the building as if it were a social entity, the 'mask' or public persona of its client. Jacques-François Blondel, the most important teacher of architects in Paris around 1750, believed that excellent buildings possessed 'a mute poetry, a sweet, interesting, firm or vigorous style, in a word, a certain *melody* that could be tender, moving, strong, or terrible'. (Blondel 1771, vol.1: 376) Just as a piece of music communicated its character through various tonal harmonies, evoking diverse states of nature and conveying sweet and vivid passions, so proportion (understood mostly as geometric magnitude and no longer as Pythagorean arithmetic ratios) now acted as a vehicle for architectural expression. Thus buildings could be made terrifying or seductive, capable of expressing their character, be it 'the Temple of Vengeance or that of Love'. (Ibid.) Notice how the inevitable mathematical and geometric qualities of architecture became subject to linguistic expression, both discursive and poetic or emotional. This early modern development constitutes the origin of our own possibilities to understand how fiction and natural language may be crucial in design.

Yet, a second consequence of the Enlightenment, with problematic future consequences, must also be noted. The association of architecture with the Fine Arts became commonplace during the eighteenth century. Arguing against Perrault, J.F. Blondel thought that beauty was immutable, and that architects, with an open spirit and keen sense of observation, should be capable of extrapolating it 'from the productions of the fine arts and the infinite variety of Nature'. (Blondel 1752: 318) This reveals a different assumption about the reception of the work from that which had operated since Vitruvius. While not totally immanent, the expression or significance of architecture was increasingly internalized and transformed into a problem of 'composition', brought to fruition through an objectified building. The temporal dimension, which was always central in architectural meaning – both emotional and intellectual and understood by the 'user' through the spatio-temporal *situation* (rituals and poetic programmes) housed by the architecture – receded in favour of the conception of architecture as 'aesthetic object.' Its potential significance could now be 'read' out of time. The ultimate accomplishment of this new paradigm, to be found only after 1800, would be an architecture reduced to a sequence of novel or exciting forms for voyeuristic visits in which linear time became an added factor, rather than being intrinsic to the situation: what would become known as the *promenade architecturale*, a place for tourism often better understood through 'pictures', rather than for genuine participatory experience. Buildings could then be conceived as literal frameworks for 'discursive' writing, like Labrouste's *Bibliothèque Ste. Geneviève*, or generated as forms motivated by fictions, yet incapable of transcending their status as aesthetic objects.

Continuing the insights of earlier character theory, two late eighteenth-century French architects, Claude-Nicolas Ledoux (1804) and Nicolas Le Camus de Mezières (1780) sought alternatives to this sort of objectified aesthetics and tried to reintroduce a temporal dimension to architectural meaning, emphasizing the emotional 'space-in-between' the inhabitant and the building, the space of action, one never before theorized, articulated through *open* narratives kindred to much-later surrealist techniques and cinematographic montage. The very nature of theoretical writing about architecture was also questioned. This implied a new concept of transmission and education, one that could no longer depend on the assumption of theory as *techne* or applied science. Boullée, Ledoux and Viel de Saint-Maux declared the need for a new architectural discourse capable of transcending the limitations of what they, mistakenly yet justifiably in view of Perrault's interpretation, perceived as the prosaic scientific prescriptions of Vitruvian theory and its reincarnation in Renaissance and Neoclassical treatises. Thus, they thought, the intentions of a new poetic architecture

could be better-articulated engaging narrative forms. Narrative and emplotment gave architects such as Ledoux the tools to imagine an architecture that no longer simply reflected the conventional order of society, like the 'masks' of the earlier eighteenth-century architecture, now fully in the realm of both human politics and fiction, devoid of intrinsic transcendence, acknowledged new responsibilities. Ledoux understood that it had become necessary for architecture to project a better future for society, and that this project issued from the critical imagination of the architect/writer, and not from rational analysis or mere societal consensus. His ideal city of Chaux, described in exquisite literary form in his lavish *L'Architecture considérée sous le rapport de l'Art, des Moeurs et de la Législation* (1804), proposes life as lived in new institutions, formally innovative yet always seeking a reconciliation with the natural world, a 'space of appearance' for the 'new man' of the French Revolution. The new political subject could not dwell in the old classical architecture. Drawing from Rousseau's understanding of historicity, Ledoux was keenly aware of the fact that the new humanity was irremediably other than that of the *Ancien Régime*. Thus he designed places for freedom and responsibility, and his literary description discloses the ethical and moral consequences of living in this new world.

Personal expression became a condition for this poetic possibility – a retrieval of the universal *in* the creative soul of the architect. This realization corresponds to the nascent paradigm of Romanticism. Nicolas le Camus de Mezières imagined the inveterate space of desire transferred to the experience of the private home, shifting the emphasis from the exterior to interiority, in search of 'limits' that could no longer be found in the infinite, homogeneous space of natural science, increasingly identified in European cultures with actual lived space. Employing descriptive narrative in his treatise *Le Génie de l'Architecture* (1780), he illustrated the manner in which architects must seek to design rooms, 'qualitative' spaces characterized by appropriate moods to specific focal actions, paradigmatic or harmonic environments, joined and modulated as if in a theatrical experience, in a way that the house itself seduces and becomes a poetic image of dwelling. Every space has its appropriate colours, light, ornaments, textures and iconography, and prepares the inhabitant for the adjoining room, ultimately leading to a sense of recognition and wholeness in the *boudoir,* literally a space apart, the uncommon sacred place that was the space for love. This is the first instance in the history of architectural discourse in which the *quality* of space becomes the subject matter, and atmospheres and moods are conveyed not through mathematical proportional relationships – like harmony in music – but through poetic words. This is indeed the inception of the modern concept of *Stimmung* or atmosphere, a term that would be used by Romantic philosophy and later passed on to phenomenology and architecture, as for instance in the works and theories of Peter Zumthor. At the time when place, as an intersubjective cosmic *topos*, was being obliterated from the public's memory, Le Camus sought to retrieve it *in discourse*, in the hope of actualizing it.

Literary Language as Architectural Tool

Australian philosopher Jeff Malpas has demonstrated how *place* is a condition of consciousness in perception (2007). Giorgio Agamben, commenting on Heidegger, adds that mood or *Stimmung*, the appropriate atmospheric quality we seek in architecture, 'rather than being itself in a place, is the very opening of the world, the very place of Being' (Doussan 2013: 22-23). Agamben elaborates that mood appears as the fundamental existential mode of *Dasein*, not in the ontic but in the ontological plane, 'neither within interiority nor *in* the world, but at their limit'. (Ibid., citing Agamben, *Language and Death*, 2006) One may recall the fundamental phenomenological context of these observations, already expressed by Buddhist philosopher Nagarjuna in the second century of our era, when he affirmed the co-dependent arising of subject, object and action as we experience the world, neither of which terms can be postulated to exist independently or prior to the other (Varela, Thompson and Rosch 1991: 221). One could then conclude that *place* is therefore present in contemporary culture, but hidden by our technological constructs, and it is the task of artefacts like literature, art and architecture to retrieve our attunement. Malpas has further pointed out that *place* emerges with language, one that we must qualify carefully. As I suggested, it is not language as commonly assumed by constructionist linguists, as an arbitrary code of more or less transparent signs that could be improved and left behind by some universal Esperanto, but one that is understood as our fundamental human expressivity, inherently poetic, indicative, polysemic and open, in continuity with the body's own expressivity and gestures; language as our connection to others in view of our primordial social being, and therefore connected to cultural habits. Properly understood in this way, language is not arbitrary: it has the capacity to speak about the world through us, and it comes to fruition in dialogue, through the voice, *Stimme*. The nature of poetic language, which is humanity's original speech, is that it can be translated out of time and place: like the work of art.

Thus, as we come back to consider the relationship of poetic language and architecture, the central concern of this book's essays, we can immediately identify some crucial issues. Regardless of whether modern and contemporary fiction can truly play the role myth did in pre-modern cultures, as Louis Aragon thought possible in his 'antinovel' *Paris Peasant*, we may expect poetic fiction to function as much more than vague inspiration. Acknowledging its role in design, both in the elaboration of programmes and in the disclosure of atmospheres, we can assume that it may further an architecture that gives *place* to significant human action, resonating with the purposefulness that characterizes our biology, even while acknowledging our generalized nihilism and the fact that contemporary man does not generally believe in the efficacy of ritual as a form of participation through action (one whose results are not necessarily the responsibility of those that act). Most of these questions were first acknowledged by Romantic philosophers who believed the novel was the central form of artistic expression, capable of addressing our modern existential questions better than any other form of discourse; concerns that were taken into the twentieth century in the writings and works of surrealist artists. Poetic language is the privileged medium of moods and atmospheres, *Stimmungen*, and the expression of *Gemüt*: the Romantic concept of emotional consciousness that anticipated the current neuro-phenomenological understanding of embodied, emotional cognition.

Paul Ricoeur (1978), Richard Kearny (1988) and Elaine Scarry (2001), among others, have suggested in their own ways that the human imagination is primarily linguistic. Furthermore, we also know through neurobiology that mental images are not picture-like, but rather literal re-enactments of scenes, necessarily operating through language (Thompson 2010: 278-279). All this poses a fundamental challenge for architects, often consumed as we are by pictures and their iterations.

Understanding the importance of literary language to architecture also entails, fundamentally, grasping the crucial importance of literature to disclose the nature of urban contexts with all their cultural complexities, essential for an ethical and poetic practice of architecture and urban design. This is something that scientific mapping and statistics can never accomplish. Let me emphasize: this is language in continuity with phenomenology, as part of the flesh of the world; language therefore in the sense defined by philosophical hermeneutics, inherently at odds, as Merleau-Ponty points out, with the so-called language of algorithms and its desire for absolute clarity and its unambiguous function as sign (Merleau-Ponty 1964: 5). This represents a paradoxical inversion of the conditions that characterized Classical architectural theory with its symbolic mathematical proportions and geometries, necessitated by the changing conditions of culture resulting in what Dalibor Vesely (2004) has called, the age of divided representation.

It is plainly obvious that some of architecture's traditional cultural roles can no longer be implemented. The crisis affecting the profession since the beginning of the European nineteenth century has been well documented. Durand was explicitly responsible for asking architects (for the first time ever) to bypass what he believed were irrelevant issues of linguistic expression in their design, and simply to solve a functional problem in a way that would repeatedly produce pleasure, seeking biological homeostasis rather than *attunement*, which is by necessity a *concordia discors*. He thought that extruding the building from its plan would bring about meaning automatically: the mere expression of a sign. Such a mathematization of design processes is still with us in all our contemporary fashions and infatuations with the computer. City planners prevailed over architects and urban designers, adopting the values of the engineers in the service of political power and economic expediency: reason, utility and efficiency became the determinants of the physical environment, assumed to communicate, if needed, clear semantic messages, unencumbered by emotional intentionality. Confronted by the inability of traditional forms and processes to engage new materials and express modern values, architects had no option but to experiment, engaging creative processes to find novel, emotionally charged forms. Like other artistic disciplines engaged in poetic making – a making that attempts not imposition but disclosure, the revelation of something that is *already there* and is thus familiar and habitual to a culture while being also new – architecture has suffered during the last two centuries the limitations of potential solipsism and near nonsense, the syndrome of architecture made for architects, *particularly when detached from language* and not framed through appropriate critical questions. This has prolonged the crisis, some would even claim, the agony of the discipline. Yet the fundamental existential questions, to which architecture traditionally answered, the profound necessity for humans to inhabit a resonant world they may call home, even when separated by global technological civilization from an innate sense of place, remain as pressing as always.

At this juncture, the call for a careful and multi-layered consideration of poetic and hermeneutic language in the generation of architecture and the built environment appears pressing. Narrative forms should be engaged for their fundamental capacity to orient ethical action, this is a call for history as interpretation through stories about the past, one that acknowledges the deep roots of our questions in the history of the Western world. Stories are also important for their unique ability to map architecture's urban context, increasingly synonymous with the human environment at large; they are crucial to set *in place* human actions, as in Ricoeur's narrative model of *prefiguration, configuration and refiguration* (Ricoeur, 1987-1990). This schema might suggest for architecture a narrative understanding of site as *prefiguration*, form and atmosphere as *configuration*, and lived programme as *refiguration*, accounting for the nature of the project as an ethical promise, communicating through emotion and reason. Engaging hermeneutic and poetic language in this fashion we can imagine how architecture could offer better alternatives to reconcile the personal imagination of the architect with an understanding of local cultures and pressing political and social concerns, beyond obsessions with fashion and form: the crucial dilemma we have inherited along with our modern condition.

Furthermore, in view of the poverty, neutrality and even hostility of much of our post-industrial environment, literary mediations of urban space in the form of novels that reveal possibilities for significant human life keep acquiring growing significance for any architectural practice that may seek to resist the pressures of consumerism, banal functionalism and ideological imperatives. Examples could be drawn from works by authors such as Bely, Joyce, Robbe-Grillet, Murakami, Soupault, Breton and Sebald, among others. Even literary science fiction, like Michel Houellebecq's *The Possibility of an Island* has the capacity to show, much better than the theory of technology, what might happen to our humanity if we finally get rid of death and desire: the limited place of intersubjectivity that has always been the gift of architecture.

Architects today, with the help of digital media, are capable of proposing all sorts of novelties. In our pathological urban contexts, it does not suffice to make contorted buildings constructed with unfamiliar materials to house the same shops and fashionable Italian designers. It is not enough either to merely disrupt habits through effects, without proposing attuned alternatives for human action. Self-edification, the architecture that completes us and lets us dwell, recognizing our human condition, will not issue from this pictorial, formal acrobatics. The problem of historical and ethical responsibility is often buried in a postmodern culture of pastiche and instrumentality. The literary imagination, drawing from language that is our being, forces an acknowledgment of ground, crucial for architecture both literally and metaphorically, in a time when designing and building complex structures for their own sake has become the leading fashion of practice.

The Semiotics of Timelessness

Reading 'Mythic' Architecture

Nadia Sels

> *A plain amidst the hills, composed of meadows and trees in rows, traversed by large clearings, on a September morning, when a little bit of fog lifts everything slightly above the ground. This scenery captures your attention by the evidently sacred character the place must have had in the past. . . . Here, on the brink of sky and tree trunk, a god could appear.*
> (Pavese 1946: 209)[1]

These are the first sentences of the essay 'On myth, symbol, etcetera' by Italian poet and writer Cesare Pavese. In this short but beautiful text, he connects the special atmosphere of certain places with what he calls 'mythical' significance. Pavese here evokes the image of a mostly natural landscape, but it goes without saying that architectural sites, too, can have this special kind of suggestiveness of meaning – and not only sacred locations, for that matter. It is this idea of the 'mythic' dimension of architecture that I would like to explore. Following Pavese's lead, I will look for the connection between the phenomenology of a space and the workings of myth and symbolism. But before returning to Pavese, I will first discuss the not necessarily obvious connection between 'myth', in its meaning of story, and architecture.

Let us start with the etymological origin of the word. In ancient Greek, the word *muthos* originally simply meant 'speech act' or 'story', but in later ages the term acquired a more specific meaning. Under the word 'mythology', modern literary science and anthropology study the corpus of traditional stories of a specific culture that express a certain cultural understanding of the world and its origins that is deemed fundamental to this particular society. Myths are nodal points of cultural significance; their meaning is never unambiguous because they can combine many functions. By narrating the lives of gods and heroes, they can propagate certain values or behavioural patterns, strengthen the communal spirit, construct a cultural identity – and often they do this all at once. This multifunctional and structuring character of myth is one of the reasons why mythology can be paralleled to architecture. Architecture, too, can perform all of these functions. And as with myth, these functions are never clear-cut, and ultimately everything depends on how its sign-system is interpreted, is used. Both the intricate webs of mythology and architecture provide a society with an infrastructure that can shape actions and thoughts.

And this brings me to a function of myth that I have not mentioned yet, although it is probably the most vital one: to provide us with a fundamental orientation on an existential level. When I use the word 'mythical', it is first and foremost this dimension that I want to address. I would like to illustrate this existential dimension of both myth and architecture by recounting the conclusion of Homer's *Odyssey*. This hugely influential mythic narrative not so coincidentally also contains the oldest testimony in Western literature of an architect of his own work. The architect in question is Odysseus himself, the Greek hero who was to become the epitome of intelligence and cunning. The Odyssey tells the story of his ten-year journey home after the Trojan war. While Odysseus wanders the seas, constantly thrown off course by the wrath of the sea-god Poseidon, in his homeland Ithaca his faithful wife Penelope desperately awaits him, surrounded by suitors who try to force her to remarry. When Odysseus at last does reach Ithaca and kills off the suitors, Penelope barely dares to believe that this man is really her long-awaited husband. Equally as shrewd as her husband, she then comes up with a trick to test his identity. Instead of warmly welcoming him home, she coolly instructs the maidservant to make up Odysseus's bed for him outside the bedchamber. These words deeply disturb the normally self-possessed hero, who immediately asks how the bed could possibly have been removed. Odysseus then proves his true identity by telling the secret story of the bridal chamber: he elaborately describes how he himself built this room, the core of the house, around an ancient olive tree. It was on the trunk of this tree, firmly rooted in the earth, that Odysseus built his marriage bed. Hearing him tell this story, Penelope finally dares to believe her eyes, and both are reunited in the bed. Indeed, the very marriage bed, which has of course remained as unmovable as Penelope's loyalty to Odysseus.

The rooted bed, however, is not simply a metaphor for marital fidelity. It is quite literally the centre around which Odysseus's universe is structured, both spatially and existentially. The Odyssey is a story about the order of the universe reaffirming itself, about the victory of harmony over chaos. (See also Austin 1975: 7) Chaos and the unpredictability of the world are symbolized by the boundless and treacherous sea, while the concentric circles of homeland, house and bridal chamber represent an inherent social and cosmic order. Odysseus's olive tree recalls the archetypal image of the *axis mundi* or world tree that connects underworld, earth and sky. In his book *Existence, Space and Architecture* (1971), Christian Norberg-Schulz has pointed out how architecture in ancient times had the primeval function to express or even create such a cosmic order. He refers to the 'navel of the world', the sacred *omphalos* that was situated in Delphi, the Roman conviction that their capital was the *caput mundi*, and the *Ka'aba* in Mecca that still functions as the centre of the Islamic world. (Norberg-Schulz 1971: 22) Giving a centre to the world meant giving meaning to it, as well as to our dwelling and wandering within this world. As Greek poet Cavafy wrote about the travels of Odysseus: 'Ithaca gave you the marvellous journey.' (Savidis 1992: 36) Norberg-Schulz argues that in pre-modern times, every simple construction symbolically echoed this idea of a cosmic meaning and structure: 'The world, hence, was understood as a large house, as something built, ordered and articulated. And thereby the house helped man to dwell, not only in the house itself, but in the world at large.' (Norberg-Schulz 1971: 108)

For Norberg-Schulz, the failure of 'orthodox modernism' lay in the fact that it neglected this existential function. Inspired by phenomenological philosophy, he argued for the creation of new meaningful, holistic environments through the 'aspects' of identification and orientation. This ambition, of course, is far from unproblematic. Few will challenge the idea that architecture can be used to communicate and even create meaning on an existential level. But critics have often reproached Norberg-Schulz as being naively nostalgic, and negligent of the fact that disorientation and confusion might not only be more authentic expressions of existence in postmodern times, but even of the human condition as such. Even Norberg-Schulz himself remarked that attempts to repeat the significant structures of the past might lead to a kind of superficial historicism. (Norberg-Schulz 1971: 135) It is not my intention here to participate in this discussion on the reception of Norberg-Schulz.[2] What I would like to do, is to pick up on the question of whether there is some timeless symbolism to be found that, applied in architecture, can help to give meaning and structure to our lives. Myth theory – and more in particular the work of German philosopher Hans Blumenberg – has some interesting insights to offer on this idea.

Blumenberg's theory on myth is particularly relevant because he shares some important preoccupations with Norberg-Schulz – which has everything to do with the fact that he, too, is strongly influenced by German phenomenological philosophy, and Heidegger in particular. Blumenberg, too, stresses the inherent need of man to orient himself in the world. Not only architecture, but every form of culture, and myth in particular, is first and foremost an attempt to structure reality, to make it inhabitable. Blumenberg, however, frames this need in the context of a philosophical anthropology that is remarkable darker in tone than Norberg-Schulz's rather optimistic humanism. Borrowing the term from Arnold Gehlen, Blumenberg sees man as a *Mängelwesen*, a 'creature of deficiency'. The deficiency referred to here is man's lack of instincts: while animals cope with their environment through fixed stimulus-response patterns, man has lost this kind of immediate and preordained relation to a certain habitat. Symbols and concepts, the sum of which can be called 'culture', gradually take the place of the instincts in mediating and structuring man's relation to the world. (Blumenberg 1999: 115) This unique capacity for symbolic and hypothetical thinking is man's blessing and his curse at once. On the one hand, it gives him the freedom to choose and create his own life world – both physically and symbolically. But on the other, these symbolic structures by which he orientates himself in the world will always ultimately be arbitrary, artificial. Underneath every significant order we impose on the world looms what Blumenberg calls *Wirklichkeitsabsolutismus*, 'absolutism of reality': the naked confrontation with the indifference and chaos of reality that finds its ultimate expression in the inescapability of death. (Blumenberg 1990: 3-7) Man by nature has no fixed purpose or place in the world, and will ultimately be erased by it. Myth, for Blumenberg, is what keeps the paralyzing anxiety of the absolutism of reality at bay. By personalizing the threatening powers of the world in the shape of spirits and gods and by relating their names to places and stories, he makes these threatening forces addressable, manageable. Gradually, this animistic worldview makes way for a scientific perspective. But even then, every cultural attitude that somehow implicitly endows the world with purpose, order and intention – with existential significance, in other words – at its core stays 'mythic', for Blumenberg.

Blumenberg's idea of 'existential' significance differs from that of Norberg-Schulz in the sense that he stresses the fact that no mythic orientation or identification can ever definitely reconcile the *Mängelwesen* with its life world. At best, our symbolic culture provides a makeshift raft that keeps us afloat on the sea of *Wirklichkeitsabsolutismus*, a raft that we must repair and reconfigure to keep it from falling apart. This is why Blumenberg's major work on the subject is called *Arbeit am Mythos*, '*Work on Myth*' (1990): mythology is not a corpus of stable images and stories with fixed meanings, but the slow and constant organic process of reshaping and reshuffling our existential symbols and metaphors. Odysseus's Ithaca must constantly be rebuilt, reclaimed. And speaking of Odysseus: it is symbolically significant that the Odyssey has an open ending. Lying in their marriage bed, Odysseus immediately tells Penelope about a prophecy that will force him to leave on a long journey once again.

Now how is Blumenberg's myth theory relevant to the discipline of architecture? First of all, his anthropology supports Norberg-Schulz's argument for an existential architecture. But on the other hand, it warns us that we can never take for granted the power of ancient narratives and imagery as such, and that an ineradicable alienation from the world lies at the core of our very need for significance itself. Blumenberg's central statement is that myth is not a product, but a process. The existential comfort and support of mythical images and stories is not an effect of their visual or narrative patterns as such, but lies in the fact that these patterns allow us to leave our passive position in relation to the world, and to *actively* shape and recreate its significance. Translated to the discipline of architecture, this means that we cannot simply reproduce ancient patterns in the hope that they will reconcile us with our existence. Rather, we have to engage ourselves with them and creatively adapt them to fit into our lives.

But does that not contradict the idea of the mythical as something significant, independent of any particular context, something that has become traditional precisely because of its timelessness and universality? This brings us to the core of the question. The idea of tradition and timelessness are indeed important to Blumenberg's conception of myth. But the interesting thing about his theory is that it situates the 'mythical' precisely in the paradoxical overlap between cultural tradition and innovation. In the case of mythology, the idea of timelessness has always been immensely compelling. Even scientific literature often talks about the fact that Greek myths in particular survived because they are carriers of some kind of 'eternal' truth (and in the worst cases also feel authorized to point out exactly what truth this is). Blumenberg, however, turns this logic upside down. He reminds us that the stories that we now know as 'myths' evolved in oral storytelling and were subject to an unsparing process of 'natural selection', which Blumenberg in fact calls the 'Darwinism of words'. (Blumenberg 1990: 159) It is this process, rather than any innate and original human endowment, that gradually gave them their special kind of meaningfulness. Blumenberg calls it *Bedeutsamkeit* or *Pregnanz*, pregnancy of meaning.

Blumenberg, however, stays rather vague when it comes to defining these terms: he states that these concepts 'can be explained but cannot, in the strict sense, be defined'. (Blumenberg 1990: 68) The closest he comes to a definition might be the phrase 'it already means, without any what' (page 75): even before these stories or images are explicitly interpreted, they possess a certain meaningfulness that is even all the more powerful because of its indeterminacy. This has everything to do with the fact that in their age-long evolution, they have amassed and interwoven such a number of associations with universal bodily patterns on the one hand and other cultural signifiers on the other that they have become extraordinarily suited to *suggest* order, *invite* meaning. But at the same time their indefiniteness is all-important: the fact that not one interpretation or association can exhaust them, allows them to transcend every single interpretation in itself and gives them their timeless character. Mythic significance, thus, needs to grow organically from a long cultural tradition. Indeed, Blumenberg claims that myth's pregnancy of meaning is dependent of the fact that 'it has no nameable author . . . it comes from afar and does not lay claim to a particular chronological position.' (Blumenberg 1990: 75) 'Equipping something with significance is not something that we can choose to do,' he states. (page 68) But what we can do is inscribe our own creativity within a certain tradition to harvest this mythical potential. We can think of the advice Zumthor claims to give his students: 'Make it typical, then it will become special.'

For some final remarks on the paradoxical nature of mythic significance, we can finally return to Pavese. Although I cannot recapture the poetic beauty and accuracy of diction of his text here, it is possible to summarize its main points in a few closing remarks. Pavese starts out, as we have seen, by describing the extraordinary mythic appeal of a certain location. But he then immediately goes on to stress that nothing about these places is extraordinary as such, except for the fact that they have been separated from the rest of the world by a certain event – a 'consecration' Pavese calls it – that gave them a unique and at the same time universal significance. To explain himself, Pavese refers to the special aura of places from our childhood memories:

> *The parallel with the childhood years immediately makes clear how the mythical place is not so much a single particular space, the sanctuary, but the common, universal name: the meadow, the forest, the cave, the beach, the house, that in its indeterminacy evokes all the meadows, forests and so on,*

and endows them all with its symbolic tremor. In our childhood memories as well, the meadow, forest and beach are real objects as many others, but at the same time they are the *meadow,* the *beach like they have revealed themselves in their absoluteness and have given form to our imagination. . . . A myth is in fact the norm, the pattern of an event that has occurred once and for all, and derives its value from this absolute uniqueness that lifts it out of time and consecrates it as a revelation. For this reason, it is always at the origin, as in childhood: it is out of time. The man who appeared one day, who knows when, on your hills, who asked for the twigs of a willow and braided a basket, and then was gone – that man would be the most simple and genuine civilizing hero.* (Pavese 1946: 209-210)

In Pavese's view on the mythical there is much that dovetails with Blumenberg's insights: the way Blumenberg sees myth as something that is created by the overlap of tradition and personal reinvention can be clarified by Pavese's paradoxical statement that the universal as a category only comes into being, only becomes imaginable, by a very personal experience – an experience that for him is typically situated in our childhood years. To quote him one last time:

If we think back of any one moment of ecstatic emotion in the face of anything in the world, we find that we are moved because we have been moved before; and we were moved before because one day something appeared to us as transfigured, separated from the rest of the world, a fable, a fantasy that spoke it and contained it.

In other words: the concepts of the mythical, the timeless and the universal only become meaningful, tangible for us through experiences, stories and images that are personal, unique and subjective. These paradoxes of course offer no recipe for the difficult task of creating images or buildings that possess these qualities on an intersubjective level, of course. Pavese, in fact, concludes his text by remarking that only the most devilish characters succeed in objectifying and analysing the mythical without destroying its enchantment. But Blumenberg and Pavese's insights on myth can help us to read and appreciate mythic architecture in its paradoxes. To see the traditional in the innovative, the personal in the universal, and vice versa.

1 Here and elsewhere where I quote Pavese, I use my own translation.

2 I will limit myself to referring to some key articles on the subject: Cacciari 1980, Heynen 1999 and Pérez-Gómez 2007.

Writing the Renaissance Villa

Yvonne Elet

> *For just as you had a villa noteworthy for its frescoing, inlaid work, and handsome mosaic floors, but thought it was not fine enough until its walls were adorned also by your writings, so I, that it might be farther adorned with fruit . . . am sending this to you, recalling as I do the conversations which we held on the subject of the complete villa.*[1]
>
> Varro, On Agriculture, III, 1, 10

Since antiquity, the villa has been the element of the built environment most closely associated with writing and literary production, as the dedication of Varro's first-century BCE treatise perhaps reflects. This association is consonant with the ideology of *otium*, or cultivated leisure, to foster study and learned conversation in shady villa groves, removed from the responsibilities of city life. Authors from ancient Rome and Renaissance Italy to Georgian England celebrated country life, ideology and design in many literary genres, including poetry and prose panegyrics, ekphrastic description, letters, dialogues, architectural treatises, agricultural and husbandry texts, and rhetorical exercises. The evocative first-century letters of Pliny the Younger describing two of his estates provide the *sine qua non* of villa literature, but their renown has overshadowed the extensive array of ancient texts studied by later humanists and writers.[2] There has been little recent attention paid to the relation of villa literature and architecture, either by literary scholars or historians and theorists of architecture.[3]

From the study of Raphael's late masterwork, the early sixteenth-century Villa Madama in Rome, has emerged a little known literary mode involving the dialectic of villa architecture and literature: prescriptive poetry.[4] Several poets visited the construction site of the partially built villa to record their impressions and envision future glories, which evidently emerged as a significant genre in early modern Italy.

Elsewhere, the author has shown how humanists and poets played an important role as collaborators in the architectural design process for this villa from its earliest stages, providing rare and specific glimpses of Raphael's working methods. That study proposes that for Raphael and a variety of associates, design was a dynamic, collaborative process that incorporated different systems of knowledge. This article presents a microcosm of the project, offering first a brief background about Raphael and his villa, before turning to poetic descriptions that open up a genre of Renaissance literature used as a tool of architectural design.

Raphael, who rocketed to prominence as the foremost artist of Renaissance Rome, created a new system of design and a new visual language that would parallel humanist verbal attempts to proclaim the renewal of ancient empire for papal patrons. He deployed his brilliant formulation of this new visual rhetoric in many media, from landscape to tapestries, most notably as painter of the Vatican stateroom frescoes and chief architect of St Peter's. The modern separation of art- and architecture-historical studies, unfortunate for the early modern period in general,[5] especially limits and distorts our understanding of such a polymath. Moreover, Raphael was also unusually engaged in extra-artistic epistemes, active as an archaeologist and in scenographic, philological, and literary projects. An important aspect of Raphael's success lay in his aptitude for collaboration, not only with fellow artists and architects, but also with patrons and literary colleagues. That humanists served as advisors and propagandists is well known, but we have scant knowledge of how they worked with artists and especially with architects, or how ideas that could be verbalized were transformed into visual and spatial forms. Considering architectural design in broad cultural and social contexts allows a new and holistic perspective on Raphael's work, and offers a rare portrait of architectural invention in early modern Rome.

Villa Madama, begun in 1517, was a rare opportunity for Raphael and his associates to conceive architecture and decoration together from the start, and a unique chance to design a new, freestanding building and its landscape. Conceived on a colossal scale, it was to be the first villa to present a Rome of revived ancient grandeur. And had it been completed, it would have looked something like Bénard's visualization (fig. 1), a Palestrina-like complex of building and gardens, terraced down the hillside of Monte Mario in north-western Rome to the Tiber. Commissioned by successive Medici popes as a pleasure villa and also a pastoral Vatican satellite in which to house foreign dignitaries, this significant villa would be one of the most closely watched projects in Renaissance Europe.

Raphael wrote a well-known letter describing his villa project, a Plinian pastiche in which he bodily walks the patron through the proposed complex, describing the extraordinary amenities planned for dining and bathing like an emperor, stabling and watering hundreds of visiting horses, and strolling through extensive gardens. Although the project was interrupted by the artist's death in 1520 and later events and only about half built, it is nonetheless a rich and fascinating ensemble, integrating architecture, landscape and waterworks with a rich decorative programme of sculpture, ancient spoils, stucco reliefs and frescoes (figs. 2, 3.) And as Raphael's partially-completed masterwork, it has continued to be an object of study and pilgrimage for centuries of architects, artists, writers and urban designers, from Serlio and Palladio through Grand Tourists and Prix de Rome winners, down to today.

In addition to Raphael's well-known epistle, several little-known poems describing the villa while it was still a construction site were written by humanists ranging from the famous – for example the legendary improvisatory poet Antonio Tebaldeo and the so-called 'Christian Virgil' Marco Girolamo Vida – to the obscure curial humanist Francesco Sperulo. Of particular interest is Sperulo's 400-line Neo-Latin poem written

in dactylic hexameter in 1519, titled *Villa Iulia Medica Versibus Fabricata* (The villa of Giulio de'Medici constructed in verse). Strikingly, Sperulo's poem is among the most extensive of Renaissance villa descriptions: it is both more detailed and more specific to the actual building than is typical of classical or Renaissance descriptions.

Through various literary devices, Sperulo asserts his own prophetic ability to envision the completed Medici villa before it is built – a kind of prolepsis. The poet also claims to be an overseer, doing the tasks he attributes to his authorial voice, Father Tiber: choosing marbles for the villa from among the ruins, transporting them to the site, directing their placement, managing the site, and proposing decorations. The poet spins long *ekphrases* of mural paintings that he wants added by the painters, and he apostrophizes Raphael, challenging him about the placement of a proposed statue. This all sounds like poetic rhetoric, but it emerges that Sperulo really was an advisor and significant contributor to the project. Moreover, as this article proposes, the basic function of his proleptic poetry was as a conceptual proposal for architecture and decoration – an example of a genre that emerged in the Renaissance, and which is herein called hortatory *ekphrasis*.

It is clear from internal evidence in Sperulo's poem and Raphael's letter that the poet was privy to Raphael's plans, and part of the circle of villa planners. (In fact, the two writings were probably complementary, and perhaps coeval.) Sperulo's formulation

Figure 1. Reconstruction of Villa Madama, after the drawings of Henri Jean Émile Bénard, 1871. Héliogravure, J. Chauvet. (Collection and photo: author)

Figure 2. Villa Madama, Rome. View of the rear façade of the building, adjoining the gardens. (Photo: author)

of visual imagery focuses on proposed paintings and the disposition of sculpture; he describes several particularly significant marbles, for each saying where he got it, what he wants to do with it, and what it signifies. In one case, an entire elevation of the villa was indeed designed around a significant marble described by the poet, confirming that he was involved in the placement of sculpture, and during Raphael's lifetime.[6] This is one of several examples found by the present author in which Raphael, Sperulo and other planners generated early-stage, conceptual programmes that could be realized in spatial, functional and decorative aspects of the built environment.

Of course, poets since Pindar have claimed to build with verse, but here we see a poet doing just that, in an unusually literal way. Sperulo applied his literary skills to a real-life project and did so with a remarkable degree of specificity: his poem pitched in the high diction of Virgilian hexameter was used for the nuts-and-bolts purpose of designing and decorating a building. Sperulo's claim to build the villa in verse was both metaphor and coded proposal, readily accessible to its Renaissance audiences. Moving beyond literary analysis of this poem to consider its function and agency reveals the work's importance as a kind of white paper in Neo-Latin, the *lingua franca* of this circle of Medici patrons and Curial humanists working with Raphael. Thus, Renaissance poetry, in this mode of hortatory *ekphrasis*, could be a utilitarian design tool, used not only for presenting and disseminating plans, but for working out ideas. The agency of wordsmiths is striking in this context; in the mode of praxis, the dialectic of architecture and literature is not an abstract concept, but a mode of thinking, a working discourse.

Conceived in this dynamic, visual-verbal matrix, the Medici villa demonstrates how notions of *ut poesis architectura* were embodied in practice. This is precious evidence, since architectural thinking in early sixteenth-century Italy remains something of a black hole. Virtually no writings survive by the chief architects of the Roman high-Renaissance – Bramante, Raphael and Peruzzi – leaving a major lacuna between the fifteenth-century treatises of Alberti, Filarete and Francesco di Giorgio, and the mid-sixteenth-century works of Serlio and Palladio. But it emerges that early sixteenth-century architectural thought encompassed a broader epistemological scope than was later codified by mid-century writers. (Pérez-Gómez 2006: 155-157)

The notion of a 'programme' in architecture – how verbal ideas may be translated into architectural design – has proved problematic. Manfredo Tafuri addressed the production of meaning in early cinquecento Roman architecture, acknowledging the shared mind-set of architects and humanists, but cautioning against 'naively' assum-

Figure 3. Charles-Louis Clerisseau (1721-1820), Interior of the Villa Madama, c. 1750-1755. (State Hermitage, St Petersburg. Photo: Art Resource)

ing any direct influence of humanist ideas on painters or architects.[7] James Ackerman challenged architecture historians to consider what he called programmes that 'bring architecture into being' – programmes framed by the visions, needs and desires of patrons operating in a specific social and cultural context, their ideas springing from ideologies of which they often were not even conscious (Ackerman 1991: 453-454.) Focusing on Giannozzo Manetti's late-fifteenth-century writings about Florence Cathedral and Pope Nicholas V as a builder, Smith and O'Connor demonstrated the power of architectural *ekphrasis* to convey a patron's goals and visitors' reactions, and thus to give a building meaning (although they are not discussing proleptic *ekphrasis*). But the notion of an architectural programme in Renaissance building remains elusive. At the Medici villa, planners generated early-stage, conceptual frameworks, variously based on ideological, literary or archaeological sources – from basic notions of peace and just rule, to specific points of Leonine ideology – that could be deployed in functional and spatial aspects of architecture. Sperulo was proposing concepts that could be embodied in paintings and the placement of sculptures, as well as spatial constructs, and Raphael's planning encompassed ideas that could be verbalized in addition to traditional architectural concerns of structure, space and style.

Contemporary ideas about the relation of architecture and language figured in other aspects of architectural design as well.[8] This linguistic matrix was important for the development of new architectural vocabularies in the early sixteenth century by Michelangelo in Florence (Elam 2005). And Raphael adapted literary methodologies of creative imitation and selection, articulated by his literary colleagues Pietro Bembo and Baldassare Castiglione, to his design practice (Aurenhammer 1994, Hemsoll 2001 and 2009)[9] Mid-century theorists would focus on parallels between rhetoric and design, equating the *maniere del dire* and the *maniere del edificare,* including Daniele Barbaro, patron of Palladio and editor of Vitruvius, who likened crafting a speech to designing a building.[10] These discussions focus on issues of style, especially the use of ornament and the Orders (ideas canonized by Serlio, who codified sixteenth-century architectural thought), using linguistic analogies or metaphors of architecture. The present study, by contrast, is not focused on analogical theorizing, but on processes of ideation and design for an actual building. It shows that Raphael's rhetorical visuality was not just a matter of linguistic analogy; and in the case of Sperulo's poem, text was not only metaphorical architecture, but also a proposal for creating the real thing. Patterns of invention evidently arose from the practical modality of artists and architects working with humanists.

These proleptic villa descriptions are a fascinating example of the epistemology of the imaginary shaping the real, which has been articulated from Aristotle to Paul Ricoeur.[11]

Figure 4. Jacopo Bertoja (1544-c. 1574), Construction of a Round Temple, study for fresco decorations, Sala d'Ercole, Villa Caprarola depicting its architect, Vignola, in discourse with humanists at a construction site.
(Paris: Musée du Louvre, Cabinet des dessins. Photo: Art Resource)

The Renaissance capacity to think in terms of poetic, fictional architecture was partly shaped by literary traditions: notional *ekphrases* of fictional places from Homer and Virgil to Ariosto; imaginary sites described by Petrarch and Boccaccio; Filarete's description of Sforzinda, blurring the lines between the visionary, the fantastical and a plan for action; and the *Hypnerotomachia Poliphili*, with its rich archaeological and philological sourcebook, and fantastical conflation of a dreamscape with real world places. These sources were an important spur to creative descriptions melding the actual and imagined. Moreover, for Roman humanists, poetry was a social activity; its production and presentation encompassed the collaboration and competition of a talented group, who honed their craft through interaction with each other. Raphael and his humanist collaborators may have recited their villa descriptions in convivia with their Medici patrons, perhaps on-site at the rising villa, their *ekphrases* staged as a kind of performance art, in addition to more informal exchanges, characteristic of this collaborative oral culture (thematised in fig. 4.). There were specific parallels between the way poets' and artists' prophetic fictions were given visual form, in this intellectual culture attuned to plays on reality and illusion in many epistemes. Artists, architects and poets engaged in a meta-conversation about the nature of vision, invention and

the relative powers of word and image to express them; at the same time, their creative visualizations could be harnessed to shape reality.

Especially in Rome, the imaginative encounters of artists, humanists and archaeologists with the fragmentary physical remains of antiquity fostered a culture of re-membering, and of virtual completion. Verbal restoration was a form of imaginative visualization. Additionally, the image of Renaissance Rome came to include not just ancient ruins, but 'new ruins' as well – unfinished building projects, from the Belvedere courtyard to St Peter's.[12] Contemporaries grasped the parallel condition of half-extant ancient and modern works, in ambiguous states of decay or growth, renovation or construction. Conditioned by the physical and conceptual parallel between old and new ruins in Rome, poets could look at a half-extant structure or a fragmentary figural sculpture and bring before the eyes a completed work in perfect form. Thus, it emerges that ekphrastic completion was a literary mind-set, further deployed as a practical tool of architectural planning. It was practiced by humanists accustomed to working with artists and architects engaged in physical restoration as well as the creation of new forms. At the Medici villa, the power of artistic *techne* was coupled with that of ekphrastic agency to bring the villa into being.[13]

Broadening the view of the architectural design process to encompass professionals from different disciplines reveals shared thought patterns. In this collaborative modus operandi, the tools to accomplish the job included words, hexameters, metaphors, drawings and ground plans. At Villa Madama, verbal and visual modes of ideation were not parallel, but inextricably connected. That is not to say that word and image were directly cognate intellectual processes; artists and wordsmiths each had different tools, and separate areas of expertise. But we see them working in tandem throughout the long design process, as ideas and forms evolved dialectically. Nor should we take the design process at Villa Madama as normative; patterns of ideation varied from artist to artist, and even between projects of a given artist, or elements thereof. But this study reveals new possibilities for thinking about the design process, from ideation through representation and building. In an age before architectural drawings were complete technical specifications, words could also be a tool for the projection of ideas. In fact, this scenario demonstrates that architectural drawings could not completely express the idea of a building in this milieu.

This study demonstrates how architecture could embody discursive ideas, including philological and poetic modes of thought. Pérez-Gómez has long called for more attention to the poetic and metaphorical character of architectural thinking and design.[14] At one level, the mutual dependence of architecture and humanism was a legacy of Alberti, who functioned as a counsellor of humanism as much as an architect himself.[15] But here, different patterns of knowledge were harnessed in the service of praxis. This case study illustrates that connections between language/text and the history of architectural design remain a fertile ground for exploration.

These findings prompt an ontological re-conception of Renaissance architectural design as a temporal process incorporating different systems of knowledge. Adopting methodologies applied to texts by Editorial Theorists, we may problematize notions of 'original' or fixed-stage plans, as well as ideas of authorial intention: rather than approaching ground plans and documents as static decrees of intent fixed at an initial point, or any other given moment, we may think of a transformative model of planning, which allows for the collective processes of design, construction and decoration, with evolving, even conflicting visions along the way.[16]

Moreover, the interactive invention of ideas, words and visual forms was a valued cultural matrix in itself: the design process was not simply a means to an end, but part of a larger cultural discourse. The coming-into-being of the villa as an architectural and literary edifice was recorded in proleptic villa descriptions thematising ideation, revealing that this process was considered a narrative worth recording. Beyond practical exigencies, this practice reflects the fundamental importance in Renaissance thought of the Aristotelian notion of the arts, especially architecture, as a process of bringing-into-existence, or *poiesis* (ποιησις). The notion is consonant with the Italian sixteenth-century metamorphic mind-set, indebted to theological as well as natural historical beliefs about the world continually in the process of formation.[17] The present study develops a view of architectural design as a dynamic, collective process that is also self-reflexive, opening a new view of the relation of discursive thought, language and architecture in early-modern Rome, where Raphael and his humanist colleagues collaborated to write, as well as build, the paradigm of the complete villa.

1 'Cum enim villam haberes opere tectorio et intestino ac pavimentis nobilibus lithostrotis spectandam et parum putasses esse, ni tuis quoque litteris exornati parietes essent, ego quoque, quo ornatior ea esse posset fructu . . . haec ad te misi, recordatus de ea re sermones, quos de villa perfecta habuissemus'. See also Fleming for the importance of parietal writing in the early modern period: Juliet Fleming, *Graffiti and the Writing Arts of Early Modern England* (London: Reaktion Books, 2001).

2 Especially the villa poetry of Statius. On villa ideology and classical literary sources about villas, the fundamental source remains Ackerman (1991: 453-494); see also Bernhard Rupprecht, *Villa: Zur Geschichte eines Ideals* (Berlin: De Gruyter, 1966); Sonia Maffei (ed.), *Paolo Giovio: Scritti d'Arte: Lessico ed Ecfrasi* (Pisa: Scuola Normale Superiore, 1999), part I; Littlewood (1987); and Perrine Galand-Hallyn and Carlos Lévy (eds.), *La villa et l'univers familial dans l'Antiquité et à la Renaissance* (Paris: PU de Paris-Sorbonne, 2008). Ancient writers who described villas in verse included Horace, Statius, Martial, Ausonius, Fortunatus, Catullus and Sidonius; and in prose, Horace, Seneca, Cicero, Pliny the Elder, Pliny the Younger, Plutarch, Sidonius and Gregory of Nyssa. On cultivated leisure in villas, see Sara Myers·*Docta otia*: Garden Ownership and Configurations of Leisure in Statius and Pliny the Younger', *Arethusa*, no. 38 (2005), 103-129. On Pliny's villa descriptions, see Pierre de la Ruffinière du Prey, *The Villas of Pliny from Antiquity to Posterity* (Chicago: University of Chicago Press, 1994).

3 In her studies of fifteenth-century Italian villas, Amanda Lillie has problematized the notion of the humanist villa, and called for a nuanced reading of the relation between literary framework and Renaissance villa architecture. See: Amanda Lillie, 'The Humanist Villa Revisited', in: Alison Brown (ed.), *Language and Images of Renaissance Italy* (Oxford: Clarendon Press, 1995). This has been answered most recently by Aksamija (2011: 127-191); Paola Modesti, *Le Delizie Ritrovate: Poggioreale e la villa del rinascimento nella Napoli aragonese* (Florence: Olschki, 2014); and Maria Teresa Sambin de Norcen, *Il cortigiano architetto: Edilizia, politica, umanesimo nel Quattrocento ferrarese* (Venice: Marsilio, 2012).

4 This notion, and the points in this article, are expanded in the author's book in press: Yvonne Elet, *Architectural Invention in Renaissance Rome: Artists and Humanists at Raphael's Villa Madama* (Cambridge and New York: Cambridge University Press, 2016).

5 Discussed by Alina A. Payne, 'Architectural History and the History of Art: A Suspended Dialogue', *Journal of the Society of Architectural Historians*, no. 58 (1999), 292-299; Rykwert (2008); and Kathleen Weil-Garris Brandt, 'The Relation of Sculpture and

Architecture in the Renaisssance', in: Henry A. Millon and Vittorio Magnago Lampugnani (eds.), *The Renaissance from Brunelleschi to Michelangelo: The Representation of Architecture* (Milan: Bompiani, 1994), 74-99. For shifting boundaries between architecture and the representational arts in modern and postmodern art, taking off from the work of Rosalind Krauss, see: Spyros Papapetros and Julian Rose (eds.), *Retracing the Expanded Field: Encounters between Art and Architecture* (Cambridge, MA and London: MIT Press, 2014).

6 For detailed analysis of the poem and its relation to specific marbles, see: Yvonne Elet, 'Papal *Villeggiatura* in Early Modern Rome: Poetry, Spoils, and Stucco at Raphael's Villa Madama', PhD dissertation (New York University, 2007), and Elet, *Architectural Invention*, op. cit.

7 '... an almost precise correspondence can be established between the aesthetic ideas expressed in *The Courtier* and the artistic achievement of the circle in direct contact with the persons who appear in the dialogue. Obviously one should not force the analogy. It would be naïve to propose an *influence* exerted by the ideas of Bembo or Castiglione on painters and architects; nor can the respective aesthetic theories elaborated by these intellectuals be discerned by observing works of art [which presumably express them]. Rather, we can best explore this terrain by using the concept of diffuse mentalities as our guide; metalanguages that obliquely traverse the spaces of architectural language, conditioning their organization and liberating their potentials.' Tafuri (2006: 7).

8 Among many recent works on the subject of *ut lingua architectura*, see especially Alina A. Payne, *The Architectural Treatise in the Italian Renaissance: Architectural Invention, Ornament and Literary Culture* (Cambridge and New York: Cambridge University Press, 1999) and *Ut poesis architectura:* Tectonics and Poetics in Architectural Criticism Circa 1570', in: Alina Payne, Ann Kuttner and Rebekah Smick (eds.), *Antiquity and Its Interpreters* (Cambridge and New York: Cambridge University Press, 2000), 145-158; Clarke and Crossley (2000); Pérez-Gómez (2006); and Eriksen (2001), who presents a 'topomorphic reading' of spatial patterns in the composition of poetry.

9 Cf. Guido Beltramini, 'Pietro Bembo e l'architettura', in: Guido Beltramini, Davide Gasparotto, and Adolfo Tura (eds.), *Pietro Bembo e l'invenzione del Rinascimento* (Venice: Marsilio, 2013), 25, who invokes Tafuri's caution of the risks of direct translation from one discipline to another.

10 Although as noted by Van Eck (2007: 37-46 and passim), Barbaro's analogy is an abstract one, with the ultimate goal of rationalizing architecture as an Aristotelian *scienza*.

11 For the phenomenology of fiction as 'productive' or 'reality shaping', see: Ricoeur (1979: 123-141).

12 Proposed by Christof Thoenes, 'St. Peter als Ruine. Zu einigen Veduten Heemskercks', *Zeitschrift für Kunstgeschichte*, no. 49 (1986), 481-501, and discussed by Suzanne B. Butters, 'Figments and Fragments: Julius II's Rome', in: Jill Burke (ed.), *Rethinking the High Renaissance: The Culture of the Visual Arts in Early Sixteenth-century Rome* (Farnham, UK: Ashgate, 2012); and Fausto Testa, '"ut ad veterum illa admiranda aedificia accedere videatur." Il Cortile del Belvedere e la retorica politica del potere pontificio sotto Giulio II', in: Francesco Paolo Di Teodoro (ed.). *Donato Bramante. Ricerche, Proposte, Riletture* (Urbino: Accademia Raffaello, 2001)

13 Among the vast bibliography on *ekphrasis*, see Murray Krieger, *Ekphrasis: The Illusion of the Natural Sign* (Baltimore: The Johns Hopkins University Press, 1992), 11, on the 'ekphrastic impulse' as symptomatic of the desire 'to have the world captured in the word'; and for Renaissance architectural *ekphrasis*, see: Christine Smith, *Architecture in*

the Culture of Early Humanism: Ethics, Aesthetics, and Eloquence 1400-1470 (New York and Oxford: Oxford University Press, 1992), and Christine Smith and Joseph O'Connor, *Building the Kingdom: Giannozzo Manetti on the Material and Spiritual Edifice* (Tempe, AZ: ACMRS and Brepols, 2006).

14 Pérez-Gómez (2006), and Alberto Pérez-Gómez, *Architecture and the Crisis of Modern Science* (Cambridge, MA: MIT Press, 1983), Introduction. This call has resonated with thinkers interested in the relation of history, theory and practice of architecture, seeking to understand metaphorical and symbolic aspects of architectural design in historical context and their applications for contemporary practice; see especially the essays in Soumyen Bandyopadhyay et. al (eds.), *The Humanities in Architectural Design: A Contemporary and Historical Perspective* (London and New York: Routledge, 2010).

15 Among the vast literature on Alberti, see especially Smith, *Architecture in the Culture of Early Humanism*, op. cit.; and Nikolaos-Ion Terzoglu, 'The Human Mind and Design Creativity: Leon Battista Alberti and *lineamenta*', in Bandyopadhyay et al., op. cit., on the dialectic of humanistic inquiry and design ideas in Alberti's thinking.

16 For an interesting analogue to these ideas, Goffi argues for a new paradigm uniting architecture and conservation in a diachronic understanding of a building, using evolving designs for St Peter's. She defines mnemic architecture as 'built conservation always *in-the-making*', Federica Goffi, *Time Matter(s): Invention and Re-Imagination in Built Conservation: The Unfinished Drawing and Building of St. Peter's, The Vatican* (Farnham, Surrey and Burlington, VT: Ashgate, 2013), 8; and rejects the notion of 'still shot' frozen moments, instead arguing for a phenomenological approach to these palimpsestic transformations.

17 Michel Jeanneret, *Perpetual Motion: Transforming Shapes in the Renaissance from da Vinci to Montaigne*, translated by Nidra Poller (Baltimore and London: The Johns Hopkins University Press, 2001), 197, notes the surprising number of Renaissance literary masterworks that were presented as works in progress, 'in the image of a universe in perpetual gestation'.

Fox/River/House: A Translation

Nora Wendl

Truth and Its Equivalent

On 31 December 1950, Dr Edith Farnsworth prepared to spend her first evening in a glass house. (Fig. 1)

The meadows surrounding the house were silent and white with old and hardened snow. The winter plains reflected the light of a bare, 60-watt bulb on an extension cord. Spots and strokes of paint dappled the expanses of the glass walls, and the sills were covered with ice. She made something to eat, and prepared to sleep on a couple of foam mattresses thrown on the floor. It was an uneasy night, she would later write in her memoir, due both to the novel exposure of the glass walls and to what she described as 'the architect's implacable intentions'. Though familiar to us as the Mies van der Rohe-designed Farnsworth House in rural Plano, Illinois, this is not the glass house that we know.

Begun in 1947 and completed in 1951, the glass house that we know is the one designed as a structure unlike any other. Its novel details and connections are by now familiar: I-beams that seem to float – connected to the house by a self-concealing process of plug-welds, erector seats, expert sanding and painting – and thin steel window mullions that act as tensile members to quietly connect the floor and roof. It is a house in which nothing is what it seems, structurally, so that the house appears to float five feet above its meadow. This is the glass house as historicized from the outside, looking in.

But as we look at it from the outside, it changes. The glass is sometimes clear, sometimes occluded, and sometimes it projects our own body back to us as a spectral image. This is because glass can only feign clearness, which 'is so eminently one

Figure 1. Nora Wendl (1980-), *Glass House (North Elevation) 2*, 2013. Chromogenic print, 60.96 x 91.44 cm.

of the characteristics of truth, that often it even passes for truth itself', in the words of philosopher Joseph Joubert.[1] The history of architecture often attempts to be that glass. But how can we account, within history, for the non-objectivity of architecture, its plasticity and fluctuation? Through what opening does one draw out of architecture the words that might express it? Better, perhaps, than calling what we will write about architecture after its construction and its inhabitation a history, is to call it a translation.

Within architectural discourse, 'translation' is typically used to describe each successive leap from one form of representation to another – from sketch to drawing board, from orthogonal representation to three-dimensional model, until we arrive at 'the final step . . . the translation from representation . . . to the thing proper, to the architectural object in its full materiality . . .' (Rykwert 1998: 67). But translations have no end, and after architecture come words – the very materiality of history. These words must do more than trace built form. Alberto Perez Gomez and Louise Pelletier write towards 'the possibilities of building architecture as a poetic translation, not a prosaic transcription, of its representations', suggesting that even in the final iteration of these

successive leaps, the final architectural form is, itself, still a translation. (Perez-Gomez and Pelletier 1997: 8). If we believe that architecture is the result of myriad translations from one form of representation to the next, and that each translation retains some semblance of its original meaning, then we must believe that even in its built form, we have not reached the end of architecture's translatability. Architecture must still carry some truth beyond form.

This truth is not an equivalent truth. For instance, the translation of a poem is not a word-for-word obligation. It 'consists of converting, turning (*convertere, vertere, transvertere*)', taking the original un-literally. (Derrida 2001: 180). The most essential quality of a translation is to transmit the essence of the original. And '[d]o we not generally regard as the essential substance of a literary work what it contains in addition to information – as even a poor translator will admit – the unfathomable, the mysterious, the "poetic," something a translator can produce only if he is also a poet?' (Benjamin 1969: 70). In a translation, we seek an elusive truth – one that can survive the transmission from one medium or language to another. (Fig. 2).

Seeking truth beyond form is precisely the reason translations are feared. *Traduttore, traditore*, translator, traitor.[2] Every translation is, indeed, a necessary corruption of the original. A translator's note at the beginning of a translated text will acknowledge this: 'Any errors found in this text are my own.' A translation is a truth that is always

Figure 2. Nora Wendl (1980-), *Glass House (Porch with Fu Dog)*, 2013. Chromogenic print, 60.96 x 91.44 cm.

doomed to being dirtied by the hands of the person doing the converting. But why fear the loosening of a few joints in the act of translating architecture beyond its built form? Why fear a translation of architecture that begins from the interior, from a woman making soup on a hot plate, under the blank stare of a 60-watt light bulb, alone in a glass house? It has already been established that a translator, an intermediary body who is *not* the architect, is required in the production of architecture, in the leaping from translation to translation, which cannot be accomplished by the architect alone. In writing the myriad histories of architecture, let's accept the task of the translator. Let's accept that we have always been instruments of converting buildings from one form to another, and that in translating built form into language, we have always been implicit in the result, the translation, the *turned* words, regardless of how they are named: history, fact, truth, fiction.

Edith Farnsworth: Translator

In the 20 years that Dr Farnsworth spent in her glass house, she dedicated herself to translating the work of several Italian poets into English – Penna, Pierro, D'Annunzio,

Sbarbo, Ungaretti, Montale and others. By the end of her life, she had produced a manuscript comprised of these translations – *Fifteen Italian Poets of the Twentieth Century*. Rejected by a publisher shortly before her death, it never reached an audience.

The images that Farnsworth rendered in these unpublished poems could easily be attributed to the Farnsworth House and its context – whether physical, or even socio-historical, if one chose to draw from the rumors of Dr Farnsworth's unsubstantiated romantic relationship with Mies van der Rohe. A survey of themes in these poems reveals nature as seen in the form of

> 'a renascent moon, attenuated sky, swallows, dawn, the twilight and the night.'[3]

Animal life in

> 'a shivering of wings.'[4]

Distanced love –

> 'Never did you think of leaving behind
> some trace of you in prose or verse,'[5] –

and domestic confinement:

> 'what sorrow, knowing you to be alone and closed
> within your fragile house open
> to the eyes like glass.'[6] (Fig. 3).

Figure 3. Nora Wendl (1980-), *Glass House (Entrance)*, 2013. Chromogenic print, 60.96 x 91.44 cm.

However, what is featured most prominently in the poems that Farnsworth translated are themes of the object and its reflection – which appear as both literal constructs in the poems and as theoretical constructs, as in her introduction to the poems of Eugenio Montale:

> *See the ricochet of rings, the subtle shift of dimly glimmering life from external to internal and then outward again, of eyes looking from outside inward before they alight like moths upon the poet's dark window and become 'you' to lean out toward a light now cosmic and burning low.*[7]

Where else could this ricochet of rings be more possible than in a glass house? Who is 'I' and who is 'you', when speaking to a figure in a glass house on top of whose image one's own is mapped? Parallel to 'I' is the elusive 'you', which in each poem, like a reflection, seems to alternate meaning – from the distanced lover, to the impossible-to-obtain love interest, to the dead loved one, to the person observing from a distance. In Farnsworth's words, this is the great conundrum:

> *. . . the 'tu,' the 'you,' the inspiration at the same time of both poetry and life. 'You' is one or it may be all; it is the companion, even though . . . it may be personally unknown. It is the creature, or the essence, to be adored, the loss of which is the most intolerable . . . and yet, although 'you' elicits a high poetic intensity in many poems, it is hard to think of an example of a love poem in any previously accepted sense. And once in a while, by a fulminating ricochet, 'you' becomes evil . . . By another rebound of paradoxes 'you' may become 'I' . . .*[8]

What does the translation of these poems, many of which are in fact love poems, have to do with the matter of architecture? Extending from 'I' to 'you,' the love poem makes tangible the space between us, between 'I' – the builder of love's language – and 'you,' the inhabitant, (willing or not) of that space. In a love poem the poet constructs a world in which the beloved is absent – and the love poem operates to either entice the beloved's inhabitation of the interior of the poem (and thus of the poet's world), or it mourns the impossibility of the beloved ever inhabiting that space. The love poem is a proxy for inhabitable space, poetry at its most spacious. The well-constructed love poem either convinces the beloved to inhabit the poet's world, or erects a (unoccupied) monument to love's demise. Such, perhaps, was the Farnsworth House.

Whether Dr Farnsworth thought of herself explicitly as a translator of the glass house is unclear. It is clear from the dozens of folders in her archive, the countless reams of

Figure 4. Nora Wendl (1980-), *Glass House (Voyeur)*, 2013. Chromogenic print, 60.96 x 91.44 cm.

paper and careful calculations of words from English to Italian that pepper her journals that she did think of herself as a translator of poetry. And it was to this effort that she dedicated much of her time in the Farnsworth House. And yet, despite her fluency in Italian and her correspondence with many of the authors to ensure her translations were accurate, Farnsworth acknowledges her own limitations in her introduction to the unpublished collection: '. . . This volume does not pretend to be a complete listing, or a perfect one,' she writes.

Neither complete, nor perfect: perhaps this is the most accurate way to refer to the translation of knowledge from building into text, from text into the narratives that comprise history. What follows is such a translation of archive into architectural history: original statements found in Farnsworth's archive, including a myriad of manuscripts, correspondence, journals, memoir and poems, are mined for phrases and statements, then assembled into a poem that approximates Farnsworth's history with the design, building and inhabiting of the Farnsworth House from 1947 to 1971. (Fig. 4)

Fox/River/House, *a translation of the Farnsworth House* [Excerpt]

1.
It lies with the translator to dim the neon lights and return us to the mysteries of our nature and our past.[9]

2.
There is no error of nature, no deadlock of the world
no failed link, no thread which disentangled
could draw us into the midst of truth.[10]

3.
My impression is
detail, probably too much

all my life is in my eyes[11]

rotting clapboards   house and farm buildings
two black sugar maples   hackberries, lindens   black walnuts
rippling river   milk-white heron

how much he understood remained problematical. We moved back to the sitting room.

The house
like a storm, flood, or other act
of God.[12]

4.
I make only pilgrimages
and know them to be such.[13]

slip in
between the swelling roots

below, infinite dark
darker
more infinite, and a familiar pain
massive, beneath feet.[14]

5.
The human desire for beauty is as inevitable
as the desire for sex or religion and the history of art
is the chronicle of its redefinition.

When you understand all about the sun
And all about the atmosphere
and all about the rotation of the earth
you may still miss the radiance of the sunset.

We still seem to need temples
Of one kind or another.[15]

6.
I came across modern
houses hanging
over cliffs and ravines or built out over water
on shelves
and coffee tables.[16]

Machines for living
so slow
in an out-of-the-way spot.

7.
Soft, and strange to the ear
  arrhythmic cells
      form comes
      by division, and division

    a cavity appears, and soon
    the equated pushing of two sides
    a bilateral symmetry of scattered islands
    come to view and fuse
    to make the vital vessels

a single-chambered heart.[17]

8.
We studied various
and drove tentative
stakes.[18]

9.
The man we see might be considered 'the visible,'
that exceedingly small segment of the spectrum which lies between
the ultra-violet and the infra-red
the rest of his being recedes, infinitely,
into the shorter rays of his deep, his unconscious, his past life
his predecessors

longer and longer waves of seed.[19]

10.
    already
I
    tremble with thirst
And am afraid

I'd fling myself upon you
I'd suck
in one long gulp
without ever drawing breath,
like a drunk[20]

11.
We can be absolutely certain
only about things
that we do not understand.[21]

12.
I was distressed that the hand-made trees gave the observer no idea of the great lindens, maples, and hackberries with which it was to stand. But it was the pivotal point of the exhibit, the prototype of new and important elements in American architecture.[22]

13.
we face each other talk modules, proportions, modules
proportions. His glass in place half-cloud eyes, his face
impassive as a landscape or a past life[23]

14.
a man wants to know
about his hopes for immortality
snowflakes on the window salt crystals on the dinner table
'I want to know what I have to expect after death.'[24]
What story do you want?
you climbed, you suffered and you conquered
it made a hero of you,
you transcended.
But now something has happened.
Leopards broke into the temple.[25]
Listen instead to the story of the
wall of bricks accidentally fused in the kiln[26]
solidarity transcending
the familiar castes of the dead.

15.
I have been having some shadowy doubts concerning the sanctity of the rectangle.[27]

16.
We
  trailed around
upon the lower of our two horizontal planes,
observing the potential
promisingly
trees and meadows,
as we saw them from our stone shelf,
faded into a vision.

In the sky something strange began –
there floated a pink celestial body
like some pale moon,
supremely large.

We stared
slipping out of orbit

after so many years in the same one
floating beautiful
uncanny
over the meadow
the unfinished building.[28]

17.
Certain details which could not be laid to modern technology bothered me.
The absence of a second door or of any window.
I couldn't
without an open window
I wouldn't
without at least one window
two ways of getting in or out
In case of fire, or
  glass trap.
the 'open plan':

he, or she, could sleep on a sofa
or
I would spread a mattress on the travertine floor.
We would cohabit a sort of three-dimensional sketch,
I in my 'sleeping space'
he in his
lest discomfort and depression
should drive us together.[29]

18.
In the end I got
caught between two horizontal planes.[30]

19.
Do you remember the story of the oil slick –
in the Baltic, wasn't it? –
that trapped the seagulls so they couldn't get off the surface,
and the boys who stoned them from the shore.[31]

20.
The abyss
        a familiar concept
        a feature of the backyard.

We could have paid more loyal attention
    defended resolutely our independence
    and clarity of mind
        kept something of what had been learned.

        In this climate
                we have been easy to control.[32]

21.
Something has happened to nature.
Possibly, science has laid calculated hands on her
Possibly her gods have died. She rubs
her muzzle on the windowpane,
domesticated.

And love –
Everybody knows what happened there.
It died from exposure.

These are grave deterrents.[33]

22.
It shouldn't be this way, but I'm afraid that this story is going to end badly.
Perhaps he is not clairvoyant
but simply more

    than anybody I have ever known.
Perhaps it was never a collaborator
so to speak
that he wanted.[34]

23.

The telephone rang.

It would have been easier to face
the raw house
the seamy flood-meadows
the young moon over black river.

How quick a river can rise

and flood the barn
where you stand on the rafters
catching fish
with a pitchfork.[35]

24.
Does the river see the house

    where this body lives?

If driven from the house
I will come to you,

slow river.[36]

The few small words which I address to you
seek to be new, but they are ancient.[37]

25.
I looked about me
        it seemed to me that a long hand
        would stretch out from the ceiling
        and draw me up into the dark
        like a feather snatched by the wind.

        By morning
        I had forgotten everything.
the sun was tangling in the trees.[38]

The day gave out no sound
but the stones, whistling.[39]

26.
The first fire lights bring out the shadows of swelling buds.[40]

27.
            soften these stones
            open my eyes
                        blind
            as a ball of coal
            and   full of thistles
                        (s)he's going blind
                        they said.[41]

28.
The simpler of those that came to look
expected to find the glass box afloat;
moored to mystic columns
enclosing mystic space

all the walls turned to air

rotting in an August noon.[42]

29.
Space
is dark, windless, leafless and unblooming
in the micro-universe.[43]

30.
House
is a memory
I reached once on foot.[44]

31. pages
have a limiting finality.
Yet it gives me little consolation
to know that,
close together or apart
we are one thing.

still the fact remains
that something happened, perhaps some trifling thing
which is everything.[45]

32. You've come
and brought me a fine thing,

these pins of light which blind me.[46]

1 This observation is found in Maggie Nelson, *Bluets* (Seattle and New York: Wave Books, 2009), 48. Here, Nelson describes Joubert as 'the French "man of letters" who recorded countless such fragments in notebooks for forty years in preparation for a monumental work of philosophy that he never wrote'.

2 It is believed that this phrase was first applied to the French by irate Italians who felt that many French-language translations of Dante were not faithful to the beauty or accuracy of the text. This clever phrase also refers, more broadly, to what is known as a 'lexical gap': the absence of a word or idiomatic phrase in translation from one language to another.

3 Gabriele D'Annunzio, 'Along the Affrico', trans. Edith Farnsworth, unpublished. Midwest MS Farnsworth. Newberry Library, Chicago.

4 Ibid.

5 Eugenio Montale, 'Xenia', trans. Edith Farnsworth, unpublished. Midwest MS Farnsworth.

6 Albino Pierro, 'What Labored Breath', trans. Edith Farnsworth, unpublished. Midwest MS Farnsworth.

7 Eugenio Montale. *Provisional Conclusions: A Selection of the Poetry of Eugenio Montale*, trans. Edith Farnsworth (Chicago: Henry Regnery Company, 1970), n.p.

8 Ibid.

9 Edith Farnsworth, 'Introduction to Albino Pierro', in: *Fifteen Italian Poets of the Twentieth Century*, trans. Edith Farnsworth, unpublished. Midwest MS Farnsworth.

10 Eugenio Montale. 'The Lemon Trees', trans. Edith Farnsworth, unpublished, no date. Midwest MS Farnsworth.

11 Camillo Sbarbo, 'Pianissimo', trans. Edith Farnsworth, unpublished, no date. Midwest MS Farnsworth.

12 Edith Farnsworth, *Memoirs*, unpublished. Midwest MS Farnsworth.

13 Edith Farnsworth, 'From Out the Eucalyptus', unpublished, no date. Midwest MS Farnsworth.

14 Edith B. Farnsworth, 'To G.W.', in: *Northwestern Tri-Quarterly* (Fall, 1960), 8.

15 Edith B. Farnsworth, 'The Poet and the Leopards', in: Ibid., 7.

16 Edith Farnsworth, *Memoirs*, unpublished. Midwest MS Farnsworth.

17 Edith Farnsworth, 'Birth of the Heart', unpublished, no date. Midwest MS Farnsworth.

18 Edith Farnsworth, *Memoirs*, unpublished, no date. Midwest MS Farnsworth.

19 Ibid.

20 Albino Pierro, *Nu Belle Fatte: Una Bella Storia: A Beautiful Story*, trans. Edith Farnsworth (Milan: All'insegna del Pesce D'oro, 1976), 42.

21 Edith Farnsworth, *Memoirs*, unpublished. Midwest MS Farnsworth.

22 Ibid.

23 Ibid.

24 Ibid.

25 Edith B. Farnsworth, 'The Poet and the Leopards', in *Northwestern Tri-Quarterly* (Fall, 1960), 7.

26 Edith Farnsworth, *Memoirs*, unpublished. Midwest MS Farnsworth.

27 Ibid.

28 Ibid.

29 Ibid.

30 Ibid.

31 Ibid.

32 Ibid.

33 Edith B. Farnsworth, 'The Poet and the Leopards', in *Northwestern Tri-Quarterly* (Fall, 1960), 7.
34 Edith Farnsworth, *Memoirs*, unpublished. Midwest MS Farnsworth.
35 Ibid.
36 Cartolerie Pineider, untitled poem, trans. Edith Farnsworth, unpublished, no date. Midwest MS Farnsworth.
37 Pierro Metaponto, 'If in Paradise You Would', trans. Edith Farnsworth, unpublished, no date. Midwest MS Farnsworth.
38 Edith Farnsworth, *Memoirs*, unpublished. Midwest MS Farnsworth.
39 Albino Pierro. 'Il M_____', trans. Edith Farnsworth, unpublished, no date. Midwest MS Farnsworth.
40 Edith Farnsworth, *Memoirs*, unpublished. Midwest MS Farnsworth.
41 Pierro Metaponto, 'Love', trans. Edith Farnsworth, unpublished, no date. Midwest MS Farnsworth. Pierro Albino. 'When I Was a Child', trans. Edith Farnsworth, unpublished, no date. Midwest MS Farnsworth.
42 Edith Farnsworth, *Memoirs*, unpublished. Midwest MS Farnsworth.
43 Edith Farnsworth, 'Arsenio', unpublished, no date. Midwest MS Farnsworth.
44 Pierro Metaponto, 'The Vigliotte', trans. Edith Farnsworth, unpublished, no date. Midwest MS Farnsworth.
45 Eugenio Montale, 'Xenia II', trans. Edith Farnsworth, unpublished, no date. Midwest MS Farnsworth.
46 Pierro Albino, 'You've Come', trans. Edith Farnsworth, unpublished, no date. Midwest MS Farnsworth.

3 OPENNESS

Narrative Experiments in Architecture

Narrative as an Educational Approach

Literary Methods in Architectural Education

Wim van den Bergh and Mark Proosten

> *Art, be it painting, literature or architecture, is the remaining shell of thought. Actual thought is of no substance. We cannot actually see thought, we can only see its remains. Thought manifest itself by its shucking or shedding of itself: it is beyond confinement.* (Hejduk 1988: 340)

With these philosophical words John Hejduk[1], by then the Dean of the Irwin S. Chanin school of architecture of the Cooper Union, concluded a short story that he used as a preface to *Education of An Architect*, a book illustrating the educational methods used at the Cooper Union. In fact in his own teaching Hejduk often used narratives as a kind of metaphor to convey certain key ideas to his students (as the one in this quote). The anecdotal story that he used in this preface, recalled a personal observation made when he was teaching in Texas and it reads as follows:

> *During a certain season in Texas, at dusk, some tree trunks seem to be phosphorescent . . . they give off a dull, blazing light. Upon close scrutiny it is found that the trunk of the tree is completely covered with discarded shells which were the outer body of certain insects. The startling fact is that the shell is intact; the form is exactly as it was when its original inhabitant was inside, with one difference. The inside has left, leaving the outer form which looks like an x-ray, producing the luminous effect. Suddenly we hear a chorus of sound coming from the dark leaves above. It is the sound of the insects hidden in the tree in their new metaphysical form. What is strange about the phenomenon is that we can see the insects' shell forms clinging to the tree, empty shells, a form that life has abandoned. While we fix our eyes on these apparitions, we hear the sound of the insect in its new form hidden in the trees. We can hear it but we cannot see it. In a way, the sound we hear is a soul sound.* (Hejduk: 8)

In Hejduk's educational approach this type of narratives played an important role not only to convey his own reflections (the remains of his own thoughts) to his students, but also to get them to reflect on the thoughts behind their own work in an unobtrusive way.

> *His colleague the poet David Shapiro, curious about Hejduk's way of teaching, once asked him in an interview: 'So how do you teach architecture?' And Hejduk, with his characteristic precise and meaningful choice of words, answered: 'Osmosistically, by osmosis'* (Hejduk 1991: 59).

It seems that the term 'osmosis' he used here refers to the common English expression 'learning by osmosis', which for instance means the way very young children unconsciously learn to master a spoken language simply by being immersed in their environment. So in this case osmosis would stand for 'any gradual, often unconscious, process of assimilation or absorption, as of ideas', as the dictionary informs us. What, however, did Hejduk mean when he consciously turned the phrase '*learning* by osmosis' into '*teaching* by osmosis'? The subtlety and calculation with which Hejduk chose the word 'osmosis' (from Greek *ôsmos*, to push, or to thrust) can be seen in the continuation of his answer to David Shapiro's question:

> *I never draw for the student or draw over their work and I never tell them what to do. I try, in fact, to draw them out. In other words draw out what's inside them and just hit a certain key point whereby they can develop their idea.*

By playing with the words 'draw' and 'drawing out' (as the opposite of the 'push' and 'thrust' of the Greek *ôsmos*), he not only indicated to the reversal in osmotic direction that takes place between '*learning* by osmosis' and '*teaching* by osmosis', but he also seems to allude to the root of education *per se*, which is related to the Latin verb *educere*, to bring or lead out (from *ex-*, out + *ducere,* to lead).
Accordingly, Hejduk's answer that he '*teaches* by osmosis' could be interpreted as a form of teaching that explicitly tries not to inscribe the mind (and instruct the hand) of the student with the teacher's own pre-existing knowledge (and/or skills), but rather seeks a manner of educating that tries to guide the student in awakening his own sub-conscious potential by (and of) himself. What Hejduk in his interview with David Shapiro meant with 'just hit a certain key point' is that he would take such key points and wrap them up in narratives like wrapped sweets in pieces of cellophane paper, whereby it would be the act of unwrapping, the unravelling of the narratives by the students themselves, that would *draw them out*. It is a form of teaching that regards the accumulation of knowledge to be first of all based on personal reflection and the acquiring of skill to be grounded in personal experience, that is, a way of teaching that tries to lead the student towards a direct and personal form of understanding.

A form of teaching that also the chair for 'Wohnbau und Grundlagen des Entwerfens' (Dwelling and Basics of Design) of the Faculty of Architecture at the RWTH Aachen University, wholeheartedly subscribes to.

While contemplating Hejduk's methods of using narrative in architectural education and looking for ways to employ narrative in our own teaching, we stumbled over an intriguing definition of narrative that is closely related to the idea of dwelling in space and time. It was provided to us by H. Porter Abbott, the eminent theorist on narrative of the University of California Santa Barbara. In his *The Cambridge Introduction to Narrative* he writes: 'Narrative is the principal way in which our species organizes its understanding of time.' And he further explains this definition with:

> *. . . wherever we look in this world we seek to grasp what we see not just in space but in time as well. Narrative gives us this understanding; it gives us what could be called shapes of time. Accordingly, our narrative perception stands ready to be activated in order to give us a frame or context for even the most static and uneventful scenes.* (Abbott 2008: 10)

Architecture, as we all know, has to do with the design of these spatial 'shapes of time' for 'even the most static and uneventful scenes' that Porter Abbott speaks about, but on the other hand we also know that architecture deals with designing the temporal

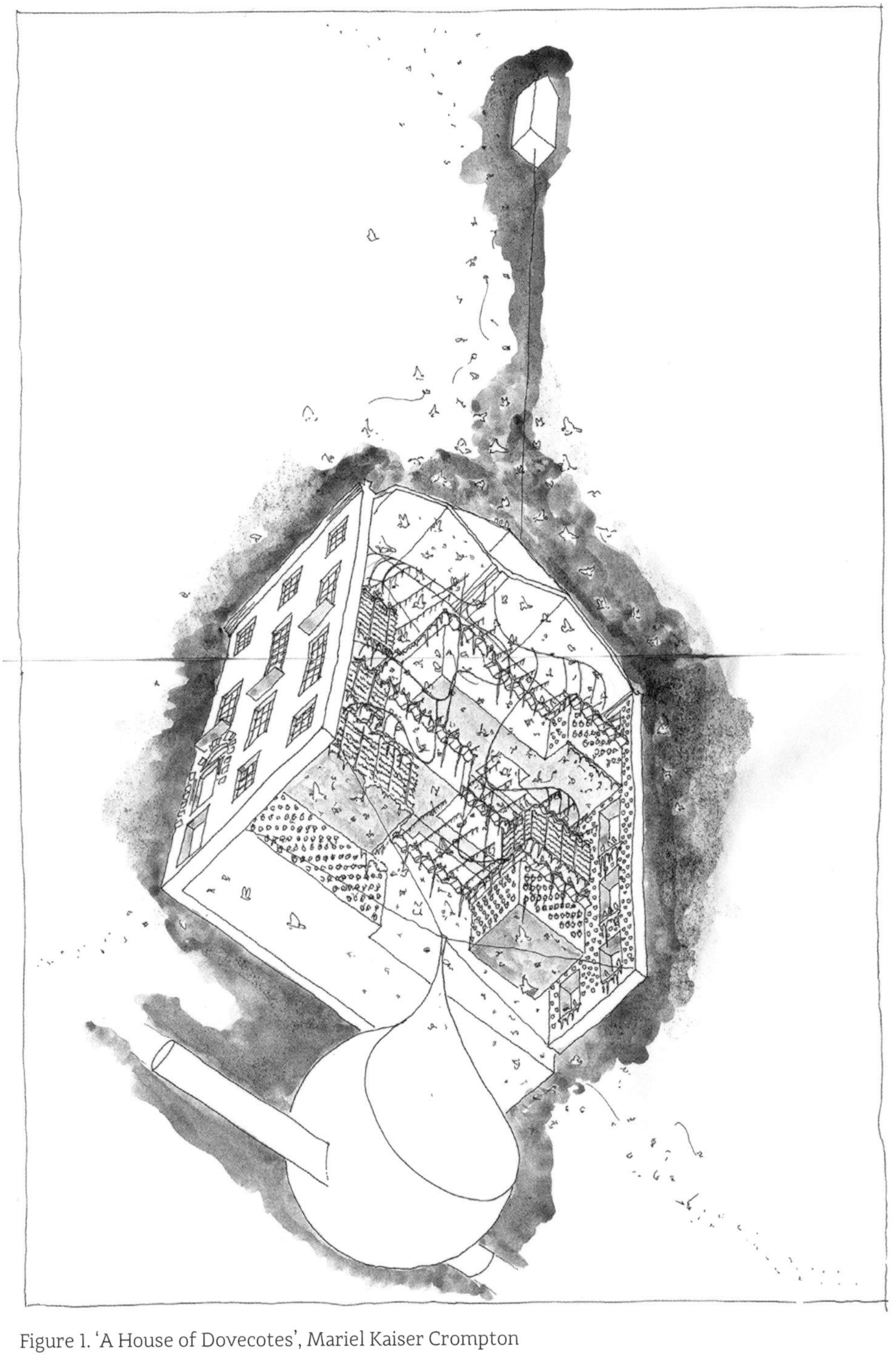

Figure 1. ‘A House of Dovecotes’, Mariel Kaiser Crompton

'frame or context' in which activities can take place. For many years we observed that students, while making a design, mainly concentrated on getting the first aspect, the 'static and uneventful scenes' right. In other words getting their spaces in terms of square metres, function and distribution organized. This would ultimately result in a kind of schematic design mainly in terms of plans with some furnishings to indicate the function of the spaces, and some sections and elevations to indicate the design's volume and form.

Such a design would probably work on the level of its distribution of functions, but on the level of 'use' it would be without any 'life', or, to use the words of Porter Abbott, without any 'shape of time' or 'narrative'.

We further observed that for the students, architecture was initially very much something external and abstracted, a kind of 'form' and not something internal, spatial and filled with atmospheres and activities.

In terms of architectural education, getting this first aspect sorted out would be fine for a student's first steps in learning how to design. Thus, in a matter of learning by doing, acquiring the basic skills for solving a small programme in terms of a spatial design that has to house specific functions. But too often one sees that beyond this initial point in learning how to design, the student would only be confronted with design tasks to house evermore complex functions and programmes.

In terms of architectural education this might further develop the student's basic skill in doing so, but it is not going to develop the student's understanding of the second aspect, that is architecture as the spatiotemporal 'frame or context' for 'use', or, to use Porter Abbott's words again, to understand architecture as 'shapes of time', or architecture as that which houses *narratives*,

We deliberately use the distinction between 'function' and 'use' here, since the first, 'function' (at least for us) entails a very mechanistic and one-dimensional concept of space and time, while the second, 'use' harbours a much more complex and multidimensional concept of activities and narratives taking place in both space and time.

So to also develop a student's understanding of architecture as a spatiotemporal frame or context for 'use', we started to develop design tasks that involved narratives. And as such to encourage the students to immerse themselves into spaces not as a kind of abstract form, but spaces as a frame or context of atmospheres and activities.

Probably the most important thing we learned over the years for ourselves was that it is necessary that the concept of such a design assignment also entails a specific expressive technique by means of which the students have to communicate their design and present their end product (for instance collaging, drawing and imaging

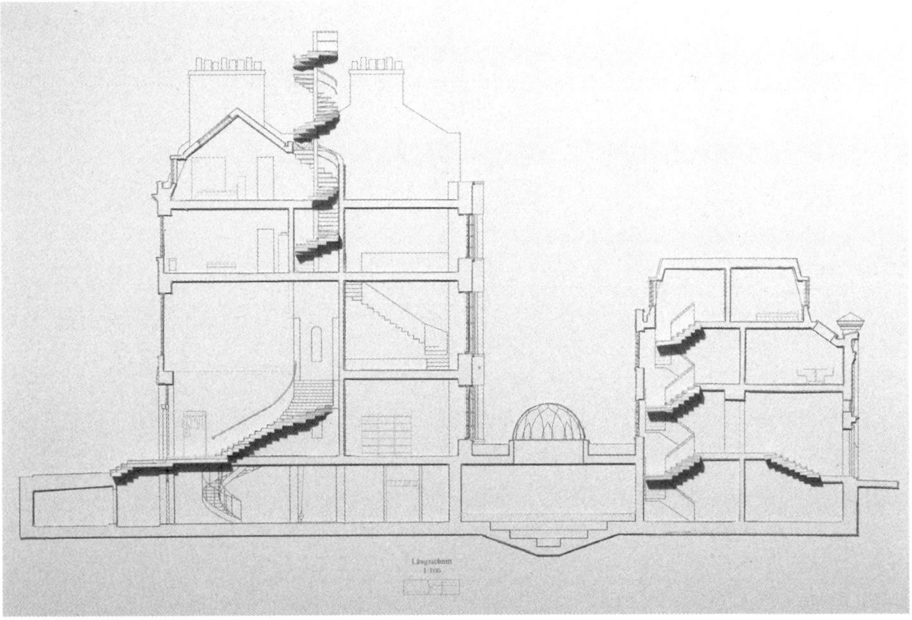

Figure 2. 'The coincidence concealed within the discovery of the stars', Stefanie Oßenkamp

techniques, or scenographic and model-making techniques). Only by the use of such techniques can the assignment provoke the necessary precision in expressing and developing their skill in producing thoughtful designs. That means designs that not only deal with architecture as a set of *static and uneventful scenes* for 'functions', but also architecture as the spatiotemporal *frame or context* for 'use'. Or, in Hejduk's words, architecture as a 'shell of thought' left by the student's simulation of 'life' in the form of its own narrative.

Within this educational context we should not forget that as educators we can transmit knowledge and skills, but that (like experience) we cannot transmit understanding, since understanding is something the students have to acquire themselves (as they also have to have their own experiences). What we are able to do is to plan the design tasks in such a way that they become a sort of educational game, by means of which the students, if they play them seriously, can acquire understanding. It also is in this sense that the term narrative is interesting, since it not only comes from the Latin *narrare,* to tell, relate, recount, explain, literally to make acquainted with, but also from *gnarus,* knowing, having knowledge of a thing, being acquainted with a thing, being skilful, being practiced. Derived from the Proto-Indo-European suffixed zero-grade *gne-ro-*, which again comes from the root *gno-* or *gneh-,* to know. So the etymology of the term narrative as such already seems to incorporate both the knowledge side and the skill side of the educational 'coin' called understanding. Before giving you a few examples of how my team and I now try to use literary methods in architectural education at RWTH Aachen University, allow me to start with an example from the early 1990s. This will not only bring us back to John Hejduk's Cooper Union, but will also show you in an anecdotal way that both the conception and the delivery of such a design assignment needs meticulous preparation.

Collage

As a guest professor at the Cooper Union in New York, I was asked by John Hejduk to direct a kick-start workshop with the theme 'collage'. Collage was something I had never dealt with myself, and to be honest I didn't really like to deal with collages made by students as such. Since my experience at other schools was that when you asked the students to express something by means of a collage, what you would see is that they took some magazines, ripped some obvious images out of them and then, without much thought or composition, glued them together. Such collages, in my opinion, pay very little respect to the material, to the precision and craftsmanship, and to the technique of montage to generate meaning or imagination in a collage. And for me these were the aspects I valued, since they are what links this theme of collage to architecture.

Figure 3. 'Memories of Julia Parker', Annika Reddemann

In order to challenge the students to understand these aspects in relation to design, I had to develop this kick-start workshop in which precisely these aspects – respect for the material, for the precision and craftsmanship, and for the technique of montage – would appear as a key to understanding the broader and deeper meaning that this theme of 'collage' might incorporate for them and later for their design project.
I started off with a lecture on the technique of montage as used (and described) by Russian film director Sergei Eisenstein, and I tried to show to students the precision and craftsmanship used by Eisenstein to express specific emotions and meanings via the technique of framing, of cutting and piecing together, thus montaging.
In a second, seminar-like lecture, I showed them a set of collages done by Max Ernst, and pointed out the precision of his cuttings and his carefully constructed compositions of lines and images done in such a way that in the end the collage didn't look like a collage made of parts pieced together anymore, but more like the image of a single (surreal) engraving. And I tried to explain to them how this whole could be interpreted as a narrative told by the pieces, and the way one could interpret the relationships of the pieces to one another and within the totality of the image.
As a next step I gave each student a very short story from a book with the title *Mirror in the Mirror: a Labyrinth* by Michael Ende, a German novelist normally known for children's books such as *Momo* and *The Never-ending Story*. *Mirror in the Mirror*, however, is not a storybook for children; it is a collection of 30 very short stories inspired by the paintings of his father, German surrealist painter Edgar Ende. The stories in *Mirror in the Mirror* are very spatial in terms of their architectural setting, and the task for the student was to read the story and imagine it as being a scenario (for a theatre play or a film), and then to design its scenography. The technique to be used was that of the collage (and the montage) – that is, cutting out and piecing together.
The only material I allowed the students to use, however, was a real $100 banknote in its entirety (by means of which I tried to force them to be very economical and precise in the use of their material). Both sides of the bill could be used for complete images or pieces of them, in order to build structures by using lines, surfaces and patterns. Finally, they had to bring it together in a collage cum montage in such a way that it would become the backdrop for the scenes of their story.

You can imagine the initial reaction of the students when I told them that the only material to be used was a real $100 banknote. So I reassured them that they could practice with copies, but that in the end I only wanted to see collages made of one real $100 banknote. I also told them that they could always get their money back if they took the collage to the National Bank, but that of course the whole point of this exercise was for them to give the banknotes added value by means of their work. And

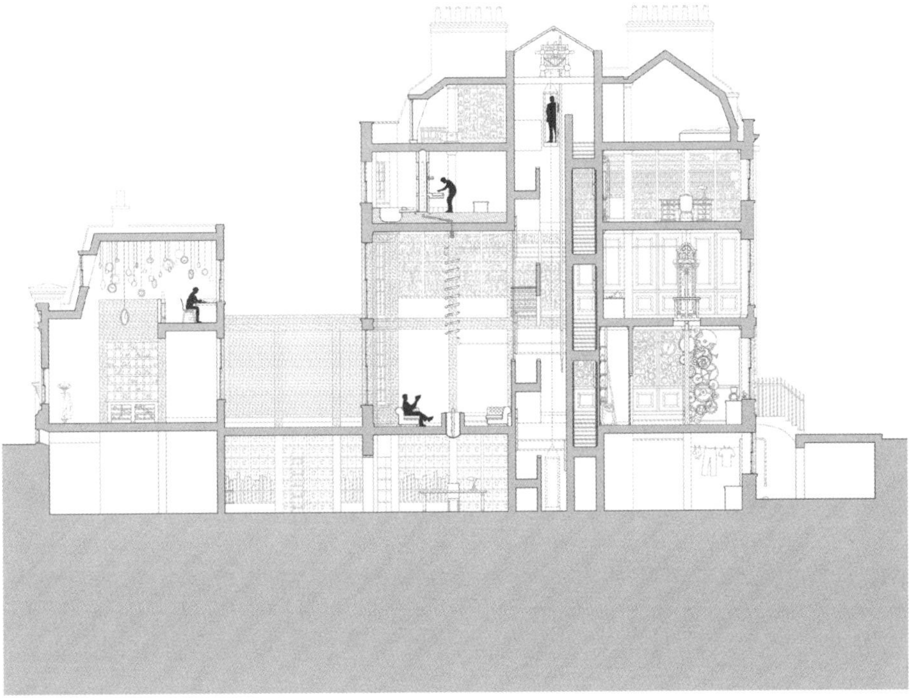

Figure 4. Section, 'Living in a Clockwork', Melanie Brügger

that if their work resulted in a well-made collage, they would never exchange them for a new banknote.

As you can also imagine, I was absolutely unsure of what the results would be after the three days they were given to work on it. I simply had to rely on my tutoring skills. Since I also didn't really realize from the beginning that a $100 bill is actually relatively small, the presentation was done by means of an endoscopic camera (linked to a large screen) that the student would have to move over the collage, or zoom in and out of it, while at the same time another student would read the corresponding story aloud.

The results were absolutely amazing, and it's a pity that I don't have any images to show you, but those images as such would not say much anyway without also publishing the corresponding story from Ende's book (which would go beyond the scope of this article).

However, what I achieved in just a view days was that the students started to understand that architecture, besides providing *static and uneventful scenes*, also provides the spatiotemporal *frame or context* in which narratives take place. In this case we started with the narratives of Ende that evoke both a spatial context and a temporal structure for their 'use'. The expressive technique of collage and montage was here not only a mere means to communicate their design and present their end product, it also tried to teach them something about narrative time (in terms of montage) and the precision of narrative relationships between things (in terms of collage). And last but not least that material has value and that precision and craftsmanship can (and should) not only add value to it, but also express the often invaluable part of an idea.

Wohnbau Aachen

At the chair for 'Wohnbau und Grundlagen des Entwerfens' of the Faculty of Architecture at RWTH Aachen University, this line of thinking about and practicing architectural education is continued.

Although in English the chair's title officially is 'Housing and Basics of Design', the German term *Wohnbau* interestingly entails more than just 'housing', literally translated in English it would be something like 'dwell-build' or 'dwelling-building', which from Heidegger's point of view would be a form of a pleonasm.

In essence, the term *Wohnbau* deals with more than just the design of houses, it envelops the whole idea of dwelling, 'as men's way of being on the world' to use Heidegger's words.

Dwelling is a verb, an action that is inspired by its cultural circumstances and as such forms the basis of any dwelling's form and its architectural expression. So within our design courses my team and I try to make the students more aware of these cultural

Figure 5. Entrance, 'Living in a Clockwork', Melanie Brügger

circumstances and the narratives that determine the idea and expression of human dwelling. To do so we consciously try to plan design studios that address dwelling as a verb, that is 'use', while simultaneously adopting narrative and expressive techniques that demand precision in communication and expression, in such a way that the students acquire some understanding of the complexities of architecture as the spatiotemporal *frame* or *context* in which 'use', that is 'life', takes place.
For instance in a project called 'Herberge', our colleagues Thomas Schmitz and Alexander Bartscher used drawing and imaging techniques to first build up spaces in terms of atmospheric elements and narratives of 'use', before fusing these spaces into the totality of a design.
Mark Proosten and Stephanie Brandt used scenographic and model-making techniques in a design project called 'Wunderkammer' to achieve a scenography within existing spaces, as Mark Proosten and Hans von Bernuth also did in using notational scenographic techniques in their instant design exercises called 'Haustheater'. Both are described below.

Wunderkammer

Taking narrative architecture as a principle theme for a design project in the Master phase, we confronted the students with the task of contemplating the space of a dwelling as a kind of *Wunderkammer*, or cabinet of curiosities. These predecessors of public museums originally were the 'private spaces' in which the aristocracy and the rich bourgeoisie collected and displayed their collections of extraordinary objects (often existing of obscene and exotic entities). In fact, as collectors the bourgeois inhabitants dwelled in and among their own private collections, which, as one will understand, had a significant influence on the way they inhabited their houses and as such on the spatial layout of each of these collector's homes.

We asked the students to design cabinets of curiosity which had to fulfil the daily activities of dwelling in relation to a self-defined protagonist/inhabitant/collector and his collection. The collector and the collection had to be accommodated in one of the typical upper-class residences that form the southern side of Bedford Square in London. The assignment allowed complete adaptation of the houses to the wishes and demands of the inhabitant/collector, as long as the brick façade facing Bedford Square remained untouched.
In replacing the programmatic brief by the self-formulated narrative of a protagonist (inhabitant, user), the students had to develop their own set of rules, customs and collection of curiosities that would determine the spatiotemporal qualities and outcome of the design, while being restricted by the existing building typology and

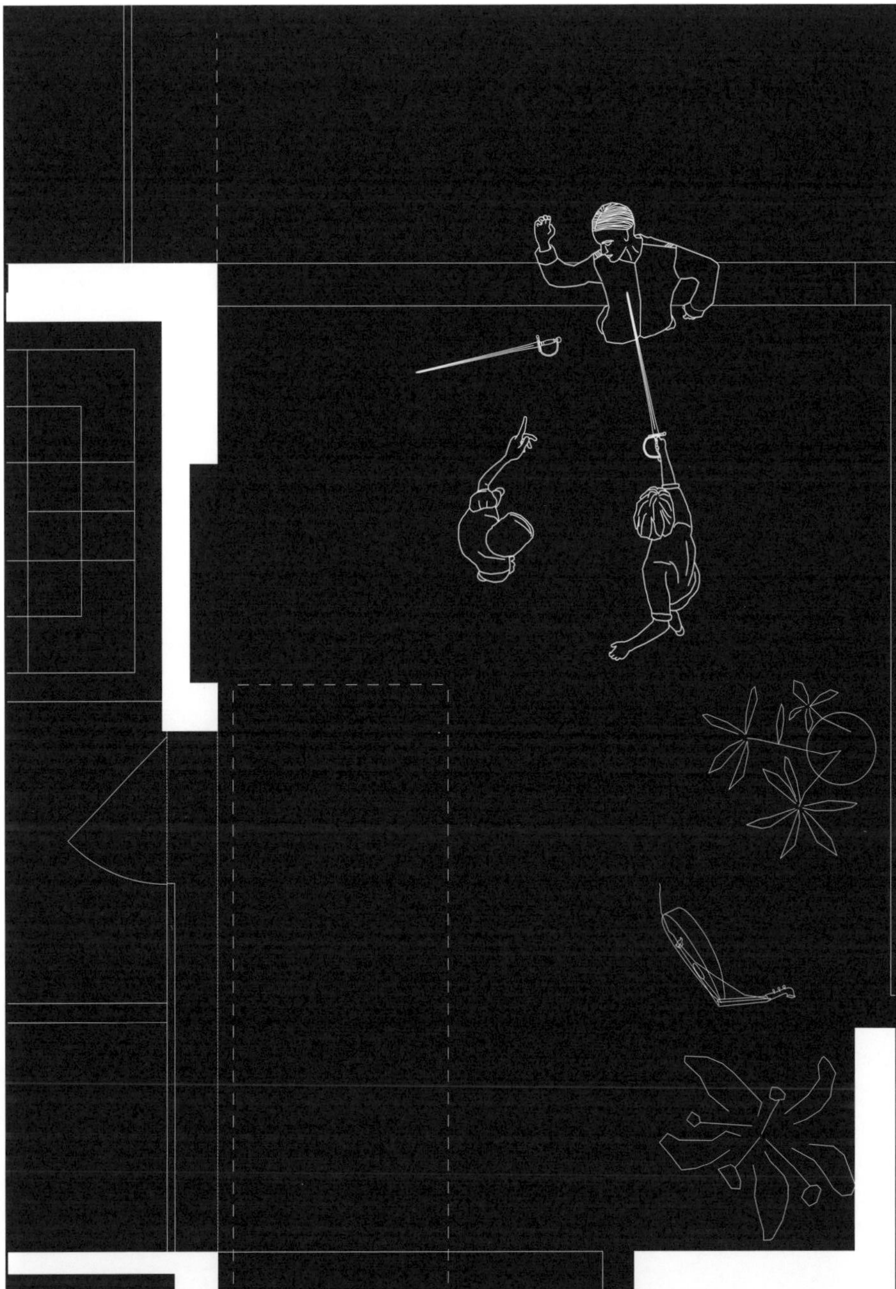

Figure 6. 'Casa Biachi, M. Botta starring in *Faust*, J.W.V. Goethe', students Amelie Kulassek and Paula Frasch

the size of the given houses on Bedford Square. This context posed boundaries that at first sight did not seem to be apparent, but would strongly influence the design in terms of 'use' and the scale of the collection, like every strong architectural 'frame or context' would do. The sheer size of the houses not only created possibilities, but also demanded a radical approach towards the role and design of the collection. A simple family life and a cabinet with objects would not fill the available space with 'use'.
As a result the designs were not simply structured by programmatic square metres and a typical programme of purely functional demands, but by a self-written narrative about the house's different uses. In this design task, narrative, dwelling, life, collection and home had to be integrated in one consistent design. Like the protagonist of a novel, who's thoughts and actions advance within the story, every decision that the student made in his narrative produced new spatial organizations, which helped to build up a complete and useful character that could fulfil the spatiotemporal demands of the house. From several psychiatrists, a hatter, a pigeon fancier up to an astronomer, all protagonists created an unexpected and an outcome not imagined beforehand.

 During the project the students were also introduced more theoretically to some of the narrative qualities of architecture. Starting with a seminar entitled 'Image Building' and an excursion to London, followed by several workshops, and ending with the symposium 'Against the Grain'.
This programme aimed at getting them more acquainted with alternative methodologies within architectural practices, research and education. By introducing them to different techniques, from scenario writing to collages and architectural drawings to models, we offered the students a varied set of tools that could help them to express their protagonist/collector and their design. Here again, it is not the educator's task to determine the outcome in advance, but the student's task to search for the mix and match in which the complexity of a self-created narrative can be explored and communicated.
The protagonist in fact played the role of an invisible incalculable force that, week by week, crystallized a bit further in the student's project. This open mode of experimenting meant opening new doors and following unmapped routes. By sending the students in different directions between the scheduled presentations they had to figure out for themselves and their protagonist which path or technique would best represent their ideas. Here the use of literature and especially the novel was favoured and recommended to the students.
As a guiding principle, the narrative strengthened the fictional reality of the project and the experience of ourselves as being mere observers. Through the structure of

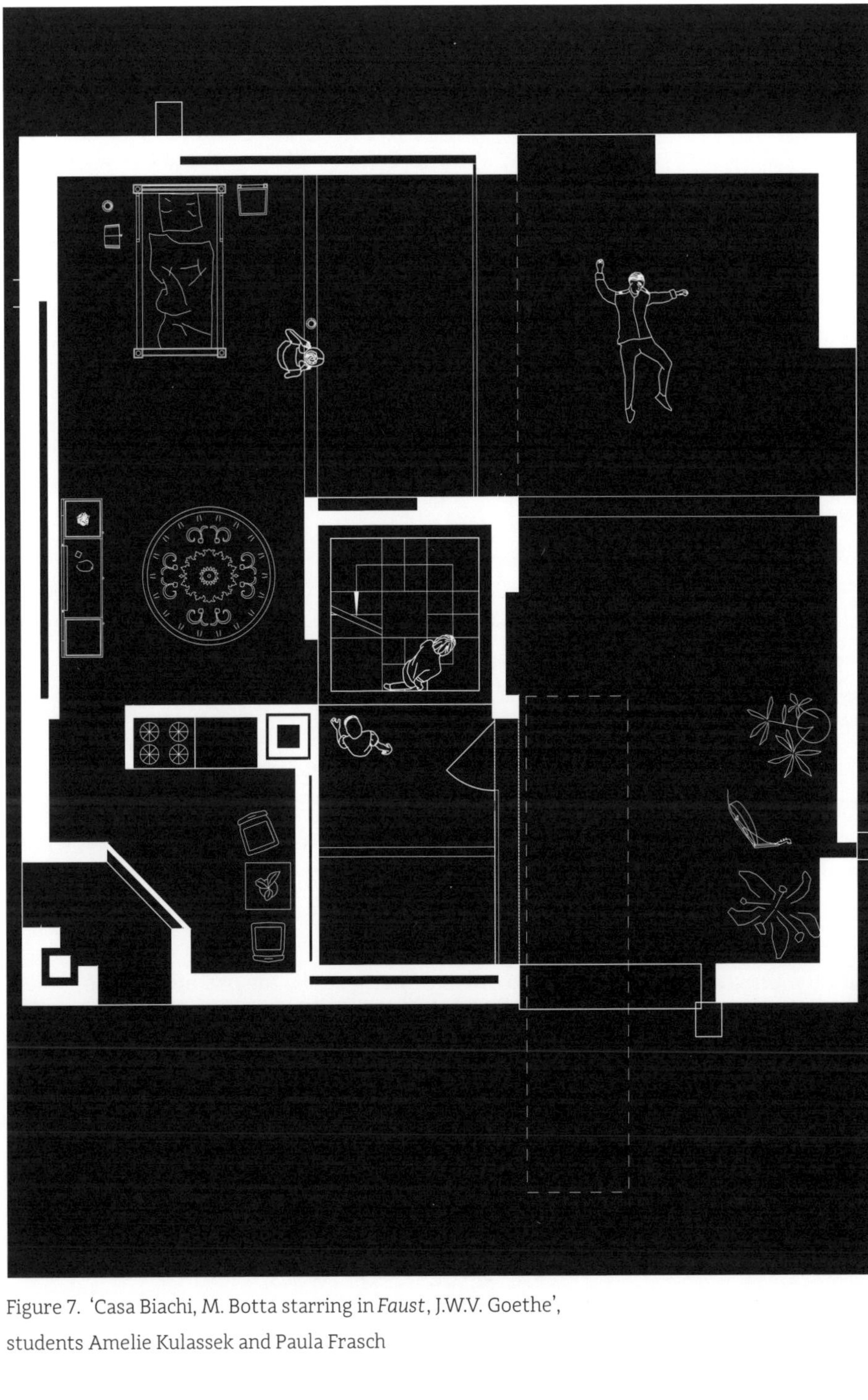

Figure 7. 'Casa Biachi, M. Botta starring in *Faust*, J.W.V. Goethe', students Amelie Kulassek and Paula Frasch

the narrative, we were forced to simultaneously enter the imaginative fiction and the framework created by the student. By focussing on the narrative qualities of their fictions, drawings and their respective (large-scale) models we as educators shifted from a mere aesthetic or functional approach towards a sensibility of 'use' and 'shapes of time'. Instead of evaluating the empty shells, the narratives formed the key element to give us insight into the thoughts and ideas of the students.
Working within the structure of a narrative, we also noticed a shift from the mere visual design position towards a multisensorial experience. The students became very sensitive to sound, smell, tactility and other sensorial qualities that were triggered by the characteristics of the collections. A clockmaker's house distinguished by the many sounds generated by the different timepieces, the different rhythms of the many staircases within the astronomer's dwelling, and the tactile properties of the numerous green objects in the refurbishment of a psychiatrist's office and dwelling.

Haustheater

Another project that takes narrative as a starting point is a yearly recurring instant-design workshop entitled 'Haustheater', a combination of the German word for house and theatre. Within this workshop that is a bit inspired by the Cooper Union collage workshop described above, the rules and preparations are simple: we set up two bowls with paper cards, one containing world-famous houses, the other a selection of theatre plays. So the combination, determined by picking a card from each bowl, resulted in a random selection of houses with plays. These plays had to be staged, meaning a selected scene of the theatre play had to take place within and/or around the house. The only expressive means the students were allowed to use was the plan drawing; so they not only had to draw the plan of the house as a *spatial collection of static and uneventful scenes*, but as a plan in 'use', *a frame or context* in which the selected scene was taking place.
Thus, the programme of the assignment is determined by the narrative of the selected play and the spatial possibilities of the house. Since the combination of both house and play was generated by a random selection, the first mission of the students was to bring these two together in a coherent way. This meant reading the play and selecting a specific scene parallel to analysing the possibilities of the house. Besides that they had to prepare the architectural plan of the house as first being an organized set of spaces, so a set of *static and uneventful scenes* which will then form the basis for the eventual outcome. From the start the students were confronted with a programme determined by the limitations of the narrative of the play, the spatial possibilities of the house and the aforementioned methodology of a one-to-one experience and its spatiotemporal notation.

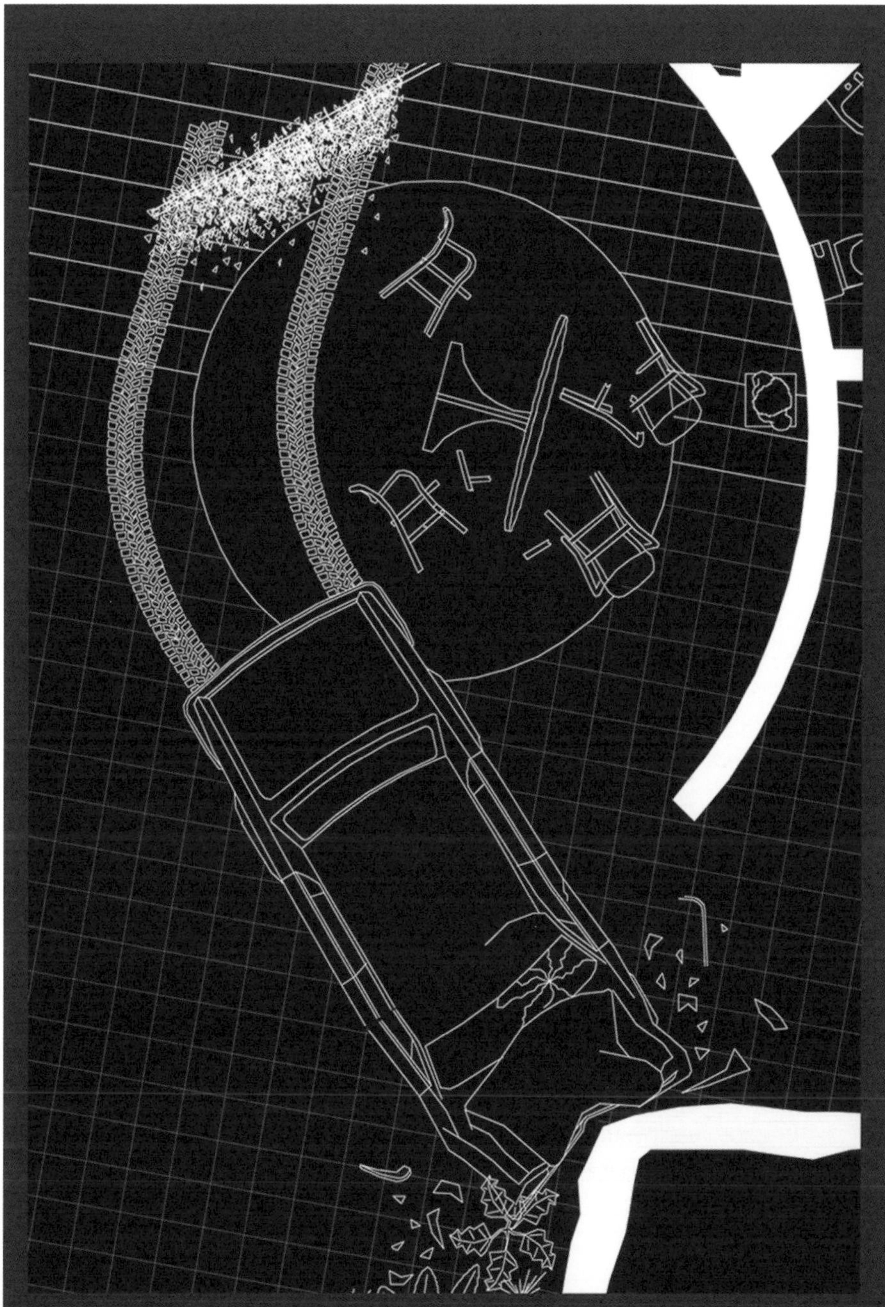

Figure 8. 'Niemeyer House, O. Niemeyer starring in *Death of a Salesman*, A. Miller', students Sonja Kellerman, Lisa Mühlnickel

As an intermediate step, the students had to perform the chosen scene on a temporary stage created within the university. On this stage the theatre act had to be presented by means of a verbal presentation simultaneously supplemented by the projected drawing of the floor plan. The architectural drawing of the plan of the house had to be used in its most elementary form, just the plan in white lines on a black background. During the performance, actions and movement had to be indicated by changing the projected viewpoint and/or scale of the plan. Thus, during the performance of the act, turning specific places on the initial plan into a spatiotemporal set of scenes in which the different acts were montaged together. This of course then had to result in plan drawings that were completely staged and equipped with furniture, attributes and protagonists, activating the plan of the house and as such indicating its possible 'use'.

After an evening of theatre performances, the students were asked to convert their presentation into a small booklet. Within each booklet the text of the theatre act and fully equipped plan drawings had to be placed next to each other, thus creating a new stage adaption for the play. As within every project, results vary but the average outcome exceeded our first expectations.

We found out that in setting the fully equipped architectural drawing of the plan to be the final result of the project, the students knew beforehand what was expected of them. And although the time they could spend on such an instant design workshop is very limited, the educational results, in terms of the use of narrative to acquire understanding of the spatial possibilities of a house as a spatiotemporal frame or context for 'use', were very promising.

Since most of the houses we selected are widely used as references in literature and lectures, students tend to think they know these houses. But there is a difference between recognizing a house and really knowing a house. Again, by focussing on the house as a temporal frame or context for 'use', the act of staging, or so to speak the introduction of a narrative, forms the basis for a thorough investigation into its architectural characteristics. The students had to make use of, or counteract upon, the static and uneventful scenes of the initial plan with the narrative of the play. For instance, the voids within Maria Botta's Casa Bianchi became a part of the deadly scene in Goethe's *Faust*. The stone in the Niemeyer house took a leading role in the end scene of *Death of the Salesman* and the Eames house became a battlefield in Karel Capeks' play *R.U.R*.

Our goal is not to create strange and uncommon events within houses. Our aim is to introduce the students to the complex activities and dialogues that occur within dwelling. Take, for example, Wladimir and Estragon waiting for Godot at Frank Lloyd

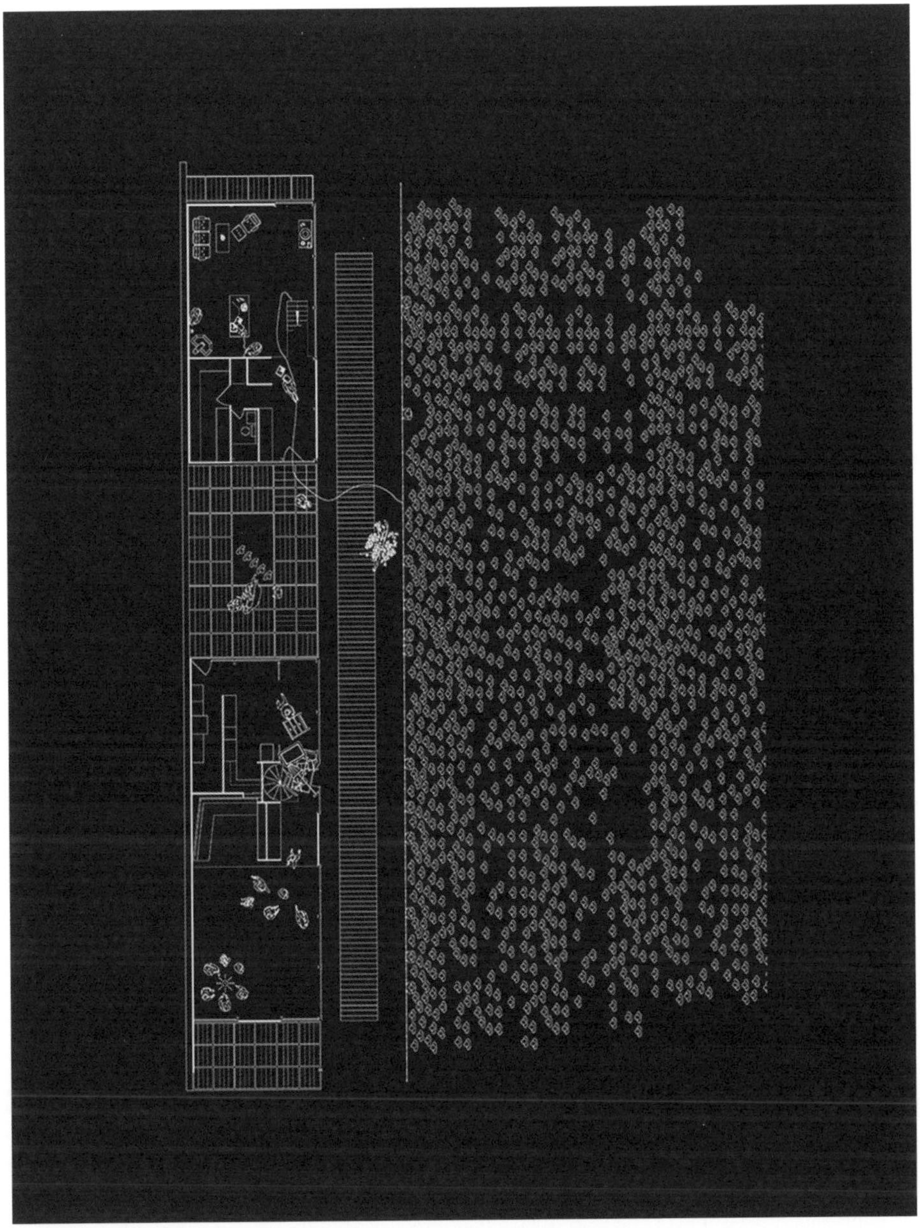

Figure 9. 'Eames House, C. and R. Eames starring in *R.U.R.*, K. Capek', students Niklas Gröhl, Sebastian Natge

Wright's Jacobs House. An uncommon event that students never expected to stage within a house. The inhabitant and the dwelling as such act upon and counteract each other. Dwelling is not static, predetermined or given. It is a complex activity that demands an empathic attitude of the students, one that can open up imagination.

Conclusion

To us, architecture and in particular the design of housing is much more than the disposition of private and public spaces or architectural elements like stairs, floors and walls. A house is a stage, a spatiotemporal frame or context in which the act of dwelling takes place. Dwelling as stated before is a verb, one that is culturally motivated, personalized and above all understood as an activity. We therefore introduced narrative and 'use' instead of 'function', which is rather uncommon, but as such triggers the students imagination. In doing so we try to transcend a purely formalistic, stylistic or functional approach towards design. By triggering a student's imagination we try to compel the student to use his own experience and understanding.

In general, we should be aware of the fact that with every architectural design, we project new possible perspectives on a landscape, an urban plot or a building. We therefore always operate in a fictional reality, in which we have to communicate our shell of thought with a broader audience. To realize this, the traditional architectural tools of drawing, model and eventually rendering might not be sufficient. The empty shell in itself is not enough to justify the design. We need tools, like a narrative, that can communicate our shell of thought by triggering the imagination.

How is it that the author of a novel is able to bring the spatial qualities of a context across in only a few sentences? We think that while reading, we substitute the authors description with our own experiences. Therefore by making use of literature and narratives in general, we have discovered a methodology that shifts the student's focus of the design from something external and abstracted, a kind of outside 'form', towards something more internal, spatial and filled with atmospheres and activities. One could say that by using narrative we try to make the invisibility of (architectural) thought more tangible for us as educators, but mostly for the students themselves.

1 John Hejduk was one of the most inspiring innovators of post-war architectural education. Along with Bernard Hoesli, Colin Rowe and Robert Slutzky, Hejduk was part of the so-called Texas Rangers, a group of young and enthusiastic architecture teachers who in the second half of the 1950s worked closely together to build a new curriculum for the University of Texas in Austin. From there, their new ideas about educating architecture spread along with their founding fathers to the ETH Zürich, the Universities of Cornell and Yale, and of course the Cooper Union.

Archives, Narratives and Bricolage

More Themes from The Manhattan Transcripts

Ioanna Angelidou

In 1981 Bernard Tschumi published his book *The Manhattan Transcripts*. Structured like a detective story that unfolds in sequences, it functioned both as a theoretical project and a mediated archive wherein new ideas and old projects were repeatedly intertwined, deconstructed and reassembled. In his introduction Tschumi writes:

> *Books on architecture, as opposed to books about architecture, develop their own existence and logic. They are not directed at illustrating buildings and cities, but at searching for the ideas that underlie them. . . . The books may read as sequences, but they do not necessarily imply narratives. They can be theoretical projects, abstract endeavours aimed at both exploring the limits of architectural knowledge and at giving readers access to particular forms of research.* (Tschumi 1981c: 6)

Deploying scrutiny and juxtaposition, the format of the architectural concept book entailed the creation of an invisible space and thus, it became architecture in its own right or, in Tschumi's own phrasing, 'a discontinuous reality where fragments are less important than the spaces between them'. (Tschumi 1990: 9)

Notation of Event

The disciplinary universe characterized by a multiplicity of references, conceptual devices, representational methods and operative platforms that Tschumi describes bears affinity to Claude Levi-Strauss's discourse on bricolage. According to Levi-Strauss, the practice of bricolage is based on the application of a conceptual inventory. Rather than a compromise like pastiche, bricolage entails the potentiality of surprising and being surprised. Levi-Strauss stresses the importance of process, noting that the bricoleur's language is articulated as much through things as the medium at hand. (Levi-Strauss 1966: 21) Consequently, a project of bricolage is not to be considered finite, but as one proliferating in creative suspension, because even the debris of a 'failed' attempt can potentially provide intellectual ground for a new concept.

A similar black-box continuum was a theme in the production of *The Manhattan Transcripts*. Hence the particular title, and specifically the word 'transcripts', implies not only a sequential development – as if working on a text whose narrative unfolds word by word – but also the articulation of a language as conceptual narrative, a literary-cum-architectural style so to speak, whose gradual emergence is being documented primarily in order to be further dissected. The book employs the format of a fragmented story told through four New York archetypes, which are illustrated in three simultaneous levels of reality. The archetypes explored are 'The Park', the story of a crime in Central Park; 'The Street', an agonising stroll (or indulgent chase) from the East River to the Hudson via 42nd Street; 'The Tower', a fall from the window of a downtown hospital, jail or asylum; and 'The Block', a series of dispersed incidents simultaneously taking place in the courtyards of an urban block in Manhattan.

These stories can be 'read' individually or as a compilation, the one gradually leading to the other via increasing graphic complexity. In each story/archetype the architect uses an iteration of a representation technique (photograph, plan, diagram) that corresponds to a disjuncture in a tripartite mode of notation. For example, in 'The Park' photographs extracted from films and newspapers are used as found objects to represent the event, original architectural plans are used to denote the space, and re-created diagrams of sport manoeuvers or theatre choreographies are used to represent movement. Tschumi continued developing the idea to produce the other instalments that explore both the limits of his multi-layered notation system as well as these four Manhattan urban clichés. (fig. 1)

Once immersed in the potentiality of graphic representation, he started undertaking quick exercises by testing techniques borrowed from cinematography in order to determine their architectural equivalent. Simultaneously, he reformatted each brief exercise into text by extracting its essence in a theorem to be demonstrated.[1] Pieces fell into place, one idea led to the next, each exercise was executed again and again, each iteration was valued, evaluated and reworked. This process eventually gave birth to a concept – a kinetic, cinematic and sequential book of architecture. The concept, in turn, culminated in a project – not just *The Manhattan Transcripts* as a book, but also the actual space of Parc de la Villette.

Archiving as Narrative

Art historian Tom McDonough has made an interesting observation regarding the choice of 'The Park', 'The Street', 'The Tower' and 'The Block' as spaces of action and conceptual terrain for *The Manhattan Transcripts*. A park, a seedy street, a public institution and the interior of a block are all urban spaces that play with the duality of privacy and publicness or, in other words, with social stratification. According to McDonough, a story of murder and desire set in Central Park triggers a whole repository of bourgeois fears connected to a mythology of illegal and illicit acts in 1970s New York. At a time when financial and social crisis was escalating into the late-capitalist desire for control, architecture was responding with designs that favoured interiority and asserted limits of space. (McDonough 2002: 119-120) Disciplinary transgression presented a way of questioning the postmodern condition for a young architect who was sceptical of this strange alliance between architecture and institutionalization.

Much has been written about Tschumi's interdisciplinary influences and his attempts to stimulate metadiscourse through the realm of art.[2] (Martin 1990: 33) However, what such analyses omit to emphasize is precisely the element of translation – the process of transformation from literary theory to design – something that Tschumi himself alludes to when referring to 'hidden codes and excesses hinting at other definitions, other interpretations'. (Tschumi 1980: 36)

In the three instalments of his curated column 'Architecture and Limits', which was published in *Artforum* between 1980 and 1981, he argues for the existence of recurring architectural themes that defy the disciplinary schism between functionalism

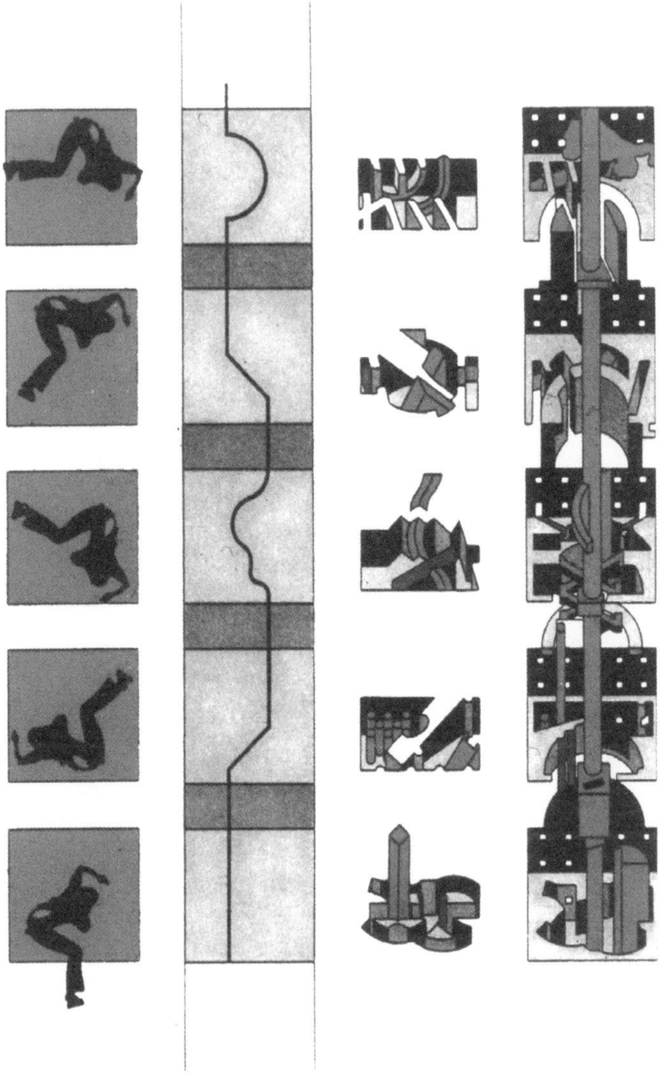

Figure 1. 'The Tower' from *The Manhattan Transcripts* (1976-1981).
Image courtesy of Bernard Tschumi.

and style. Such reductionist battles were never absent from architectural discourse; on the contrary, they were established with the advent of the modern project. The Vitruvian triptych of beauty, structural stability and utility has been questioned and transformed, with the concern for beauty and efficiency of structure gradually waning as industrialization led to the idealization of machine aesthetics and subsequently also its reverse condition, namely the aestheticization of construction. But what about utility, the architectural embracement of the body, the accommodation of experience?

> *Space is not simply the three-dimensional projection of a mental representation, but it is something that is heard, and is acted upon ... Bodies not only move in but generate spaces produced by and through their movements. Movements are the intrusion of events into architectural spaces. At the limit, these events become scenarios or programs, void of moral or functional implications, independent but inseparable from the spaces that enclose them.* (Tschumi 1981a: 45)

From this excerpt of 'Architecture and Limits II' we can extract three terms that shape the narrative that would eventually become fully articulated in *The Manhattan Transcripts* and through which we can unpack the project's genealogical complexity. These key terms are representation, event and programme; suggesting a process of creative documentation they provide evidence of a historical trace that foreshadows the construction of an intellectual, conceptual and operational depository and resembles Paul Ricoeur's definition of the archive, coincidentally contemporary to the *Transcripts*. This is not to claim that Tschumi's theoretical trajectory was necessarily informed by Ricoeur's writings, but rather that both – each making use of his own discipline's tools and devices – were critically responding to a broader theoresis regarding the definition of events, the notation of their course, and the disjunction between present and past. In Ricoeur's words:

> *We must turn towards the notion of a document (or record) contained in the initial definition of archives and to the notion of a trace implicitly contained in the notion of a deposit. In the notion of a document the accent today is ... placed on the support, the warrant a document provides for a history, a narrative, or an argument. This role of being a warrant constitutes material proof, what in English is called 'evidence,' for the relationship drawn from a course of events.* (Ricoeur 1966: 116-119)

Certainly, it is interesting to note that both Ricoeur and Tschumi revert to the term narrative and attempt to position it within a creative context. Let us now turn to another definition of the narrative that Tschumi has explicitly admitted to have drawn influence from. Roland Barthes writes in 'Introduction to the Structural Analysis of Narratives':

> *Either a narrative is merely a rambling collection of events, in which case nothing can be said about it other than by referring back to the storyteller's (the author's) art, talent, or genius – all mythical forms of chance – or else it shares with other narratives a common structure which is open to analysis, no matter how much patience its formulation requires. There is a world of difference between the most complex randomness and the most elementary combinatory scheme, and it is impossible to combine (to produce) a narrative without reference to an implicit system of units and rules. Where are we then to look for the structures of narrative? Doubtless, in narratives themselves.* (Barthes 1978: 80-81)

The theoretical premise that Barthes sets for the operative platform of narrative is one of duality, a subject matter of either self-referentiality or interconnectivity. This twofold nature of the narrative in Barthes' writings is connected to Levi-Strauss through the idea of combinatory schemes – in other words, the practice of bricolage. In *The Savage Mind* Levi-Strauss writes that 'the bricoleur is adept at performing a large number of diverse tasks' employing a universe of instruments representing 'a set of actual and possible relations, "operators" that can be used for any operations of the same type'. (Levi-Strauss: 17-18) Tschumi understands architectural narrative as a system dependent on temporality and language, the latter constructed via analogies:

> *Is there such a thing as an architectural narrative? A narrative not only presupposes a sequence but also a language . . . The ability to translate narrative from one medium to another . . . suggests architectural equivalences, equivalences that are not made by analogy to an architectural strip of course, but through carefully observed parallels.* (Tschumi 1983a: 36)

It is on these 'carefully observed parallels' that one should focus in order to decode the dual nature of the archive Tschumi constructs in *The Manhattan Transcripts*. The first layer of this archive is one of sequence – let us call it a meta-manifesto – an internal process of calibration and self-criticality. The second layer is that of language, a combinatory process observing practices of other disciplines but also of other historical contexts, which it critically dissects and reassembles. These two layers together register the emergence of a new, utterly theoretical mode of architectural operativity: the architect as bricoleur.

Modern Bricolage

In the third part of 'Architecture and Limits' Tschumi unveils himself as a modernist bricoleur by claiming that architecture found a new base in the modern theories of literature, music and the visual arts. He is sceptical about the reductive interpretation of the modern programme as either a functional or a stylistic endgame that refutes the interaction of space and event and describes architecture as the meeting place of temporality and experience. (Tschumi 1981b: 40) In a later article titled 'Illustrated Index: Themes from The Manhattan Transcripts' Tschumi unpacks his modernist library by offering a detailed user's manual with specific references: the documentary quality of photography and film as employed in the collage techniques of the constructivists; Oskar Schlemmer's diagrams of the Gesture Dance as movement notation; and Sergei Eisenstein's multi-layered montage and sequence annotations including camera placement, sound tracks, musical scores and movement. (Tschumi 1983b: 64, 74)

The conceptual and technical transpositions from these references are easily distinguishable in the 'Screenplays', an exhibition project in the form of a visual manifesto immediately preceding the *Transcripts*. The first experiments are simple enough, with the use of a two-frame sequence from a film in lieu of a diagrammatic terrain for the action movements combining devices from techniques such as fade-in/out, repetition, juxtaposition, superimposition and distortion. (fig. 2) This process of conceptualization and subsequent visualization implies a reciprocal relation between the spontaneous nature of experiencing space through movement and the perceptual tactics of engineering an event.

Experience and Space

Tschumi has described the production of the 'Screenplays' as an essay in preparation of a novel, indeed a convenient yet somewhat cryptic metaphor for *The Manhattan Transcripts*. (Tschumi and Walker 2006: 33) By equivalence we could claim that the theoretical projects preceding the 'Screenplays' would be notes that eventually transform into an essay. Upon entering the New York gallery Artists Space in April 1978, one would encounter a series of rooms that, according to the exhibition press release, were 'conceived as an exploration into real and fictitious spaces'.[3] This exhibition titled 'Architectural Manifestoes' was Tschumi's first major project and to that end, it

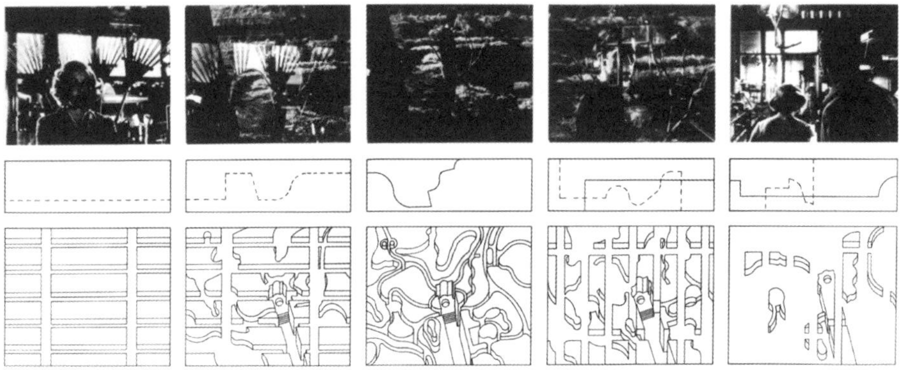

Figure 2. Screenplays (1978), technique 3: fade in/out with frames from Alfred Hitchcock's film *Psycho* of 1960. Image courtesy of Bernard Tschumi.

employed architectural drawings as evidence to his theoretical investigations.

In 'Architectural Manifestoes' each of the devices of his tripartite notation system finds an early spatial manifestation in the three rooms comprising the exhibition. The first room, 'The Space of Manifestoes', was a simple space with a series of fake advertisements for architecture – an 'ironic propaganda' that Tschumi had created to illustrate his writings. This room could be perceived as the equivalent of the photograph in his collages, because it bears the factographic quality of documenting events and projects materialized in the immediate past.

The second room, 'The Manhattan Transcripts', was much larger and on two of its walls were mounted the collages 'The Park' and 'Border Crossing'. (fig. 3) The 'Manhattan Transcripts' room could very well serve the same role as the movement diagram in the tripartite notation system.

The third and final room, 'The Space of Space', contained small installations and abstract objects whose presence was meant to alter the experience of the space itself. The latter, contrary to the other two rooms, was not an incomplete space of representation, but a fully articulated environment anchored in imagination. At the same time, it helped the visitor unpack what had already been triggered by the gradual transition from the Manifestoes room to the Transcripts room and ultimately in the Space room – a sequential experience of space, movement and event.

Sequential Meta-Manifesto

The 'Architectural Manifestoes' exhibition at Artists Space was accompanied by the publication of a small black booklet of the same title. This catalogue chronologically unfolds eight manifestoes, four of which were exhibited in the three rooms of Artists Space. However, a year later, when 'Architectural Manifestoes' was exhibited in the gallery of the Architectural Association in London, the catalogue was revised to include a new, ninth manifesto: 'Screenplays.' As a matter of fact, all other revisions in the second edition trace a path back to the conceptual underpinnings of the entire repository of projects that underwent a critical enrichment between the two instalments of the exhibition. It is the composite nature of 'Manifesto 9: Screenplays' and the discernible references to the other manifestoes that make an initial strong impression. Yet a closer reading unveils a much more interesting conceptual complication, with 'Screenplays' as the latest stage in a project constantly under development.

The first manifesto of the series is 'Fireworks', a brief polemical text from 1974 and a

Figure 3. 'Manhattan Transcripts' room, 'Architectural Manifestoes' exhibition, Artists Space gallery, New York, 1978. Photograph by Bernard Tschumi. Image courtesy of Bernard Tschumi.

photograph from a fireworks show created for the book exhibition 'A Space: A Thousand Words'. The strike of a match, according to Tschumi, is an act of pleasure that defies space, words and images. If the history of architecture has been structured around writings and drawings of space as much as their built translation, would not an act that negates or even destroys them become an architectural revolution against a selective kind of historicism that seemed to be the prevalent critical approach at that time?

The second manifesto was the performance *Questions of Space*, staged in the Royal College of Arts Gallery in 1975. The third was 'Advertisements for Architecture', the ironic propaganda Tschumi had devised in lieu of conventional illustrations for his articles in the journals *Architectural Design* and *Oppositions*,[4] and which were presented in the 'Space of Manifestoes', the first of the three rooms in Artists Space. The fourth manifesto was 'Joyce's Garden', extracted from the unit brief Tschumi taught at the Architectural Association in 1977, the premise of which was that in architecture fiction could replace function by borrowing a set of literary practices. Manifesto five was titled 'Birth of an Angel', a potential book that would give unbuilt architecture an existence of its own. Manifestoes six and seven were the drawings and diagrams titled 'The Park' and 'Border Crossing', which were presented in the 'Manhattan Transcripts' room at Artists Space.

Finally, manifesto eight was 'The Room', a real space rather than a spatial representation and as such the exact reversal of the other pieces in the catalogue. 'A real space cannot be printed on a page,' we read in the midst of the otherwise blank last page in this first catalogue. Yet, a year later when 'Architectural Manifestoes' was exhibited at the Architectural Association, the new edition of the black booklet contained a revised version of manifesto eight now titled 'Rooms' instead of simply 'The Room' and accompanied by a photograph of 'The Space of Space' installation in New York. Tschumi had even updated the text for the particular manifesto: 'Objects determine, qualify, modify, reinforce the purpose of a given space, while their own purpose affects their common 'type': operating table; dissecting table; communion table; gaming table; dining table . . .' (Tschumi 1979: 16)

This is not the only change in the second edition of this small catalogue; 'Birth of an Angel' changed to 'Little Books'. 'The little books are not sets of architectural drawings, not books on architecture, but books of architecture,' Tschumi writes before elaborating the theoretical premise of a book in the making under the potential title *Events*. (Tschumi 1979: 9) 'Birth of an Angel' is still there, but only as yet another booklet in

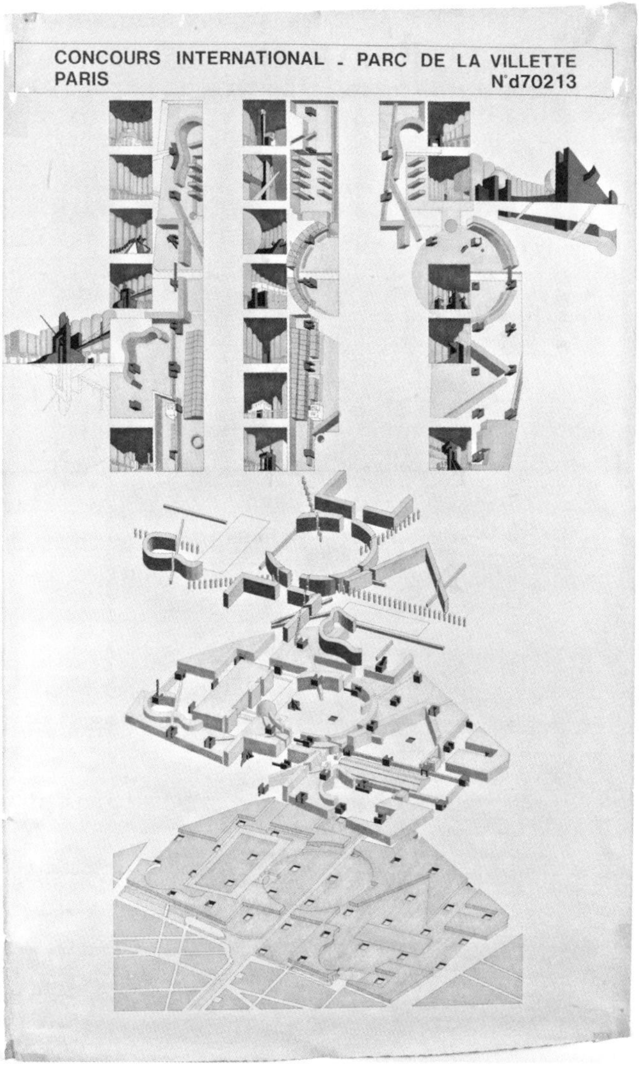

Figure 4. Parc de la Villette exploded axonometric (competition board 1982). Image courtesy of Bernard Tschumi Architects.

this potential series. Manifestoes six and seven – 'The Park' and 'Border Crossing' – both bear a subtitle, 'Transcript 1' and 'Transcript 2' respectively. Obviously, this change echoes their combined presentation in 'The Manhattan Transcripts' room at Artists Space.

It becomes apparent that once a stage of the project had been formulated and visualized adequately, the earlier projects were revisited and calibrated accordingly in order to articulate a new overarching narrative that could act as connecting matter. As Tschumi writes in *Architecture and Disjunction*:

> *In my case, theoretical writing had for its aim not only to expand architectural concepts but also to negotiate the relationship between the cultural practice of architecture and the interrelated spheres of politics, literature, or the arts. . . . Whether texts, drawings or buildings, each mode of working provided further means of exploration. This is indeed one of the great characteristics of architectural work: you can also think through it.* (Tschumi 1996: 19-20)

It should come as no surprise that the fundamental elements of the 'Screenplays' would keep emerging in future design work and writings by Tschumi, neither would it prove a challenge to recognize fragments from 'Joyce's Garden' in the conceptual scheme of Parc de la Villette. (fig. 4) The perpetuation of the New York diagram series from Artists Space to the Architectural Association gallery catalysed their transformation and development. The two editions of the 'Architectural Manifestoes' catalogue and the respective exhibitions operated in a similar way. The printed object was a mediating platform employed as a collected architectural manifesto in its own right.[5] These manifestoes and the infinite search for a common denominator among them delivered an early concept book, practically an avant-propos for the 1981 publication of *The Manhattan Transcripts*. The latter, as Tschumi would not hesitate to confess, was the conceptual basis for the competition entry that would eventually win him his first major project, the Parc de la Villette.

1 The idea of the theorem and comparison of architecture with mathematics on this basis is a recurring theme in Tschumi's discourse. In an interview with Cynthia Davidson he says: 'The interesting thing about math for me, however, is something else, is its procedure, its devices, the montage of math – that is, the hypothesis and its demonstration. I find the notion of the theorem absolutely fascinating because it is so close to the notion of the

architectural concept. Architects can propose a concept and then demonstrate it in the same way in which a mathematician can demonstrate a theorem. One must demonstrate that it is applicable.' Bernard Tschumi, 'Modes of Inscription,' ANY 0 (1993), 51.

2 Louis Martin offers a quite comprehensive analysis of how Tschumi's theoretical work has been shaped by the writings of critical theorists such as Barthes, Bataille, Bachelard and Derrida, among others. Yet, written in 1990, around the time that this sort of discourse had become common ground in architecture – particularly the American East Coast academia of which Tschumi had become a central figure with his appointment as Dean of the Graduate School of Architecture, Planning, and Preservation at Columbia University – it lacks the argumentative connection between the theoretical aspect of Tschumi's work and the one pertaining to visual/formal explorations. See Louis Martin, 'Transpositions: On the Intellectual Origins of Tschumi's Architectural Theory', *Assemblage* 11 (1990), 33.

3 Press release for the exhibition 'Architectural Manifestoes' by Bernard Tschumi, held at Artists Space in New York City, 8-29 April 1978. Material retrieved from Fales Library, New York University, The Downtown Collection: Artists Space Archive, Series I: Exhibition Files, 1973-2009, box 5, folder 13.

4 The 'advertisements' that accompany Tschumi's article 'Architecture and Transgression' in a 1976 issue of the journal *Oppositions* depicts Le Corbusier's Villa Savoye in a derelict state, circa 1965 and before it underwent preservation. Above one of the images is written in bold font: 'The most architectural thing about this building is the state of decay that it is in.' Tschumi draws a comparison between the Corbusian whiteness and formal austerity of modern architecture and Georges Bataille's studies of eroticism. Bataille, as Tschumi observes, pointed out that the fundamental prohibitions of mankind were centred on the polar opposites of life and death, reproduction and decay. If Bataille's observations were a response to the social taboos of his time, wonders Tschumi, couldn't their contemporary (modern) architecture be another spectrum through which to look at them? And if erecting modern buildings was an erotic act for some, couldn't their death through decay equal pleasure for others? See Bernard Tschumi, 'Architecture and Transgression', *Oppositions* 7 (1976), 60. See also: K. Michael Hays (ed.), *Oppositions Reader* (Cambridge, MA: MIT Press, 1998), 360; and Bernard Tschumi, *Architecture and Disjunction* (Cambridge, MA: MIT Press, 1996), 73-74. For Tschumi's references to Bataille's theories of pleasure and desire see Georges Bataille, *Eroticism* (London: Calder, 1962).

5 Manifesto five or 'Little Books'/'Birth of an Angel' of 1977. See Tschumi, *Architectural Manifestoes* (New York: Artists Space, 1978), 18-19; see also Tschumi, *Architectural Manifestoes II* (London: Architectural Association Press, 1979), 10-11.

Exhausting the Narration / Exhausting the Architecture

Esteban Restrepo Restrepo

Every architecture houses infinite potential narrations, in the same way that every narration houses infinite potential architectures. We could say that architecture is *in potency of* narrations as the narration is *in potency of* architectures. Thanks to the invariable materiality of the building, the contingence of human dwelling can have a place. The building remains the same while countless events occur in it. On the other hand, the narration allows us to *invoke* individual images in our minds, even if its materiality, the writing, remains the same. This is not different when the narration refers to a building, a house or a room. Each reader *imagines* that architecture in a different way; that imagined architecture is, in fact, a personal reaction between the written architecture proposed by the text and the personal experience and *encyclopaedia* of the reader him/herself. Nevertheless in the work of Samuel Beckett a hybridization or a synthesis of these two conceptual definitions, architecture as a potency of literatures and literature as a potency of architectures, takes place through the technique of *exhaustion*, a technique that philosopher Gilles Deleuze uses to understand how Beckett multiplies the otherness of objects, words, voices, images and spaces, taking them to an indeterminate ontological condition or state. Architecture does not remain immune to Beckettian *exhaustion*. Architecture and narration trouble each other, one over the other, when they are affected by *exhaustion*.

Indeed, architecture becomes troubled within the work of Samuel Beckett from its very basis. All architectural notions – dwelling, function, form, symbol, proportion, scale, and so forth – become troubled by the state of deterioration in which the bodies of his characters are found. Because of this state of being blind, amnesiac, paralytic or schizophrenic, Beckett's characters conceive and experience architecture in their own and singular way. A way that is radically different from ours (in our healthy, normal bodies). And as Diderot says in *Letter on the Blind,* if 'the state of our organs and senses has an enormous influence over our metaphysics and moral',[1] (Diderot 2004: 27) we could say, then, that architecture within Beckett's work, far from our optical, mnemotechnical and locomotive epistemological *construct,* proposes, with its own sensorial logic, an architecture of its own with its own metaphysics. The sensorial logic of this architecture refers to a permanent loss of qualities or to a certain tendency to nothingness that we could compare to what John Cage does with music, taking sound to its inaudible condition, or to what Yves Klein does with painting, taking colour to its invisible condition.

Beckett's work also becomes progressively closer to nothingness. This proximity makes it gain intensity, as when one, on the edge of a cliff, feels the attraction of the abyss, and getting closer and closer to the abyss, perceives an increase in adrenaline. Beckett, by pushing his characters, objects, words, voices, images, spaces and architectures to nothingness, then weakens them or *fragilizes* them, to use one of Sartre's terms, making them carry henceforth a possibility of non-being, reducing their guarantees of existence, which confront them with their own essence, with what is irreducible in them. But even if nothingness is the motor of Beckett's work, it is not its *telos* (finality), which is why it would be more precise to say that Beckett's work tends, not towards annihilation, but towards lessening. In his short text *Worstward Ho* (Translated as *Cap au Pire* in French) he states: 'The lesser can never be the nothingness.'[2] (Beckett, *1991*: 41) In these terms one can establish a comparison between the work of Samuel Beckett and that of Mies Van der Rohe about the notion of lessening, where what is remaining during this process becomes more reduced, more intense, more essential. Thanks to its tendency to lessening, Mies Van der Rohe's architecture evidences the essential condition of structural support, of shelter, of surface, of constructive technique, etcetera.

It is because of the attraction to nothingness that Beckettian characters have a very unstable relationship with architecture. Sometimes they seek it tirelessly when they are unprotected; sometimes, on the contrary, they run away from it when architecture suffocates them with its impositions. However, what is a constant in both cases is that Beckettian characters are apathetic and insensitive to all the structures of codes and symbols that architecture represents, as well as to the forms it imposes with the purpose of ordering life. If Beckett's characters are visibly marginal, we could say that they are marginalized from the sense of architecture and that they also marginalize the sense of architecture itself. Abandoned to the elements, or in the opposite sense, guests in a determined dwelling, Beckettian characters always wish to *architecturalize* the place where they are in order to affirm, undoubtedly, that they are in this place and not in any other. The architectural desire is spread over all of Beckett's work. Desire that takes them to elaborate elementary actions or project strategies in order to found or to base the space, that is to say, to architecturalize it. One of these strategies is *exhaustion*.

The Unnamable is the *exhausted* par excellence within the work of Samuel Beckett, the highest degree of that condition. The novel starts with three questions: 'Where now? When now? Who now?'[3] (Beckett *1953*: 7) Questioning the where, the when, and the who supposes an actual disappearance of space, time and subject. The question 'Where now?' asked by the main character of the novel, which certainly has a spatial and architectural connotation, leads him to begin an erratic search in order to find a space of his own, a definitive space that makes him stop his meanderings and allows him to start a sedentary life, guaranteed thanks to architecture. The task of the character of *The Unnamable* is to prepare for the arrival of the wished architecture. For that, he constantly elaborates series after series of hypotheses about that architecture which has not yet arrived. The exhaustion of the possibilities of that architecture still to come is the technique employed by the character of *The Unnamable* in order to attract it to him. None of the possibilities is verified or rejected; in fact, they accumulate one on top of the other without any hierarchy within the virtual space of the narration. Thus, if the bright side of the possibility is realization, the dark side would be nothingness. The postponement of a concretization or a total dissolution of this architecture still to come leaves it in a state of suspension between concretization and dissolution.

Now, exhausting is not just tiring, as Gilles Deleuze says. If the tired tires and gets tired in the realization, the exhausted exhausts and gets exhausted in the possible. If the classical architect, the one who wishes to realize, gets tired in the process of making the possible pass into the real, the Beckettian architect, the one who wishes to rest within the potential, gets exhausted multiplying the possibilities. If the tired cannot realize anymore, the exhausted cannot 'possibilize'.[4] (Deleuze 1992: 57) The maturing of the architectural project, or its tiredness, which in this case is the same thing, in any of its moments, from formal or volumetric definition to the production of a constructive detail, unavoidably deals with the loss of possibilities. According to Deleuze: 'But still the realization of the possible proceeds by exclusion because it supposes preferences and objectives that vary replacing the foregoing.'[5] (Deleuze1992: 59) Projecting is, then, the permanent action of refusing all possibilities but one, the chosen one that is supposed to enter into the real. That is why the project is also a *projectile*, an *ontological projectile* that pretends to make the idea pass into the real. The *projectile*, thus, crosses different phases or ontological thresholds that brings it closer to the real.

If the predominant projectual technique of architecture is fatigue, Beckett proposes another alternative, the projectual technique of the exhaustion of the possibles. In Beckett's work the idea of preference, exclusion or rejection is inexistent. No possibility prevails over another because there are no criteria, nor functional or aesthetic objectives, nor goals of any other order. In the work of Beckett, possibilities remain within a projectual space that no longer belongs to the order of the projectile but to the order of the orbital satellite.

But, how do we consider all those possibilities in permanent incubation without depriving them of their own existence? How could all those inclusive disjunctions survive, without being annihilated by the strength of the exclusive disjunctions, which is typical of the real? Jorge Luis Borges would create a library containing all the books that are possible to write, permuting the 27 signs of the alphabet or a labyrinth where the exit has not yet been found, making all the ways to go over it remain as possible routes to the exit. Now, to understand Beckett's exhaustion technique it is useful to refer to two cases or concrete examples: the novel *Watt*, where exhaustion is featured by the enumeration of the possibilities two characters could use to dispose of furniture within a chamber, and the work for television *Quad*, where exhaustion is featured by the simultaneity of the possible ways that four characters could travel around a space.

In *Watt*, Mr Knott and Watt, his servant, constantly rearrange the placement of the furniture within the master's chamber. They re-create the spatial system within the chamber every day. However, they do not do this because they are not convinced of the current distribution of the chamber, nor because they are looking for an ideal, definitive or perfect chamber that meets Mr Knott's criteria. What they are looking for is indifferent to the need, to beauty, to form, to use or to the function of the chamber. That is why, most of the time, they arrive at absurd configurations (absurd, for us who judge architecture within these parameters).

This room was furnished solidly and with taste.
This solid and tasteful furniture was subjected by Mr. Knott to frequent changes of position, both absolute and relative. Thus it was not rare to find, on the Sunday, the tallboy on its feet by the fire, and the dressing-table on its head by the bed, and the night-stool on its face by the door, and the wash-hand-stand on its back by the window; and on Monday, the tallboy on its back by the bed, and the dressing-table on its face by the door, and the night-stool on its back by the window, and the wash-hand-stand on its feet by the fire; and, on the Tuesday, the tallboy on its face by the door, and the dressing-table on its back by the window, and the night-stool on its feet by the fire, and the wash-hand-stand on its head by its head by the bed; and, on the Wednesday, the tallboy on its back by the window, and the dressing-table on its feet by the fire, and the night-stool on its head by the bed, and the wash-hand-stand on its face by the door; and, on the Thursday, the tallboy on its side by the fire, and the dressing-table on its feet by the bed, and the night-stool on its head by the door, and the wash-hand-stand on its face by the window, and, on the Friday, the tallboy on its feet by the bed, and the dressing-table on its head by the door, and the night-stool on its face by the window, and the wash-hand-stand on its side by the fire; and, on the Saturday, the tallboy on its head by the door, and the dressing-table on its face by the window, and the night-stool on its side by the fire, and the wash-hand-stand on its feet by the bed; and, on the Sunday week . . . (Beckett 1963: 204-205)

Deleuze says: 'Mr. Knott, without another need than being without need does not reserve any combination to a particular use that could exclude the others, of which one should wait for the circumstances.'[6] (Deleuze 1992: 61) Rather than pretending to achieve the correct chamber, Mr Knott and Watt operate a sort of *becoming chamber (devenir chambre)*, putting all the possibilities of configuring it in perpetual movement, in a condition of permanent variation, as an eternal and paradoxical architectural project, where all the possibilities of realizing it spin rhythmically, choreographically in a loop That manner defies the Aristotelian's metaphysical categories of potency and act, and the movement as the step from one to the other. In fact, Beckett creates a third category or a hybrid notion, a sort of limbo between them. In this case the potential and the actual find a type of spatiality in which the one does not exclude the other, but where they cohabitate together. This limbo is the one of the inclusive disjunctions. Within this potential space it is possible to realize the possibilities without depriving them of their potential nature

Now, after having shown how the exhaustion of the project has a place within *Watt*, it will be necessary to show what happens to the narration in order to observe how it affects architecture. The extract we just read shows us a chamber composed of four architectural elements (the door, the window, the fire and the bed, which is considered as something immobile) and four pieces of furniture (the tallboy, the dressing-table, the night-stool and the wash-hand-stand). In that moment, the narrator renounces the story of the chamber itself, focusing, instead, on enumerating all the possibilities of occupying it. He stops the narration or the progression of the story in order to pay attention to the possibilities of arranging the chamber. Here, the novel passes from a level of narration to a level of meta-narration or para-narration. That 'out of narration' belongs, in this case, to the order of architecture. It is as if the narrator stops the story to become the architect, to reflect on the architectural possibilities of the chamber he is going to narrate. 'What happens if . . .' he should ask himself. 'What happens if the chamber was like this or like that . . .' What is amazing is that if, in this moment, the narrator opens the architectural spectrum of possibilities of the chamber, at the same time he opens the spectrum of possibilities of the narration for every possibility of the chamber. Here the exhaustion exacerbates both narration and architecture Thus the novel becomes a stage, that is to say, architecture in a potency of stories, and vice versa, a story in a potency of architectures. The permutation exhausts the chamber but – at the same time – it is the way Beckett uses to give it a certain 'visibility'. The cyclic exhaustion of all the possible dispositions of the pieces of furniture within Mr Knott's chamber shows it progressively more complete and sharper. This dispositive works in a certain way as a cubist machine, where every frame would be a possibility of the chamber that, chained to the next frame, makes the univocal image of the chamber emerge. Surprisingly, while the cyclic narration of the possibilities of the chamber goes on and on, a sedimentation starts to form, in the bottom of the mind, while the act of perceiving and imagining take place; that sedimentation is the invariable of the room, its architecture. The architecture of the room emerges, in fact, as a trace that, because of repeating itself over and over again, starts to adopt a form, such as when a child's boots wears down the grass until a path is formed by crossing a prairie to go from home to school and back and with it a mark: a *geo-graphy* (in the way of Richard Long's *Line Made By Walking*).

If the exhaustion of the possibilities of Mr Knott's room is shown through the sequential condition of writing, that is to say that every single possibility is shown individually, one after the next one, in *Quad*, Beckett attempts to take the experimentation of the inclusive disjunctions already started in *Watt* to another level, this time using a different expressive instrument, the one of the image in movement. If in *Watt* we talked about a sequence of the possibilities of the chamber, in *Quad*, sequence gives place to simultaneity, exacerbating, then, again, the *exhaustion*.

> *Figure 1. Quad – The Plan*
> *Figure 2. Quad – The Diagram*
> *Figure 3. Quad – The Play*
>
> *The players (1,2,3,4) pace the given area, each following his particular course.*
>
> *Course 1: AC, CB, BA, AD, DB, BC, CD, DA*
> *Course 2: BA, AD, DB, BC, CD, DA, AC, CB*
> *Course 3: CD, DA, AC, CB, BA, AD, DB, BC*
> *Course 4: DB, BC, CD, DA, AC, CB, BA, AD*
>
> *1 enters at A, completes his course and is joined by 3. Together they complete their courses and are joined by 4. Together all three complete their courses and are joined by 2. Together all four complete their courses. Exit 1. 2, 3 and 4 continue and complete their courses. Exit 3. 2 and 4 continue and complete their courses. Exit 4. End of 1st series. 2 continues, opening 2nd series, completes his course and is joined by 1. Etc. Unbroken movement.* (Beckett 1986: 451)

In *Quad* there is no architecture, or at least that seems to be the case at first sight. There is no form nor matter nor geometry. But somehow, the four hooded characters assume and simulate these three architectural roles. They *play* the architecture of a square. They are the guardians of its geometry. Thanks to the repetition of their precise choreography, we arrive to 'see' the square. If, for any reason, they should stop their movement, the square would disappear. Now what we want to point out is that the architecture of the square appears or is stabilized thanks to the superposition of the possibilities of traveling the square itself. The square is nothing other than the synthesis, the sedimentation, of the movements of the four hooded characters.

But if in *Watt* the moment of the enumeration of the possibilities of the chamber is just a *meta-narrative* fragment or a bubble in the middle of the novel, which means that the novel, after having closed the bubble, goes on, *Quad* is the fragment that has become the whole piece. A piece, then, without narration. What happens in *Quad* is, as Deleuze sates, 'the replacement of all kind story by a "gestus" as a logic of postures and positions.'[7] (Deleuze 1992: 83)

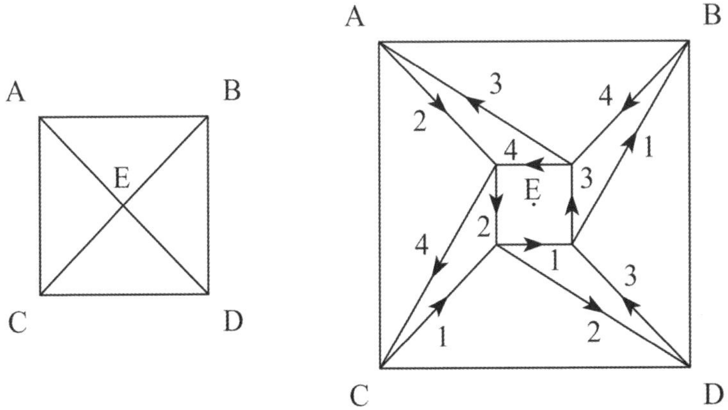

Figures 1 and 2.
Samuel Beckett, 'Quad', in: *Quad et autres pièces pour la télévision suivi de L'Épuisé par Gilles Deleuze* (Paris: Les Éditions de Minuit, 1992), 9-10.

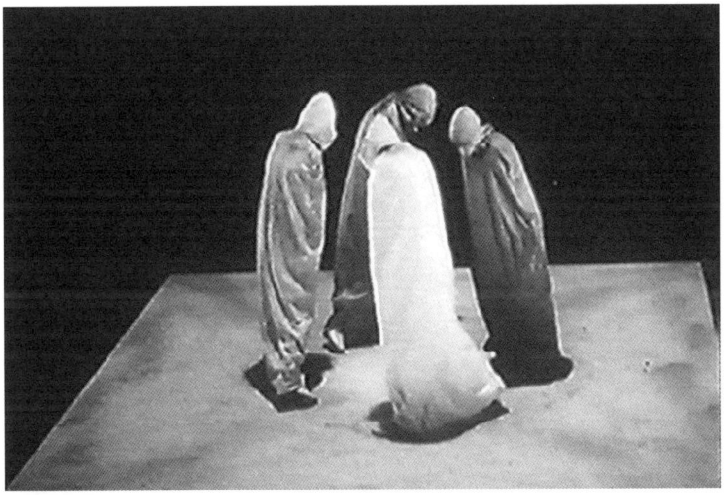

Figure 3. Samuel Beckett, *Quad I + II*, 15', Betacam SP, PAL, couleur, son, Collection Centre Georges Pompidou, Paris (France).

A multiple architecture is a heterotopic architecture. *Heterotopie*, as Foucault says, is the superposition of several spaces in a single place (Foucault 1994: 758)[8]. In that sense we could say that Beckett's architecture is a heterotopic architecture. It is given by the set of all its possibilities. One cannot consider them separately. We have to say that all possibilities, in fact, cohabitate. This architecture is, then, a schizoid architecture or, as we just said some lines up, the idea of a stage itself, a place where everything could happen: every kind of event, every kind of choreography, every kind of scenery.

1 'l'état de nos organes et de nos sens ont beaucoup d'influence sur notre métaphysique et sur notre morale.'

2 'Le moindre jamais ne peut être le néant.'

3 'Où maintenant? Quand maintenant? Qui maintenant?'

4 'Le fatigué ne peut plus réaliser, mais l'épuisé ne peut plus possibiliser.'

5 'mais toujours la réalisation du possible procède par exclusion, parce qu'elle suppose des préférences et buts qui varient, remplaçant les précédents.'

6 « *M. Knott, sans besoin autre que d'être sans besoin, ne réserve aucune combinaison à un usage particulier qui exclurait les autres, et dont il faudrait attendre les circonstances* ».

7 '*. . . le remplacement de toute histoire ou narration par un "gestus" comme logique des postures et positions*.'

8 '*L'hétérotopie a le pouvoir de juxtaposer en un seul lieu réel plusieurs espaces, emplacements qui sont en eux-mêmes incompatibles*.'

4 COMPLEXITY

Writing as a Mode of Architectural Investigation

Between Sites and Stories, Between Texts and Times

A Dialogue about Fiction and Narrative in Architectural Inquiries

Katja Grillner, Klaske Havik

KH:
To discuss 'Writing as a mode of investigation', we engaged in a dialogue: an open form that addresses different ways in which architectural research might be approached. Allowing a discussion on multiple perspectives, the dialogue is a good form with which to bring the performative capacity of writing to the fore. If a dialogue offers the possibility to place the reader 'in between' two positions, this discussion ponders the space between different temporalities, between sites and stories, between experience and different forms of imagination. Ultimately, we could discuss how literary forms of writing allow for critical and experimental architectural investigations, and how the results of such modes of investigation can be assessed.

KG:
Indeed, the form of a dialogue offers different perspectives to matters discussed within a single essay. It makes it possible to construct, or reconstruct, conversations between different positions, and to bring characters from different places and times into a temporary fictional location. This is a method I used in my own PhD thesis *Ramble, Linger and Gaze: Dialogues from the Landscape Garden*.[1] The dialogue in my thesis is situated in the landscape garden. It unfolds as the material ground on which discourse develops, and uses different layers of text around the main body of text to care for different reflexive perspectives. Textual layers such as endnotes, preface, postscript and bibliographical essay may function as such.

KH:
This reminds me of Mark Z. Danielewski's stunning novel *House of Leaves,* in which different layers of text, such as footnotes that are considered 'neutral' in academic texts, as well as layers told by different narrators, are fully played out, to the extent that the novel consists of different parallel narratives that each make full use of the space that these layers offer.[2] In a ludic way, Georges Perec also points at the possibilities of such layers of text on his first pages of *Species of Spaces*:

> *I write: I inhabit my sheet of paper, I invest it, I travel across it.*
> *I incite* ***blanks, spaces*** *(jumps in the meaning: discontinuities, transitions, changes of key).*
>
> *I write*
> *in the*
> *margin*
>
> *I start a new*
> *paragraph. I refer to a footnote*[(1)]
>
> *I go to an new sheet of paper.*

(1) *I am very fond of footnotes at the bottom of every page . . .3*

These examples show that the text offers ample space to experiment, to go back and forth to different textual layers, and thereby to include different voices, timeframes or narratives. This experimental space that the text has to offer is rarely used to its full extent in architectural research.

Your *Ramble, Linger and Gaze* also makes use of the freedom of the text to enrich the research, to make it more than a singular narrative. The use of dialogue allows different timeframes to be present simultaneously, thus showing the interconnectivity between these different temporalities and their influences on the landscape garden you investigated. It is remarkable that the possibility to jump between different timeframes, which is quite natural in literary and cinematographic narratives, seems underused in architectural inquiries. This very mediation between past, present and future is one of the main capacities of architecture. Even if an architectural design is first and foremost a projection of a possible future, and thus a fiction, every building, urban space or landscape is positioned simultaneously to history and the present. Our stories connected to place gain more depth and richness when different temporalities coexist. When introducing literary modes of writing, such as dialogues, narratives or poetry, into architectural investigations, different temporalities can come together.

KG:
I am currently working on an essay on the topics we are discussing here. Its working title is 'Enacting the Past, the Distant (or what is not here, but there)' pointing to the capacity of performative modes of writing to mediate between historical and contemporary readings of spaces and places.[4] I am, for example, now thinking of Lina Bo Bardi's SESC Pompeia as an excellent example of a project where a practice of connectivity between past, presence and future experiences as well as social and physical spaces determines the architecture as it evolves.[5] In a very literal, material sense, the traces of the past in terms of cobblestones, remaining structures from the old factory building here intermingles with the contemporary additions that in themselves are at once bold and playful – intensely alive.

On another note, the design process as orchestrated by Lina Bo Bardi embraced a dialogical perspective. When she was commissioned by SESC in 1977 to develop the new culture and sports centre at the old steel drum factory, SESC members, workers and their families were already occupying the site for leisurely activities. Lina Bo Bardi moved on site with her team, and articulated the programme of the future building through a careful survey of the technical and material conditions of existing structures

Figure 1. Photograph reminding visitors of the first SESC activities on the site before the development of the current buildings and program. SESC Pompéia (1977-1982, Lina Bo Bardi)

Figure 2. Library spaces. SESC Pompéia (1977-1982, Lina Bo Bardi). Photos: Katja Grillner.

as well as though encounters with and participation in ongoing practices and desires. Members of her team have testified to her particular collaborative method, whereby creative contributions were expected from everyone involved in the materialization of the construction. The skills of craftsmen and construction workers were particularly respected.[6] This practice formed a culture that was maintained at the centre long after the formal completion of the project. Maintenance staff, programme directors and curators shared a particular love for the site, its spaces, materials, programmes and oddities. Stories are still embedded in the daily wear and tear.[7]

KH:
Would you say that, just as in a written work of architectural research like *Ramble, Linger and Gaze*, a certain sense of dialogue or co-presence of different historical (and textual?) layers is at stake in this physical work of architecture?

KG:
They are probably very different. Perhaps some of the effects – the possibility to simultaneously experience, in juxtaposition, different pasts and presents – can be interpreted somehow as analogous. But in terms of their design the two works are very different. While SESC Pompéia is a fantastic work of architecture, one should perhaps also be careful in connecting architectural quality too strongly with its spatial capacity to tie back to a history of place as well as pointing towards a new future. The past may at particular times or places be completely irrelevant to the future, or even deeply disturbing and best forgotten. By discussing, in the current essay I am working on, the 'past' side by side with the 'distant', I would like to somehow emphasize the relativity of historical pasts. In architectural storytelling 'real' material traces of a temporal past can, for example, make immediate sense in the present, thus not at all point back towards their 'factual' past. Perhaps these traces rather stir up imaginations of an alternative future, an 'other' world. All this depends of course on the frame of reference at play, with the users and uses, current political and social contexts, etcetera. I experienced SESC Pompéia as a site that encompasses these particular qualities – playful and liberating. The past is present as an imaginary, rich with connotations no matter what you make of it. The production of meaning lies very clearly in the user herself, while material forms act as concrete gestures, some highly dramatic, others extremely subtle.

KH:
In dialogues in literature, different temporal perspectives can be shown together. Think for instance, to give an obvious example, of one protagonist telling memories to

a younger one. It is of no surprise that the interview is such a successful tool in historical research, giving voice to people's memories of places, registering oral history. Narratives, as the unfolding of events in time and space, by definition have a temporal component. Events take place in time, and the way they are narrated does not always follow a linear chronological order. In his discussion on time and narrative, Paul Ricoeur explains how in the mimetic act of the narrative 'the words "future", "past" and "present" disappear, and time itself figures as the exploded unity of the three temporal extases'.[8] This sounds cryptic, but indeed, it is within a narrative that different temporalities coexist naturally, and that the categorization between past, present and future becomes obsolete.

KG:
In his lectures on the imagination, Ricoeur distinguishes between reproductive and productive imagination.[9] Reproductive imagination refers to the notion of 'image as copy', whereby the imagination is a vehicle to imagine the real as it is: the real as original. Productive imagination, on the other hand, shifts the reference from copy to fiction – 'image as a production of a new world' – a world that did not exist prior to its realization through fiction. His essay on 'the function of fiction in shaping reality' is fascinating in its extremely concise account of the urgent necessity of fiction.[10] Reflecting back on the example I just gave on a situation where the significance of the 'real' history of a certain architectural detail may be overshadowed by its capacity to stir up imaginations of alternative futures or other worlds, this would be a case where, following Ricoeur's terminology, the productive imagination has been set in motion. The productive imagination is, in Ricoeur's thinking, linked directly to fictionality and storytelling. We need to be wary, he writes, of the simplifications that may result from an overly visual, image-driven understanding of imagination. To him the 'what if' condition that the fictional frame unlocks is an absolutely essential component of a society where change is possible – fiction, then, is essential for the 'shaping of reality'. My own interest in developing spatial modes of writing comes from a particular fascination with these aspects of architectural experience and imagination.

KH:
Strikingly, these two aspects – experience and imagination – address both ends of the spectrum of what Bernard Tschumi called the paradox of architecture:

> *... the paradoxical relationship between architecture as a product of the mind, as a conceptual and dematerialized discipline, and architecture as the sensual experience of space and as a spatial practice ... the impossibility of*

simultaneously questioning the nature of space, and, at the same time, making or experiencing a real space.[11]

In literary writing, these aspects naturally come together. In literature, we can find very accurate and detailed descriptions of architectural experience, both of real, existing architectures and of fictional ones. Poetic writing is exceptionally useful for registering architectural experience. In poetic writing about a landscape, building or urban place, the meticulous attention to details, both material and ephemeral, gains importance in grasping the different spatial as well as temporal layers of a site, and the connections between them. A simple detail may link to a larger narrative, to other times and even other places, and indeed connect, as you suggested in your working title, the present situation to a past, the proximity of the site to a distant other one.

KG:
I would like to highlight here a degree project in architecture from KTH by Malena Norlin. [12] Entitled 'to walk', the project sets up – through text, charcoal drawings, wood and plaster models – an imaginary landscape populated by literary characters and Norlin's own alter ego. Across this landscape – based on her memories of recurring walks in the mountainscape around the city of Bergen – encounters with specific characters occur in carefully selected spots. Emancipatory struggles are materialized and shared in these locations – narrated through textual episodes, through material models and through charcoal details. The resulting book and exhibition open up new imaginary worlds on their own account. From Paul Ricoeur's theory of the imagination we can tease out different aspects and functions of the imaginary thus presented: It engages utopian, emancipatory visions as well as the poetics of lived pain and material struggle. In terms of epistemological imagination the project offers, with the support of literature and feminist design theory, a ground to rethink and question the basic grounds upon which architecture is developed.[13]

KH:
In my teaching I have noticed that exercises based on poetic reading and writing greatly enhanced the students' sensibility for site-specific atmospheres. Poetic writing in particular has the power to unveil qualities that do not come to the surface when using conventional surveys and modes of mapping. For a recent site-specific analysis course with Master students at Delft University of Technology, I first asked the students to reinterpret literary modes of analysis used by architects such as Bernard Tschumi, Peter Eisenman or John Hejduk. The students were asked to critically reflect on these methods, to reinvent and apply them to the site analysis of a site completely

Figure 3: Charcoal drawing, landscape details. To walk, Malena Norlin, Diploma Degree Project, 2013.

Figure 4: To walk, Malena Norlin, Diploma Degree Project, 2013. Photos: Malena Norlin.

unknown to them, in Skopje, Macedonia. Seline Wijker, a student departing from the work of Hejduk, found great analytic capacity in Hejduk's word matrices. She also invited her fellow students to participate in an *in-situ* poetry writing session and supplemented this material with drawings of the trajectories of different characters in a dense urban neighbourhood. Altogether, her poetic exercises resulted in a rich and sensible reading of a socially and spatially complex site. The results were shared with local students in Skopje, who used it as point of departure for design interventions. The combined material of the Hejduk-inspired exercises and the involvement of local characters proved very productive. In this exercise, the focus on experience in the analysis opened ways to new imaginations. Hence, investigating experience may lead naturally to imagination – architecture as a 'product of the mind', to refer back to Tschumi again.

We can thus clearly see the advantages of using literary forms of writing in architectural education. Nonetheless, literary writing is not often acknowledged as a serious mode of operation in architectural research. In the academic environment it is considered at best 'nice' or 'creative', but all too often it is regarded as too subjective, artistic and suspicious to be recognized as a form of producing valuable knowledge. Maybe this is due to the background of many faculties of architecture as part of a university of technology, in which rational methods claiming objectivity and measurability prevail. If architecture as a field of investigation would have been rooted more strongly in the human or social sciences, would we have met less suspicion when proposing literary writing as a serious from of inquiry?

KG:

I have always felt a rather strong support for pursuing the development of alternative modes of academic writing and inquiry. This is of course thanks to my own educational background and the links I have establishing over time with likeminded writers and scholars around the world. I am actually not convinced it has to do to with which faculty or discipline architecture in the end belongs. KTH is a technical university to which architecture belongs, and yet I would say that we have a long tradition of quite experimental research in architecture theory and design. I have experienced conservative responses from academics in arts and humanities as well. This is to be expected when you challenge established norms and destabilizes conventions on, for example, how a dissertation should be composed.

Within a technical faculty, if you engage with the experimental and innovation-driven aspects of a lot of research conducted here, you can also encounter unexpected situ-

Denominator

The Thing:	ROAD	STREET	SQUARE	ROADSIDE
The Material:	ASPHALT	COBBELSTONES	NATURAL STONE	GRAVEL
What for:	TRANSPORT VEIN	CONNECTION	FOR PUBLIC BUILDINGS	FILLING
A Texture:	FLAT SURFACE	UNEVEN STONES	CLATTERING WATER	LOOSE GROUND
A Sound:	BUZZING	RATTLING	VOICES	UNOBSTRUCTED WIND
A Subject:	THE STRANGER	THE NEIGHBOUR	THE PUBLIC	THE STREET YOUTH
Dark Association:	SMOKEY AIR	LABYRINTH	CONTROL	ABANDONED
Conclusion:	BOUNDARY	INTERIOR	GATHERING PLACE	LEFTOVER

Figure 5. Adaptation of Hejduk's *Passage through the streets of Berlin* (John Hejduk, *Berlin Night* (Rotterdam: Nai publishers 1993) 20-21, for the reading of the open spaces of the urban neighborhood of Cair, Skopje. The 'denominators' were identified by the student. Seline Wijker, Master seminar project, 2015.

ations of mutual understanding. On the other hand, it is absolutely true that we find a lot of theoretical and methodological affinities with particular strands of humanities and social science research. That is where we find the philosophical bearings of our practice. Within, for example, feminist studies, ethnography and geography, narrative methodologies play an important role, not the least for practices of positioning the researcher within the research context, and affording agency to a multiplicity of research subjects.[14] What has always been helpful to me, in positioning my work in different research contexts, is to insist on a clear methodological reasoning. That is, to explain the motivations behind a specific approach: What is my argument for developing this particular mode of writing, what is it that I hope to research, and how do I explain what I find?

KH:
At the TU Delft, this is exactly what we do with our group Methods&Analysis. We challenge students and researchers to experiment with methods from different disciplines, while being aware of the purpose, limitations and capacities of these methods. These explorations are very productive and eye-opening for students and researchers alike. An important question is how to assess such explorations. For instance, in an experimental diploma project, as the one you described earlier, how much must we then expect from the reader (or examiner, reviewer) in terms of almost co-creating its critical significance? Should we expect them to be able to produce knowledge by reconstructing these imaginary worlds him- or herself?

KG:
Conventional assessment criteria in both architectural education (diploma works) and research (PhD) can be argued to be somewhat bound to reproductive imagination (referring back here to Ricoeur's theory of the imagination). This is of course an argument that demands to be teased out much more carefully than what we can do here. But, if simplifying greatly, what I mean is that an architectural design project may conventionally be expected to point to a 'real' referent (a realizable building or environment), and a research project to deliver 'real' contributions to knowledge. When we instead argue for projects that engage with productive imagination, offering alternative worlds to be explored, other modes of assessment must come into play. Often these perspectives are not conflicting – a project often engages our productive imagination, and at the same time presents us with what appears to be a realizable building design. When, on the other hand, architectural projects are found to project dystopic conditions, play with irony, or as in Norlin's case present a fictional landscape inhabited by literary characters, it may become difficult to find appropriate ways to

Constructing narratives - The daily life of Artan.

Artan

Finally the school is out. Artan is chasing Besian. Besian runs from one end of the street to the other, suddenly he disappears behind the corner. Artan follows him, there he is! He enters a door. The door swings back in its position. Artan pushes it and looks around. Where did he go? Then he sees Besian climbing the outside stairs of his house. Besian looks down to Artan and shouts: "You can't catch me!" and he disappears inside. Artan goes back to the street to continue his route. Two more streets and he is home as well. He hopes his grandmother prepared something delicious because he is very hungry. After lunch he goes back onto the street to search for Besian. He carries his football with him. They always play together in the afternoon. When it gets dark he returns home. When he enters his street Artan sees an older man talking to his granddad. He knows the man and he decides to hide behind the corner. He hears the man talking to his granddad: "Your grandson is steeling my bicycle every day!" Artan decides to walk another round before he faces his granddad because he will definitely be very angry.

Figure 6. Constructing narratives on the basis of daily trajectories of inhabitants of the urban neighborhood of Cair, Skopje. The Daily life of Artan. Seline Wijker, Master seminar project, 2015.

respond. If not projected into a desirable future, how do we interpret and assess what we encounter? In PhD theses a scientific or scholarly claim to truth, to a true (or credible) representation of a current or historical situation conventionally frames the academic assessment of the work. When the principal contribution of the thesis instead is an imaginary construction or enactment, other types of questions need to be asked and other qualities assessed.

KH:
Here, we arrive at a crucial point in our dialogue: If architecture as a discipline by definition deals with the productive imagination, inventing new realities on the basis of the existing, couldn't architectural research perform in a similar manner? Could architecture research function more in a dialogical sense, mediating between different temporalities, between the experience of real space and the speculation of possible new realities? In that case, architectural research could have a speculative component, and the assessment of architectural research would take place in a discursive manner. The criteria of such an assessment need to deal with the methodological framework, the apparent knowledge of the state of the art of the research field, and with the potential new perspectives the work opens up for critical discourse. Making full use of the space that the textual layers of an academic article or a PhD dissertation have to offer, architectural research could become more stratified, evocative and challenging. Essentially, architectural research could open up the dialogue between different temporalities, between historical facts and possible new realities, between experience and imagination. Could we state that it could be one of the key ambitions of architectural research to open up dialogues?

KG:
One could absolutely argue that we already are in this position. There are many powerful examples of architectural research that do precisely this (made quite clear by the contributions to this publication). On the other hand, I would also like to take a somewhat more humble stance. In my own engagement and interest for this particular strand of architectural research I make no claims for its relative priority. I think it is an extremely important path to pursue, yes, but, given that it is a recognized path, it is perhaps not more principal than other modes of architectural and urban design research, research that sometimes appears to fit more neatly into established knowledge regimes. My view, however, is that there is a need today to articulate more precisely the philosophical implications of what I call performative and fictional modes of architectural design and research. Knowledge appears here not as a tangible 'result', but remains situated, produced through a performative process, a writing and

the street
cardboard
closure
introversy
being pushed out
children's noise
a worried mother
melancholy
apathy
time stands still

chaos
creaking
crumbling
darkness everywhere
but
the old man
his memories
his collection
his universe

short silence
of stone and concrete
far away sounds
then children's voices
cars passing
louder and louder
peeling plaster
the creaking of wood
the swinging of cables
then again silence

moving slowly
passing by
cars and men
new meets old
sound of movements
social meetings
non-understandable voices
staring coldness

children's laugh
break
the silence
the dust
in the air
peeled off
plaster
exluded
composition
stay together

voids
everything that is nothing
personal objects
lost, chaotic
different voices
shouting
cars
swinging
strolling
the streets, the only public zone
no reference
framing the freedom

unfinished structures
entangled in wires
cars passing
growling engines
men looking
shuffling
distant minaret
voices of children
the toothless smile
of an older woman
living
life

Figure 7. Poetic site-reading of Cair, Skopje. Master seminar project, 2015.

reading process, a making, drawing and experiencing process. Thinking as produced in specific relation to the experience of reading (taking in, perceiving, appropriating) the work and conversing around, on and within it.

1 Katja Grillner, *Ramble, Linger and Gaze: Dialogues from the Landscape Garden* (Stockholm: KTH, 2000).
2 Mark Z. Danielewski, *House of Leaves* (London: Doubleday/Transworld Publishers, 2001 [2000])
3 Georges Perec, *Species of Spaces* (London: Penguin Classics, 2008 [1974]), 11.
4 For publication in Hélène Frichot and Gunnar Sandin (eds.), *After Effects: Theories and Methodologies in Architecture* (forthcoming volume from the strong research environment Architecture in Effect to be released in 2016/2017).
5 Cecilía Rodrigues dos Santos, 'SESC – Pompeia: An American Citadel', in *SESC – Pompeia Factory* (Lisbon: Editorial Blau, 1998); Zeuler R.M. de A. Lima, 'Lina Bo Bardi and the Architecture of Everyday Culture', *Places*, November 2013 (www.placesjournal.org, accessed 1 April 2016).
6 Marcelo Ferraz, 'The Making of SESC Pompéia', at *Lina Bo Bardi: Together*, exhibition and website www.linabobarditogether.com (accessed 1 April 2016).

7 Conversation with Roberto Cenni, curator at SESC Pompeía from 1980 to 2014, on a visit to SESC Pompeía on 18 February 2014.
8 Paul Ricoeur, *Time and Narrative, Volume I* (Chicago/London: The University of Chicago Press, 1990), 61.
9 George H. Taylor, 'Ricoeur's Philosophy of the Imagination', *Journal of French Philosophy*, vol. 16 (Spring-Fall 2006) no. 1 and 2, 93-104.
10 Paul Ricoeur, 'The Function of Fiction in Shaping Reality'; *Man and World*, vol. 12 (1979) no. 2, 123-141.
11 Bernard Tschumi, 'Architecture and Transgression', in: Bernard Tschumi, *Architecture and Disjunction* (Cambridge, MA/London: MIT Press, 1996), 66-67.
12 Malena Norlin, 'att gå' [to walk], (Stockholm: KTH School of Architecture and the Built Environment, 2013), M.Arch degree project.
13 See George H. Taylor on the four domains of the productive imagination, op. cit. (note 9), 94.
14 See, for example, Mona Livholts (ed.), *Emergent Writing Methodologies in Feminist Studies* (London: Routledge, 2012).

Practical Ambivalence

A Dialogical Approach to Design and Public Space

Thomas-Bernard Kenniff

How should we approach the task of designing for the public realm once we recognize the paradoxes that mark our conceptions of publics and public space? The difficulty, for critical practice, rests on reconciling the act of significantly affecting the social and built environment of others, while opening up the same process to their agency. In addressing this question, this chapter develops a framework for design and public space based on the dialogical theory of Mikhail Bakhtin. It suggests that the range of concepts Bakhtin develops from literature, linguistics and creative acts like writing, concepts related under the broad notion of dialogue (Holloway and Kneale 2000: 83), are particularly relevant when it comes to understanding design and public space as open, collective and ultimately unfinalizable processes. In this sense, dialogism offers critical insights into critical spatial practices that treat contemporary public space as an agonistic and continuing negotiation (as supported by the respective work of

Chantal Mouffe and Doreen Massey). With regards to design, the chapter suggests that the paradoxes and incongruences inherent to designing public space – that neither publics nor public spaces are ever well-defined – can be reconciled under the notion of *practical ambivalence*. This notion recognizes that if design is treated as a narrative, then its degree of ambivalence is the extent to which the narrative remains open in a dialogical sense.

The relevance of Bakhtin's work to this approach to public space is not only in the immediate connection between language and space, but in the wider breadth of dialogism. As an underlying principle of most of Bakhtin's work, dialogue relates creative activity, interpretation and communication in terms of alterity, relationships, uncertainty and unfinalizability.[1] In this chapter I focus on ambivalence since it is this quality of dialogue that allows for the co-existence of differences, between self and other, utterance and response, social structure and the everyday, but also in design between designer and user, form and function, social and material, public and private. Ambivalence significantly recognizes dialogue's 'inherent instability and incapacity for absolute signification' (Beasley-Murray 2008: 131) so that each relationship remains open and changing, without synthesis or closure. This suggests that impossible positions may be manoeuvred – say the notion that neither publics nor their spatial production (public space) can be in any way fixed and must be understood as constant dialogical processes – bridging the gap between affirmative and representative design actions and the uncertainty of use.

In developing these ideas, this chapter makes use of an extensive case study of the Barking Town Square in east London by muf architecture/art.[2] Designed and completed between 2004 and 2010 and expressive of the regeneration policies of the Urban Renaissance, the project participated in the rapid and significant transformation of the town centre and overlapped with a period of increased immigration during which a quarter of the local assembly was held by the far-right British National Party. Rebirth, in this part of London, was not without its growing pains. The Town Square project, whose design process included ideas of narrative, collaboration and ambiguity, is used here to develop a dialogical approach to public space that may have significant resonance with critical spatial practice while raising questions about the implications of practical ambivalence.

Dialogue and Public Space

The significance of Bakhtin to public space, writes Ken Hirschkop, lies in the idea that public space is less a place designed for a particular type of communication, rather than a space generated by a particular type of communication (Hirschkop 2004: 51). Bakhtin's dialogic theory has indeed been used to expand and criticize the Habermasian tradition of the discursive public sphere, particularly through the notion of the everyday and 'gross reality' (Gardiner 2004). Dialogical space is characterized by an ambivalent relation between text and context, situation and system, much like the relationship between an utterance and language (Holloway and Kneale 2000: 78). What is of particular interest, in this model, is the necessary incompleteness, or, in Bakhtin's words, unfinalizability, of the object of study. Whether it is public space in general or the act of designing for public space, each is defined dialogically by its incapacity to be fully resolved.

Design activity, in this reading, is a constant negotiation between the act of defining something (giving form to public space, for example) or someone, and the everyday reality of the same entities. 'What we did,' muf partner Liza Fior says, 'was to draw the dotted line around the boxing ring we were boxing in (interview held in 2010).' Here, the act of delineation points to the dialogical space of the project, both as physical place (the public square) and as the spatial production of a set of social relationships. Drawing a line, whether the dotted line around a boxing ring, the line separating two functional areas, or the path of a potential user across the site, is inevitably dialogical. It links the author of the act to another subject, individual or collective. Every 'creatively productive event', writes Bakhtin, inevitably occurs between two or more subjects (Bakhtin 1990: 86). Reading from Bakhtin's notion of the act as an exterior-oriented event, we can say that each design act similarly 'shapes values into form' (Clark and Holquist 1984: 10). Regardless of whether this form is a simple line or a participatory workshop, they are all acting on the polyphony of the project, propositions for particular arrangements of relationships.[3]

Designing public space, then, implies much more than a series of steps leading to a final product, but includes a series of dialogical spaces generated by the multiple meetings and negotiations that occur within the project. The practical issues we are interested in here arise when design methods are conceived in order to entertain the ambivalence and unfinalizability of these spaces.

Counter-Narratives

How, then, can the ambivalence of dialogue become a foundation for design practice? The creative act, polyphony (in the novel), the carnivalesque and speech are for Bakhtin modes of expressing and working with dialogical ambivalence. Each of these, if we follow Holloway and Kneale, can be seen to 'carve up space' (79); that is, they produce space and can be read spatially. Each will have a differentiating function, creating ambiguity between author and reader, or between a social system and its critique.

Perhaps the most indicative and direct of these modes with respect to public space and its design, and for the questions raised in this chapter, is the carnivalesque. In *Rabelais and His World*, Bakhtin draws on the phenomena of carnival and folk culture, especially its humour, the grotesque, satire and parody, to reveal the revolutionary potential of laughter itself. Laughter stands for the mechanism that dissolves the contradictions of authority and sociality in the public square. It is counter-cultural because it has the power to expose the over-seriousness of power and authority and to reveal the authoritarian-monologic nature of its discourse. A narrative, this suggests, does not exist without its own counter-narratives. The significance of carnival and laughter in the development of a dialogical theory for design is in the way that these concepts tie dialogical ambivalence to a practice and its effect.

Carnivalization, Folch-Serra writes, is 'the insertion of genres: letters, found manuscripts, retold dialogues, parodies on the high genres, parodically (sic) reinterpreted citations, and so on' (264). As the opposite of monologue, carnival abolishes the absolute difference of values 'by the conjunction of opposing values which brings forth laughter' (Zima cited in Beasley-Murray 2008: 154).

Extrapolating to design, the introduction of contradictory values can establish a dialogue between form and function, designer and user, and collage aesthetics in both social and material capacities. The meeting of two or more entities does not negate each element, but revives and supports its counterparts so that there is no resolution of the dialogue. Carnivalization in design, then, can take the form of a dialogical play between social engagement and formal assemblages for which ambiguity is central.

This was evidenced in Barking in what FAT has described as muf's method of unpacking the site and project narratives in order to rearrange them into a design proposal (60). The design proposal, in this sense, seeks to establish those counter-narratives that disconnect the possibility for a finalized and monological narrative. Commenting on the ethics of their practice, Liza Fior explains that 'by opening public space to ambiguity you open it to multiple possibilities and interpretations' (interview held in 2010). What a reading of Bakhtin suggests with respect to method is that this 'opening up' is achieved in two ways. First, by expanding the discursive space of the project whether through collaboration, participation or foreshadowed use. In Barking this took the form of parallel workshops and public art commissions that brought in local residents and technical expertise that would have otherwise been missing. Second, with ambiguous form or the architectural equivalent to open questions, unfinalized dialogues, and invitations for differing appropriations. For example, the balustrade around the planted areas of the Town Square (fig. 1) combines foreshadowed use, ambiguity and collage. 'We knowingly put [the balustrades] around the fragile ecologies so that people don't walk on the desire lines, but they're actually designed so children can climb in without saying that's what they're for' (interview held in 2009). Another example, the Folly wall (fig. 2), is the result of a public art commission and a collaboration with the local masonry college, that, as we will see later, seeks to carnivalize the narrative of regeneration.

The collaborative, intersubjective and ambiguous formal aspects of this carnival aesthetics can all be understood as facets of making ambivalence practical. The narrative created, if we extrapolate to design in general, represents, as Sophia Psarra argues, a desire to create coherence out of conflict and resolve contradictions (Psarra 2003: 388). Yet in carnival this remains unresolved and ambivalent (both a desire for resolution and its negation), a way of understanding that is both procedural and open-ended (Tappan). The introduction of these counter-narratives act on social and material relationships while keeping them unfinalized. This is crucial when discussing the design of public space, because it readily orients the act of design towards the uncertainty and otherness of the public realm. At the same time, however, the narratives or counter-narratives derived by designers are also giving sense to a series of evolving dialogues. This, in proper dialogical fashion, inevitably leads to contradictions.

The Politics of Practical Ambivalence

> *'Every act of world history was accompanied by a laughing chorus.'*
> *(Bakhtin 1984: 474)*

Bakhtin's laughing chorus is a reminder that no narrative knows no other. Irony and parody are seldom acknowledged aspects of design practices, or indeed considered serious modes of operation. However, it is not the irony of design assemblages that is the point here, but their ambivalence. Laughter, for Bakhtin, much like shock for Benjamin, is a reaction to the coexistence of contradictions and to the destabilization of monological structures (Beasley-Murray 2008: 3-4). Acknowledging that contradictions inevitably arise from constructing design narratives and/or their counter-narratives is perhaps one of the principal lessons of practical ambivalence.
What muf calls 'room for doubt', or the desire to allow uncertainty to productively

Figure 1. Balustrade detail around planted areas of the Town Square with metal cast of tree branch.

Figure 2. Folly wall by muf at the end of the Town Square's civic plaza with workers on their lunch break, September 2009.

influence design (muf 2001: 213), is a theoretical idea that can only go so far before it meets the real constraints of clients, budgets, health and safety regulations, use or affirmative design aesthetics. With respect to authorship, Bakhtin's theories in no way diminish the importance of the author in structuring the possible meanings of a work, but rather give proper weight to the collective dynamics of ever-changing interpretation and reinterpretation, particularly its contradictions and paradoxes. The interest of ambiguous details is partly in the expansion of the discursive field they support, but perhaps even more significantly in the misuse their ambivalence may attract (fig. 3).

This dynamic is perhaps most evident in Barking in the Folly (fig. 4) because it stands in for a reflection on public space whose principal qualities are ambivalence, uncertainty and incompleteness. Completed in September 2007, it was commissioned by the Council's Arts department as part of a series that would reflect the town's changing heritage and public realm. For muf partner Katherine Clarke, the wall became a counterpoint to the evolving narrative of the Town Square, the construction of another way of imagining public space. 'We made an overt sort of *mise en scène* which didn't necessarily need to be occupied but stood for a potential mythology of the public realm' (Clarke). Open-ended and ambiguous, as she describes it, it demands a response from its audience because, unlike the popular idea for a statue to local fishermen of the eighteenth century, it is 'not sure whether it is committed to tradition or not' (Clarke).'[4] In other words, it is a response to the town's transforming identity that seeks ambivalence. 'What a great job you did restoring it,' said a passing architect to the masons when the scaffolding came down, not realizing the wall had been entirely built brick by brick over the last six months.[5]

The Folly wants to be the laughing chorus of regeneration. Yet the project is funded and approved by both the Borough and the London Thames Gateway Development Corporation who in turn support the larger development of the Town Square unambiguously. The critical aspects of the Town Square project, especially its peripheral public art commissions, arise from government-supported schemes and ideas that stand in opposition to market forces, which are paradoxically supported by the same government.

This is the paradox of practical ambivalence. Every narrative is caught between centripetal forces, those that keep it tidy, and centrifugal forces, those that seek to break it, counter it and recombine it to multiply its possibilities (Bakhtin 1981:270). Dialogue and ambivalence indeed have radical roots, but may find their edges blunted against the centripetal forces of authorities – including, significantly, the authority of the

Figure 3. Dancing in the Town Square's 'fragile ecologies' during the Molten Festival, September 2010.

Figure 4. The Folly wall, fabricated entirely from architectural salvage material, covers the loading dock of high street shops.

designer who seeks openness. The lesson, in relation to designing public space, is one about the double-edged sword of ambivalence: if you want ambivalence, you must be ready to eat it too.

Practical ambivalence, to summarize, is a mode of working that celebrates the uncertainty and incompleteness of the dialogical public realm. With respect to design, it suggests that the counter-narratives tied to carnival aesthetics are potentially effective as long as they are committed to difference and alterity and willing to accept their own contradictions.

Designing public space is uncertain and risky, and should be, since there is effectively 'no last word' to the dialogical context (Bakhtin 1986: 170). Design, paradoxically, can acknowledge its own failure to resolve this. However, it may nurture and support dialogue and ambivalence by making useful and effective 'room for doubt' while simultaneously understanding the realistic limitations of critique. As Edward Sapir wrote, 'every system leaks' (cited in Clark and Holquist 1984: 14). It is the quality and effectiveness of the space for doubt that matters rather than its mere existence. Whether architect, artist, planner, developer, council official, public or local resident, each authority must be able to laugh at their own conceptions with the help of others.

1 The early essays of Bakhtin focused on the creative activity of the author. This was followed by work on the novel and its dialogical aspects and later studies on speech and language. The dialogical thread in all of his work has been described by Tzvetan Todorov as the principle that states that nothing can be understood outside of the relations that link it to the other (Todorov: 94).

2 The overall project is a mixed-use development that includes residential buildings, commercial space and a library by AHMM Architects. In this chapter I focus on the public realm contract commissioned to muf architecture/art. The case study is supported by extensive participant-observation in Barking and interviews with the square's designers between 2009 and 2011.

3 For a discussion of design processes, dialogue and ethics, see Kenniff and Sweeting.

4 Barking in the eighteenth and nineteenth centuries was one of the country's most important fishing villages. The construction of the railway marked the decline and ultimate disappearance of the fishing industry.

5 The wall was designed by muf in collaboration with a local college and constructed by professional masons out of architectural salvage pieces. The anecdote of the architect was reported by Shane Moss, the lead mason on the project.

Configuring Beirut's Vague Urbain

A Marvellous Real

Carole Lévesque

Let me begin with words by Alejo Carpentier:

> *The word 'marvellous' has, with time and use, lost its true meaning. . . . Dictionaries tell us the marvellous is something that causes admiration because it is extraordinary, excellent, formidable. And that is joined to the notion that everything marvellous must be beautiful, lovely, pleasant, when really the only thing that should be gleaned from the dictionaries' definition is a reference to the extraordinary. The extraordinary is not necessarily lovely or beautiful. It is neither beautiful nor ugly; rather, it is amazing because it is strange. Everything strange, everything amazing, everything that eludes established norms is marvellous.* (Carpentier 1995a: 101)

In an introduction to his novel *The Kingdom of This World*, he adds to this revision of what should be defined as marvellous, that the 'marvellous begins to be unmistakably marvellous when it arises from an unexpected alteration of reality . . . [a sort of] amplification of the scales', (Carpentier 1995b: 86) during which improbable juxtapositions suddenly emerge as dominant features of the real. In this novel set in French occupied Haiti, a simple cook becomes the emperor of the island who, believing that Frenchmen will try to reconquer the island, sets on building a magnificent fortress in which he and his people can outlive a ten-year siege. Twenty thousand people, men and women, built the fortress atop a 900-metre mountain, for a battle that never came. This, according to Carpentier, is marvellous. While it may appear to be an improbable heroic task, the folly of king Henri Christophe was clearly beyond reason and he built a reality that could only be possible by 'virtue of a specific history, geography, demography, and politics – not by manifesto'. (Carpentier 1995b: 75). The marvellous defended by Carpentier is one that is latent, omnipresent and always in the commonplace.

The amplification of the scales and improbable juxtapositions is also found at the scale of everyday occurrences. Similar to the proposal made by Michel de Certeau, everyday practices may embed manipulations within a given system or of an established order. (De Certeau 1990: 135) Tricks can be played, as tropes can be written, both inscribing ruses and displacements within the ordinary, revealing strange, bizarre or simply unexpected elements that provide an awkwardly real perspective on things. And according to Carpentier: 'We have only to reach out our hands to grasp [the marvellous]. [Our everyday environment] presents us with strange occurrences everyday.' (Carpentier 1995a: 107). As in this passage:

> *While his master was being shaved, Ti Noël could gaze his fill at the four wax heads that adorned the counter by the door. The curls of the wigs, opening into a pool of ringlets on the red baize, framed expressionless faces. . . . By an amusing coincidence, in the window of the tripe-shop next door there were calves' heads, skinned and each with a sprig of parsley across the tongue, which possessed the same waxy quality. . . . Only a wooden wall separated the two counters, and it amused Ti Noël to think that alongside the pale calves' heads, heads of white men were served on the same tablecloth. Just as fowl for a banquet are adorned with their feathers, so some experienced, macabre cook might have trimmed the heads with their best wigs.* (Carpentier 1957: 10-11)

Carpentier explores ways in which the marvellous augments the layers of the narrative, creating, with the addition of each exploration, a plausible sense in which every encountered place can hold the seed for the marvellous to grow. As such, Ti Noël observes how indeed, 'the morning was rampant with heads', (Carpentier, ibid.: 11), remarking on the various prints hung in front of the bookseller, picturing kings and dignitaries, until he hears the 'voice of his master, who emerged from the barber's with heavily powdered cheeks. His face now bore a startling resemblance to the four dull wax faces that stood in a row along the counter, smiling stupidly.' (Carpentier, ibid.: 15) The presence of the heads continues as Ti Noël has to carry, across town and into the plantation, a 'chill skull under his arm, thinking how much it probably resembled the baldhead of his master hidden beneath his wig'. (Carpentier, ibid.: 11). In insisting on the presence of heads and on the versatility between two- or three-dimensional, printed, powdered, with a wig, or parsley, animal or human, over a body, on a shelf or under an arm, heads are no longer the essential part of a complete being that one carries at the upper extremity of one's body, but rather become an apparatus that is at most decorative and interchangeable. As Carpentier relates the dramatic end of the colony and the eventual enslavement of Haitians by their new king, the marvellous real gains its *raison d'être* as one builds one's vision of an everyday reality that encompasses the marvellous, and trains the eye to be acute for a marvellous ordinariness that enriches what one is willing to consider as real.

A Configuring Act

Carpentier's marvellous real offers a compelling additional element for the configurational stage of French philosopher Paul Ricoeur's theory of emplotment (*mise-en-intrigue*). Ricoeur situates the configuration at the centre of a tripartite process that leads to a multifaceted reading of the familiar, and in the case at hand, of our cities, a multiple reading that can participate in challenging our preconceptions of how cities need to be looked upon and practiced.

The first part of Ricoeur's model is 'prefiguration'. He suggests that the 'composition of the plot is grounded in a pre-understanding of the world of action, its meaningful structures, its symbolic resources and its temporal character'. (Ricoeur 1983:54) In other words, the narrative, or the everyday, is practiced well before it is written. Prefigurative elements are the available material one disposes to comprehend stories: familiar things, events and places that allow us to approach narratives with a certain pre-understanding of what will constitute the intrigue.

The second part of Ricoeur's model is 'configuration'. This central and most decisive part of his model is what mediates between singular events and the narrative as a whole, giving shape to and connecting disparate elements, circumstances, means and interactions. The role of this emplotment is to hold together the various parts into a meaningful story: it is a 'temporal synthesis of the heterogeneous, [an] attempt to clarify the inextricable [and to] confront several stories against, before or after each other'. (Ricoeur 1998: 50) Ricoeur speaks of it in terms of a 'braid' that ties together events with their ways of creating actions, their causes and reasons for acting, crossed by elements of fortuity, coincidences and simple chance. (Ricoeur, ibid.: 49) The configuring act can bring closer together overlooked, unknown, surprising or marvellous elements within the realm of normative situations, allowing the latter to transform.

The process of configuring ends in the third and final part of Ricoeur's model, a 'reconfiguration' of the temporal and spatial experience. Reconfiguration is what marks the intersection of the text with the reader, where the land of interpretation opens up. The configuration thus contributes, once it comes into contact with the reader/user, to the enunciation of possible inhabitations and engagements with the physical world. What this three-part act allows is the possibility for re-reading our environments. Indeed, in his short essay 'Architecture and Narrative', Ricoeur pulls his theory of emplotment out of literature to extend it towards architecture and cities. In his argument, the prefigurative stage is linked to the general built environment because every 'lived history' happens within 'lived spaces': everyday events mark and affect spatial organizations. (Ricoeur, ibid.: 51) The configuration, which consists of a temporal synthesis of the heterogeneous, finds its architectural correspondence in a spatial synthesis of the heterogeneous. (Ricoeur, ibid.: 51) To build necessitates bringing together know-hows, context, users, history, and so on, into a cohesive, yet ever changing, built form. The last part of the model, the reconfiguration, finds its equivalent in architecture as a retaliation to building, an active inhabitation that implies an attentive re-reading and continuous re-learning of the built environment. (Ricoeur, ibid.: 51)

A Vague Urbain

Adding the marvellous real to the configuring act implies that the awkwardness of places and situations be integrated within a renewed effort for reading our cities. As such, I would like to propose a possible configuration of what I have come to call *vagues urbains*, (Lévesque 2013), that is, areas of soon to come transformation, or inhabited *terrains vagues*, (Solà-Morales 1995), well-defined areas where the marvellous real and configurations are in constant reinventions. While the grand-scale developments are busy redefining entire cities, there sometimes remain large inhabited areas completely neglected, overseen, defying and challenging how the city is to be perceived, lived and practiced. Like a literary configuration, they provide a space for dwellers to put their cleverness at play and demonstrate how the ingenuity entailed in times of need and of urban *laissez-faire* can create other possible perceptions and uses of the city. Until land and properties are sold and occupants evicted, until 'proper' replacements are built, *vagues urbains* offer the possibility for the most basic, ordinary, free activities to take place, in ways that make sense to the inhabitants, and in ways that imagination and the marvellous can find their space of negotiation.

I initiated the idea of configuring a *vague urbain* in 2010 at the beginning of a three-year stay in Beirut, Lebanon. Weaving the marvellous, the configuring act, the vague and the representation of architectural invention into a theoretical structure, it seemed an appropriate mechanism to provide opportunities for creative proposals to emerge and for neglected neighbourhoods and communities to participate in our configuration of cities. The attentive observation, description and transcription of such places suggest that there can be ways to find alternative narratives in the city within what is already there and experienceable. What this theoretical structure and project attempt to do is to propose that the configuring of such places draws to our attention possible and different ways to inhabit and suggest alternatives to standardized positions as to what is worth investigating.

My investigation began in Bachoura, a large inhabited and vibrant *vague urbain* in Beirut's city centre, standing still and resisting, for the time being, pressures from fierce investors and speculators' fashionable towers. Coincidentally, its local name, *Khandaq el-Ghamiq*, brings with it a whole alternative field: 'the deep ditch', in its English translation, suggests a world of its own, physically divided from a world further above, with the promise of never before seen combinations and constructions. If Bachoura is clearly not a space offered to spontaneous appropriations, as some would describe the *terrain vague*, (Lévesque, 'The Terrain Vague as Material': 6-7) mostly due to its political 'flavours' that more often than not trigger suspicion and surveillance, it is nevertheless a place within which de Certeau's 'ethics of tenacity' (De Certeau 1990: 46) provide the urban wanderer with a space in which to reflect upon a city's trajectory.

The project is a combination of photographic documentation, as a witness to the prefiguration, textual descriptions that are somewhere between prefiguring and configuring and drawings that run from configuration to the beginnings of a refiguration. The work captures details from the built environment and the situations encountered as a means to construct and give sense to the neighbourhood, to give non-official stories to be seen, and to value places that might appear as useless and dispensable.
From documented and described found places and situations, five nomadic and transitory personal infrastructures were elaborated, or five configuring acts if you will, that manifest essential practices of Bachoura: the practices of storytelling, of walking and filching. While storytelling acts as a spatial and temporal trajectory, as a means to create sense, memory and value, walking appears as a search and need for the safeguard of found everyday details and seeds of potential occupation. It is the act of walking that links the stories so as to understand the untamed and the resilient. And here, a practice of filching begins: the collection of stories allows for surreptitious transformations and occupations of the city, which allow, in return, the creation of urban alternative narratives. The fugitive and transitory personal infrastructures

Figure 1. Carole Lévesque, *A Room for Going Where You Don't Need to Be*, 2011. Ink on paper, 30 x 34 cm.

thus stem from found situations and events, to become, as they belong to soon-to-disappear places, people, buildings and practices, invented places without definite locations, being pushed, rolled, pulled, swung or carried in the new city as nomadic personal *terrains vagues*.

For instance, children playing hide and seek in an abandoned building located in the midst of an impromptu garden becomes a room for hiding in the shadows of a room, in which thousands of silk threads build shadows when it is in fact impossible to find shade. Men spending most of their day sitting on plastic chairs, smoking *arguileh* and drinking coffee, become a room for keeping distractions away, a machine that keeps you both in movement and in the same place by a simple reversal of gears attached to a swing. Confusion about wanting to give unnecessary directions becomes a room for going where you don't need to be, a gigantic portable watchtower that is more problematic than useful, unless where one doesn't want to be is in fact where one wishes to go (fig. 1). An old woman proud of her one-room apartment containing a complete life story becomes a room for sharing essential things, a half dome structure one carries as an oversized backpack. When a carrier meets another one, both half domes are placed on the ground to form a complete structure in which essential things, words or practices can be shared. And finally, the incredible story of a Prime Minister who sends men to tear up sidewalks in order to build a villa hundreds of kilometres away, becomes a room for carrying stones, a structure pushed through the city to collect stones and broken concrete. When the room becomes too heavy, stones are emptied for the structure to continue on, leaving behind a pile of travelled stones.

Even if these rooms seem improbable, they link the everyday creative dimensions of Bachoura, its margins, its changing context, and imminent disappearance with the possibility of infiltrating bachourian practices in the developing context and narrative of the city: when the neighbourhood is swallowed by the newly built Beirut, the infrastructures could allow for pieces of bachourian-marvellous-real to wander and glean the new landscape. By interpreting and telling practices that are not represented by the grand urban discourses, these nomadic *terrains vagues* propose that found situations contain the extraordinary and the imaginative, that they contain, in other words, a necessary urban marvellous. They also propose that the marvellous is somewhere integrated to the present, as a territory of possible actions. That is why the infrastructures are presented in orthogonal projections: their drawing builds a dialogue between the informality of a found and projected everyday, a personification of knowledge and the neutral communication of architectural drawings. In this way, the drawings introduce the informality of the *vague urbain*, as a silent reality of our cities, in the scholarly discourses of architecture and the cities it builds. The strangeness of the infrastructures and situations from which they emerge are thus associated, through the architectural drawing, to disciplinary know-hows.

Through this methodology, I hope to resonate with the words of Alejo Carpentier when he says that 'we must uncover and interpret [the world] ourselves. Our reality will appear new to our own eyes. Description is inescapable, and the description of a [strange] world is necessarily [strange], that is . . . the 'what' and the 'how' coincide in a strange reality.' (Carpentier 1995a: 106) This strange reality suggests that the city as found is something we need to be ready for and willing to imagine. Architectural configurations can provide the means to resist the short-sightedness common to many urban development visions and supply the material from which to build hopeful potentials. It also becomes possible to think that literary discourses and creative writing can collaborate with architecture to uncover value where it might not have been thought possible, and to contribute to a reconfiguration of our cities to include the vague within our telling of the city.

5 INCLUSIVITY

Towards an 'Architextural' Praxis

The Westward-Moving House and Other Stories

J.B. Jackson, Reading and Writing the Landscape

Bruno Notteboom

John Brinckerhoff Jackson (1909-1996) was among the most influential thinkers and writers on landscape of the twentieth century (Groth & Wilson; Lefkowitz Horowitz; Treib). Primarily interested in the vernacular landscape, his focus was on everyday man-made environments: rural lands, small towns, villages and farmsteads, but also the suburban houses, yards, cars, highways, gas stations, shopping malls and supermarkets that became an essential part of daily American existence after the Second World War. Jackson's main forum was *Landscape*, the journal he founded in 1951 and of which he was the editor in chief until 1968. At first, *Landscape* focused on the landscapes of the American Southwest and revolved around Jackson – he wrote the first issues almost entirely himself under a series of pseudonyms. However, the journal soon evolved into a forum for research and opinions on architecture and landscape worldwide, with contributions by emerging as well as established scholars and practitioners.

Jackson is renowned for his literary writing style. Many of his articles on landscape and architecture read like short stories, ignoring formalities of scientific writing like footnotes. In *Landscape*'s very first essay, 'The Need of Being Versed in Country Things' (Jackson 1951), Jackson hints at the relevance of literary methods to reading the contemporary American landscape: 'We have become, in the course of the last few decades, a nation of city-dwellers,' he writes; man has become ignorant of the 'lay of the land', but 'landscape is a rich and beautiful book, we have but to learn to read it' (Jackson 1951: 5). Jackson's way of reading the landscape and writing about it in an essayistic, literary way has to be situated against the background of his very own pedagogical project: *Landscape* was set up to share knowledge about landscape not only between specialists, but also with what he called 'the intelligent layman'. He was primarily interested in what he called 'the variety of man's work of coming to terms with nature', in ordinary, everyday man-made landscapes. His writing was not only an analysis of the American vernacular landscape, but also a search for a literary form, for a language in which to talk about it, a language that is, as I will argue, rooted in a *praxis* of direct observation.

Background

Quite unlike one might suspect from somebody who founded a journal on landscape and architecture, Jackson was trained neither as an architect or an urban planner, nor as a geographer. He went to college at an art school in Wisconsin and at Harvard, where he graduated in 1932 with a major in history and literature (Lefkowitz Horowitz 1997: xiii). After studying architecture at the MIT in Boston, from which he withdrew in less than a year, he spent the rest of the 1930s wandering through Europe and later working as a cowboy on a ranch in New Mexico, his first experience in living and working among common Americans. In 1938, Jackson wrote *Saints in Summertime*, a well-received novel about the effects of the political changes of the 1930s on a rural community in Eastern Europe. However, his interest in the landscape was mainly fuelled by his experience in the US army during the Second World War. As an officer in Normandy, he not only had to learn to read the landscape for military strategic reasons, he also got acquainted with French cultural geographers who wrote extensively about the relationship between man and the land. He was especially charmed by a cheap but 'charmingly written' Gallimard series edited by Pierre Deffontaines that popularized cultural geography. A couple of years after his return to the United States he was determined to set up an similar endeavour with the journal *Landscape* (Lefkowitz Horowitz 1997: xvii-xii).

The Westward-Moving House

Jackson would never write a second novel. However, with *Landscape* he created a laboratory in which to experiment with narrative forms of analysis: most of the essayistic texts he wrote for the journal read like short stories. One of the most exemplary and well-known is 'The Westward-Moving House' (1953), which tells the story of three generations of farmers ('the Tinkhams'): Nehemiah in New England in the seventeenth century, Pliny in Illinois in the nineteenth century, and Ray in Texas in the 1950s (Jackson 1953). The three chapters of the text, each focusing on one farmer, deal with a different relationship between man, the land and the house. Chapter I, 'Nehemiah's Ark', is set in an unalterable environment determined by tradition and religion. Chapter II, 'Pliny's Homestead', describes farming and homesteading as a more speculative activity; family life and the love of nature gradually replaced religion and community as a cornerstone of society. Chapter III, 'Ray's transformer', narrates how the farm became a flexible entity that 'has no organic relationship to its environment – weather topography or soil', an investment run by the latest economic and scientific insights. Farming in the 1950s was not a way of life anymore, so the story tells us, but a business, and family life on the farm could not be distinguished from the average 1950s suburban household.

By placing his analysis in the context of an intergenerational family history, Jackson helps the readers to visualize the mutually constitutive relationship between cultural ideas and the physical environment. Throughout the text, the perspective of the reader goes back and forth between that of the protagonists – as in a literary story – and the meta-narrative of socioeconomic and architectural history. For example, in a passage describing what Nehemiah feels and thinks in church, hierarchical society of the time is discussed the way it would be in a novel:

> *He did not enjoy sitting for two hours in a cold building while the Reverend Jethro Tipping expounded the significance of the Tenth Horn of the Beast, but he believed that all was well while he did so. Dozing off during the exegesis he saw the world as an enduring and majestic pyramid, an orderly succession of ranks – yeoman, husbandmen, squires; elders, deacons, ministers; heathen, gentile, elect – each one indispensable to the solidity of the structure, and helping to bear the weight of the crowing stone. (Jackson 1953: 11)*

In the third part he writes about Ray:

> *The ranch will not take every one of Ray's working hours. He hopes in time to be able to leave it to look after itself, not merely overnight but for weeks on end, while he and Shirley and the children take winter vacations in California. He even dreams of having a small business in town to keep himself occupied. (Jackson 1953: 20)*

Figure 1. Cover of *Landscape*, Winter 1965-1966.

These 'literary' parts of the texts, using the thoughts and emotions of his protagonists, provide a very effective entrance to the issue of changing domestic culture, which is as much a matter of aspirations and dreams of individual families as it is the result of historical changes. However, the narrative of the three generations Tinkham are interspersed with references to the history of architecture, such as a passage of Siegfried Giedion's *Space, Time and Architecture* on the balloon frame and books on American architecture history. Jackson uses these references not only to place these individual stories in a historical framework, but also to provide detailed descriptions of the layout of the house, the garden and the land, for example in this description of Nehemiah's house:

> *The plan of the house was equally nonfunctional as we understand the term. The ground floor had two main rooms: a combination living room-work room-kitchen with a large fireplace, and a parlor, also with a fireplace. The parlor was reserved for important guests and family religious observances. Between these two a flight of stairs led to the two bedrooms where the family slept, and above these, reached by a ladder, was the attic, where slept the servant, There were in addition several outbuildings, including a barn, all near the house. Outside the back door there was a small garden chiefly devoted to vegetables and herbs, but containing a few flowers as well.(Jackson 1953: 10)*

This kind of 'dry', factual information, what people did and how they constructed their environment was just as important in Jacksons essays as people's dreams or the larger historical framework. Jackson's narratives work in a distinctively inductive way: observations on the role of religion in domestic culture or the changing relationships between money and labour are developed gradually throughout the family history and description of the practical organization of daily life.

The Stranger's Path

The storyline in 'The Westward-Moving House' is developed through time (from the seventeenth century to the 1950s) and through space (from the East Coast to Texas). This kind of 'chronotopes' are at the basis of several of his stories and provide a strategy to understand what is going on in the ever-changing urban and rural landscape. In 'The Strangers Path' (1957), Jackson uses movement through time and space again, however in a somehow loose way (Jackson 1957). Compared to 'The Westward-Moving House', this text is less a story in the sense that it has a clear protagonist – besides 'the stranger'. The text is mostly written in the first person. Based on his own experiences – in the first sentence he calls himself 'a professional tourist with a certain painfully acquired knowledge of how to appraise strange cities' (Jackson, *Stranger*: 11) – Jackson takes the reader on a walk along the path followed by a stranger trough a fictitious city, which is an abstraction of the small American city. In contrast to the city's residential quarters, where Jackson feels 'excluded from these rows and rows of (presumably) happy and comfortable homes' (ibid.). The stranger's path is 'that part of the city devoted to the outsider, the transient, devoted to receiving him and satisfying his immediate needs' (ibid.). The stranger's path is also defined by the description of the stranger:

> *Stranger does not only mean tourist, and by and large the strangers who come to town for a day or two belong to a more modest class: not very prosperous, often with no money at all. They are men looking for a job or on their way to a job; men come to buy or sell one item in their line of business, men on a brief holiday. (Jackson 1957:12)*

The walk starts where the stranger arrives: the train or bus station, or the parking lot adjacent to it, often the most run-down part of town. However, the stranger's path becomes more respectable the further it gets from its point of origin in the course of the text: it starts out as a seedy row of flophouses, brothels, dive-bars and 'catchpenny businesses', a place where – in contrast to the suburbs visited at the beginning of the essay – no families or children live. Then it passes through a middle region that is more respectable and that is characterized by the market, the place where the countryside enters the city. Continuing along this path this middle section merges in the financial section of the city – the banks and upscale hotels – to end up in City Hall and the politico-legal centre around it. The stranger's path is all about exchange, 'exchange of goods for cash, exchange of labor for cash' (ibid. : 12), about 'bringing the city into touch with the outside world' Ibid.: 15) which brings along a particular visual experience:

> *The Path bursts into a luxuriance of colored and lighted signs: Chiliburgers. Red Hots. Unborn Calf Oxfords: They're new! They're smart! They're Ivy! Double Feature: Bride Of The Gorilla-Monster From Outer Space. Gospel Evangelical Mission. Checks Cashed. Snooker Parlor. The Best Shine In Town! Dr. Logan and His Amazing Europathic Method. Coney Islands. Fortune Told; Madame LaFay. (ibid.: 12)*

Although Jackson claims to talk about the average American town of between 20 and 50 thousand inhabitants, the images he evokes in his text are definitely cosmopolitan:

the evocation of neon signs reminds of modern *Großstadt* imagery (reflected in the drawing of neon lights that accompanies the text). Also the concrete examples (Skid Row, the Tenderloin, Hell's Kitchen, Wall Street, the Bowery) are taken from cities such as New York, San Francisco or Chicago. However, the hand-drawn scheme that illustrates the text seems to suggest the map of an American small town, but then again the grid pattern does not really suggest a size and the scheme is expandable to a large city as well. In a way this drawing does something similar to what the narration in the text does: it describes the city in a very concrete way, yet at the same time it slides back and forth between different scales, combining different cities into one narrative.

At the end of the text Jackson's description of the stranger's path shifts into a critique of modern urban planning. The bottom line is not that the stranger's path should be kept as it is – by 1957 the decline of the American inner cities had started – but it is rather the specific quality of urban public space that is lost in modern city planning. Jackson refers to the examples of the Ramblas in Barcelona or the Cannebière in Marseilles, used by a 'public that is a large cross section of the population of the city, men, women and children, rich and poor, strangers and natives' (Jackson 1957: 15).

In his description of these European examples, Jackson stresses the almost ritualistic aspect of moving through this public space:

> *To walk up such a street in to the quieter, more formal part of town, is to be part of a procession, part of a ceaseless ceremony of being initiated into the city and of rededicating the city itself. And that is how our first progress through even the smallest city and town should be: a succession of gay and beautiful streets and squares, all of them extending a universal welcome.* (ibid.)

Towards the end of the text Jackson stages a kind of dialogue with the city planner who wants to demolish these 'depressed' parts of town where the Stranger's Path is situated to erect new housing, parks and high class shops, or a pedestrian civic centre. These redevelopments, as well as the new suburban shopping malls, Jackson argues, are the exact opposite of the Path: 'Their emphasis on convenience, cleanliness, and safety, their distrust of everything vulgar and small and poor is symptomatic of a very lopsided view of urban culture' (ibid.).

Narration as Praxis

Jackson was one of the first voices in America to criticize the rigour of modern architecture and city planning. The use of narration was an important instrument in this critique, as a means to place the individual back in the centre of our understanding of

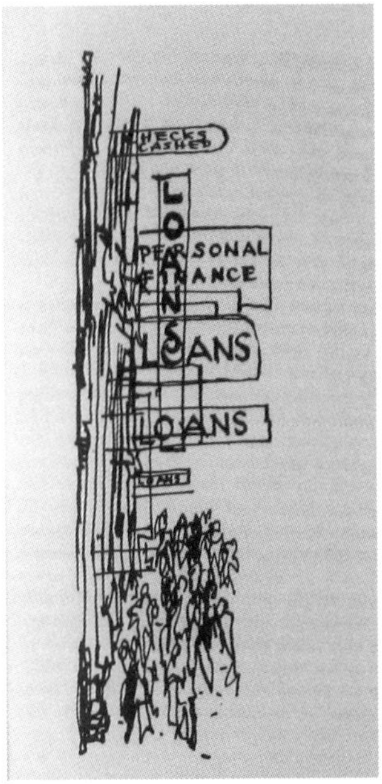

Figure 2. 'The Stranger's Path'. J.B. Jackson, 'The Stranger's Path', *Landscape*, vol. 7 (Autumn 1957) no. 1, 11-15.

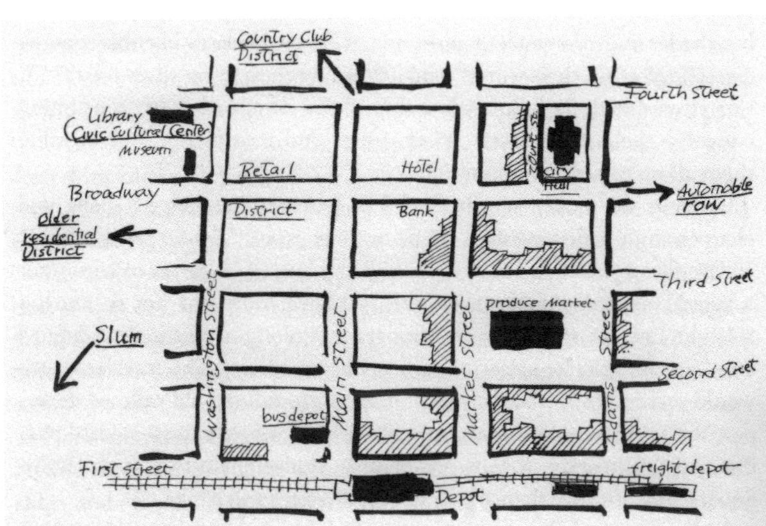

Figure 3. ' Plan of an average American city. J.B. Jackson, 'The Stranger's Path', *Landscape*, vol. 7 (Autumn 1957) no. 1, 11-15.

the environment. Although informed by a broad array of relevant literature, Jackson's narrations were in the first place rooted in his own observations. He was a fervent traveller, by plane, car or motorcycle, taking record of the places he visited and the people he met by means of sketching photography and writing. Jackson wrote 'The Stranger's Path' after travelling through the South of the United States; the writing in his travel journal is interspersed with drawings of vernacular architecture and grid patterns of the towns visited. In the published text, his observations on the American city do not only combine different cities into one fictitious city, it also blends his own experience and that of his fellow travellers in the character of The Stranger. Jackson is at the same time the narrator and the protagonist of his own story.

As opposed to classical geographic description, in which the geographer is a scientist placed outside his object of study, the praxis of narration allows Jackson to be at once inside and outside the (urban) landscape he describes, and it allows him to take on different roles: traveller among travellers, New Mexican among New Mexicans, but also publicist and, from the end of the 1960s onward, professor at Berkeley and Harvard. Observing, writing and teaching were all part of this praxis of narration. Jackson had thousands of notecards with information on aspects of the landscapes, which served as a resource when preparing lectures or a publication (Limerick 2003:134). In texts such as 'The Westward-Moving House' or 'The Stranger's Path' these various types of information were bound by the narration, a narration that had a pedagogical ambition. Author Crady Clay compared 'The Stranger's Path' with Patrick Geddes's famous Valley Section, in the sense that they are both cross sections that act as a learning tool (Clay 2003: 115-119). On the other hand, Jackson avoided the question of pedagogy (Lewis 2003: 92). His way of teaching was conversational and Socratic: his narrations were often open-ended and did certainly not develop overarching theories. Instead he stimulated students, or more generally readers, to formulate the questions and answers themselves.

The use of narrative techniques and the idea of an embedded way of reading the (urban) landscape would gain momentum in the 1960s phenomenological approach in urban analysis. Jackson was a forerunner of people like Kevin Lynch and Christopher Alexander, who published their early research results in *Landscape* (Lynch & Rivkin 1959; Doshi & Alexander 1963-1964), and Robert Venturi and Denise Scott Brown, who acknowledged that their work was indebted to him (Scott-Brown 2003). However, in 1968 Jackson withdrew as an editor of *Landscape*, wondering if the exploratory and speculative character of the journal was still widely acceptable: 'The landscape as an object of contemplation in both senses of the word – seeing and pon-

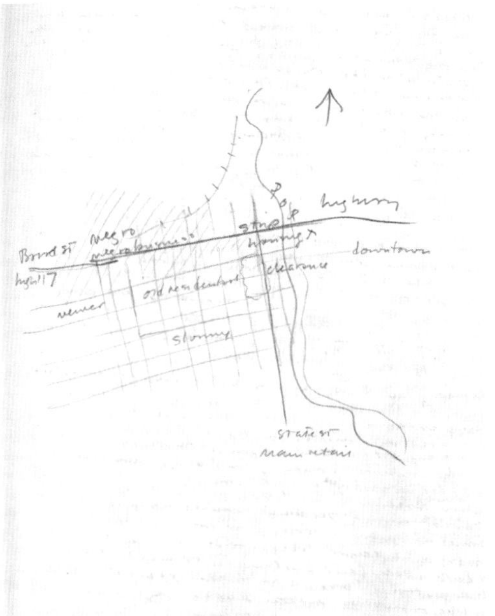

Figure 4a. Plan of Savannah

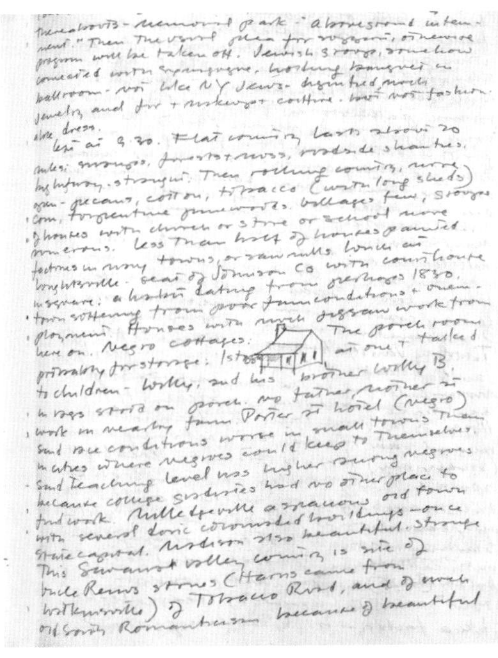
memorial park - "a [illegible] interment." Then the [illegible] plan for [illegible], otherwise
program will be taken off. Jewish group, somehow
connected with synagogue, holding banquet in
ballroom - not like NY Jews - dignified, much
jewelry and fur + [illegible] costume. but not fashion-
able dress.
Left at 9.30. Flat country lasts about 20
miles: swamps, forests + moss, roadside shanties,
highway straight. Then rolling country, more
open - pecans, cotton, tobacco (with long sheds)
corn, turpentine pinewoods. Villages few, groups
of houses with church or store or school more
numerous. Less than half of houses painted.
factories in many towns, or saw mills [illegible] courthouse
Wrightsville - seat of Johnson Co with
in square: a [illegible] dating from perhaps 1830.
town suffering from poor farm conditions + unem-
ployment. Houses with much jigsaw work from
here on. Negro cottages: The porch room
probably for storage: 1st [illegible] at one + talked
to children - Willy, and his brother Willy B.
[illegible] stood on porch. No father, mother [illegible]
work on nearby farm. Porter at hotel (negro)
said race conditions worse in small towns than
in cities where negroes could keep to themselves.
Said teaching level was higher among negroes
because college graduates had no other place to
find work. Milledgeville a spacious old town
with several doric columned buildings - once
state capital. Madison also beautiful. Strange
This [illegible] valley country is site of
Uncle Remus stories (Harris came from
[illegible]) of Tobacco Road, and of much
old South Romanticism because of beautiful

Figure 4b. Textual description with sketch of 'negro cottage' in the middle.

dering – has yielded to the landscape as a problem to be solved' (Jackson 1969: 1). By the end of the 1960s environmental studies had become the terrain of ecologists, sociologist, psychologist, economists and planners, an evolution Jackson admittedly could not – and, most likely, did not want to – keep abreast of. One of his concerns was that the phenomenological approach would lead to behaviourism, an idea that seduced architecture students, but, according to Jackson, overestimated the power of urban planning and architecture (Jackson 1967-1968). His narratives, fully exploring the complexity of how man's environment comes into being, must have been an antidote to such a conception of the discipline during his teaching years. Jackson never stopped writing and telling stories, and he received a PEN award for *Sense of Place, Sense of Time* in 1994, two years before his death at his home in La Cienega, New Mexico. His kitchen table was allegedly the centre of village life (Treib 2005: 192).

Textual Cities / Working Drawings

Rereading the Space of the Drawing

Sophia-Konstantina Banou

Textual Cities

It is common to come across the simile of the city and the text. Under the influence of the new theories of space-time and the increasing mobility and mechanization of the world since the beginning of the twentieth century, the experience of the city has been consistently understood as a deciphering of the urban fabric, an understanding expressed in approaches such as the situationist *derive*.[1] The complex negotiations between movement and perception that this understanding entails have exerted a critical pressure on the static image of the city as traditionally established by architectural representation. It is in this struggle between the static and the kinetic, between the structured order that architecture appears to impose and the microbe-like processes of everyday life that the textual nature of the city is found as a coherent coexistence between structure and event. It seems, however, that this textuality of the city is only made apparent by means of its transcription to another medium, another space; an *image* that may be either virtual (the mental image of perception) or physical (another kind of script).

In the essay 'Walking in the City', it is through the abstraction of the panoptic aerial view that we come to realize the discrepancy, the 'misunderstanding' (De Certeau 1984: 93), between what *is* and what is *represented*. Gazing at Manhattan from the top of the World Trade Centre, theorist Michel De Certeau observes how people, the ordinary 'practitioners' of the city, weave a 'curious' text; one without an author and, more importantly, one that appears to resist being read:

> *... [they] live 'down below', below the thresholds at which visibility begins. They walk an elementary form of this experience of the city; they are walkers . . . whose bodies follow the thicks and thins of the urban 'text' without being able to read it. These practitioners make use of spaces that cannot be seen . . . The paths that correspond in this intertwining, unrecognized poems in which each body is an element signed by many others, elude legibility . . . The networks of these moving, intersecting writings compose a manifold story that has neither author nor spectator, shaped out of fragments of trajectories and alterations of spaces: in relation to representations, it remains daily and infinitely other (ibid.)*

In De Certeau's terms it is by means of walking that the infinite possibilities that smoulder within the order of the urban are activated and that our spatial organizations are also largely constructed. Yet walking, that daily act which humans and animals practice almost instinctively is, in the context of this weaving, more than a simple act of locomotion. Walking becomes a practice that, even if not consciously so, involves tactics and intentions that surpass the structure that is already given.

Nevertheless, it appears that these practices remain 'other' when it comes to representation. If anything, to render them static by means of a graphic trace would mean to forget the very dynamic that makes them operative. (De Certeau 1984: 97) Not only do they then escape the boundaries of architectural representation conventions, but they also seem to be untranscribable, by default impossible to represent. Moreover, they render parts of the city illegible as they 'contaminate' the city's legible part through the movement of the bodies that enact them. Facing this textual nature of the city, from which the supposed failure of its reading paradoxically seems to derive, are urban representations forever doomed to inadequacy? Bearing in mind the nature of text not only as a weave but also as script, how can the transcription of this text without an author take place? It is then perhaps necessary to consider, not only how the city is being *read* but also the ways in which its text is being *written*.

Reading the City

What is really entailed by legibility? What does it mean to read a text and what does it mean to read a city? If the former denotes the extraction of meaning from a writing, to read the city should in turn mean to decipher, to 'conquer it' by means of stabilization, in other words to crystallize an *image* within one's consciousness that will render the city (semantically) coherent and – for the purposes of architectural design – manageable. Is it really then a matter of failure to read, or is the inconsistency between the city and its representation occurring at the process of transcription? It is the very nature of the *script* of this text that needs to be addressed in order to define this shortcoming of the transcription. Normative architectural representations propose that it is found in the matter of buildings that outlines the insides and outsides of the city. Are the criteria of inclusion in this transcription of representation those of persistence, measurability and materiality: a solid-versus-void distinction that defines the city through the 'ink' of the figure against the 'white' of the ground? Or is the space of the city concluded in the weaving that emerges from the practices of the everyday?

In De Certeau's essay, walking poses as a form of enunciation of the city's text. It proceeds through *speech acts*, utterances that, enriched by performance, have an effect beyond the purity of the text's structure. Through walking, the city dwellers do not just write but they also 'speak' the text: they *enact* the space of the city, which is thus constantly rewritten. If these *speech acts* are not part of a writing, but acts of enunciation, what then constitutes the *script* of this urban text,[2] the matter in which the city is written? What is the form that is borne out of this conjunction of the given structure and the spontaneous event? In the text of the city the human body is interchangeably called to act as more than a 'writer' or a 'reader'. It is most importantly a central character in the narrative of space, and it is exactly the compilation of an *image* that is at stake. Bodies and their movements are inevitably part of the actual, physical image of the city as they alter its materiality. At the same time, however, they contribute to shaping its virtual image(s), as they constantly reshape it by means of visual perception. The textual city then (from Latin *texere*: to weave) emerges at the weaving of these lines of movement: an interlacing that relies equally on the structure of an architectural language and the improvisations of experience and inhabitation.

In *Paris Invisible City (Latour and Hermant 2006),* sociologist Bruno Latour also negates the image of the city by contrasting the totalizing bird's-eye view of a map to the real experience of the city by its inhabitants. He maintains that the real image of the city is formed between two agents: on the one hand there are the humans while on the other are the various urban artefacts that allow the experience and comprehension of the actual city. Latour's point shifts attention from the human body as encompassing the agency of space by introducing the importance of the non-human counterparts that facilitate this configuring of the urban. As the space of the text is not only drawn by the sublime genius of an author, but also by the signs that words

Figure 1. Site-specific installation, 2013. Newcastle University School of Fine Art (UK). This installation constituted the transcription of a small urban site in Edinburgh. Focusing on the ephemeral and the transitory it stood as an architectural drawing that revealed the density of the seemingly 'empty' space of the site in a weave of lines that resisted two-dimensionality.

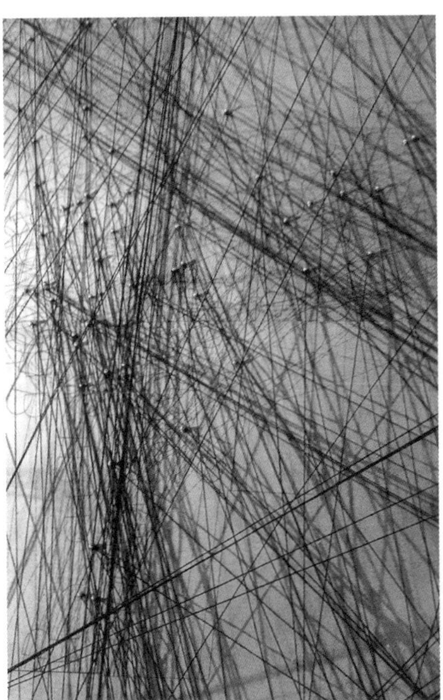

Figure 2. Site-specific installation, 2013. Newcastle University School of Fine Art (UK). Detail of the weave tying onto the planar traces.

themselves constitute (Barthes, 1967), in the same manner the space of the city is not strictly shaped by the authority of architecture, but by the negotiations that take place between the animate and the inanimate.[3] Considering this, the city and its image emerge as the result of an ever-evolving 'discourse' between its users, the architecture, and the secondary infrastructure that mediates between the two.

This interaction unfolds through events such as the twist of a key, the crossing of a street, the flight of a bird; through the informal and the ephemeral that can only be anticipated, beyond the controls of architecture. Such manifestations find little trouble in being accommodated by language, nevertheless, they are lost when it comes to architectural representations. They constitute the *infraordinary* of cities (Perec 1999) and, in turn, architectural representations: the 'banal' that, below the ordinary, remains hidden not due to illegibility but due to inattention. It is then in the infraordinary layers of the city, which escape not transcription but selection, that the elusive textuality of the city can be found. By means of performing the infraordinary, bodies form the points of indeterminacy in the text of the city: a dynamic collective weave of the multiple, ever-evolving 'cities' it entails.

Transcriptions from City to Drawing

To return then to the moment of realization of this inconsistency between reality and representation, is to return to the drawing: a tangible transcription of the urban text into a new writing. Taking into account the textual nature of the urban, it is now possible to realize the preconceptions through which this transcription has been taking effect, traditionally omitting the parts of the writing that previously escaped representation, not necessarily by being 'illegible', but mostly by being informal or ephemeral. How could drawing thus become informed by such a realization, by the consideration of the city in a textual fashion? And beyond that, how is this textuality operative to the creative process of design?

Such a reconsideration would call for an abolition of the various factors of representational bias common in architectural representations, such as scale, materiality and temporality. What becomes prominent through the textual city is the role of inhabitation, or experience, as a performative utterance of space that presents an equal agent in the narrative of the city. To sum up, representation should remain a text in itself, and by all means maintain the dynamic between structure and agency found in the original. Other than the above, there seems to be no reason to further challenge the conventions that already guide architectural representation. Despite De Certeau's hesitation about the fixation of the script (De Certeau 1984: 97), what architectural representation is after is not a duplication, but the transcription from reality to drawing: the expression of the city, a text in itself, to a new text by means of architectural notation. How is then representation anything more than a mere survey? According to Salvador Dalí, there is hardly any objectivity or even connection to reality in discriminating between the various expressions of the real. In his 1929 'Documentaries', published in the Barcelona paper *La Publicitat*, Dalí reports on a series of spontaneous observations of Parisian life, aiming to provide his reader with a rigorous and objective documentary:

> *For five minutes at eleven in the morning in the Luxembourg garden I observe the things which cross over a surface of twenty square centimetres, traced with a stick in wet sand. In order of succession I see: the heel of a man's shoe, the tip of a woman's shoe – after an interval of four seconds – a little boy's or a little girl's hand, three little boys' or three little girls' hands . . . (Dalí 1998b: 106)*

What is he anticipating by attempting this degree-zero writing?[4] (Barthes 1995: 5) A writing that is almost clinical at describing the mundane, that which is happening there and then, without any attempt to sublimate the real through mannerisms of language. Is he denouncing creative initiative altogether? On the contrary, it appears that Dalí is seeking in the real a 'lyricism' that is not deliberate and therefore subjective. He is relying on the peculiar powers of reality in the same manner that Robin Evans Evens 1997: 154) proposes reliance on the 'peculiar powers' of drawing.[5] Dalí thus proposes that *lyricism* is already inherent in the everyday:

> *In effect, documentary and the surrealist text coincide from the outset in their essentially anti-artistic and more particularly anti-literary process, since not the slightest of intentions, be they aesthetic, emotional, sentimental, etc. – essential characteristics of the artistic phenomenon – enter into this process. The documentary notes things said of the objective world anti-literarily. In parallel fashion, the surrealist text transcribes with the same rigour and as anti-literarily as the documentary, the REAL free functioning of thought, of events which occur in reality in our mind, thanks to psychic automatism and to other passive states (inspiration). (Dalí 1998a: 93)*

It appears that there is therefore no need for any invention. The 'narrative' already exists and awaits to be found, to be excavated. For if our cities are textual, it should be expected that their representations would be textual also, able to excavate the surreal out of the code of representation.

Unlike the processes dictated by architectural convention that are concerned with dissecting space in the orthographic manner of a plan or a section, Dali's transcription relies on spontaneous visual observation, at times constituting the ephemeral visible and hence infusing the transcription with the memory of movement and change. Instead of adding to the subject, the focus of the transcription is shifted to the transitory, setting aside the static manifestations of space traditionally found at the core of architectural representation. This representation[6] is still partial, however, it is charged with an attention to detail that expands the possibilities of both space and representation through its inclusiveness. It does not propose a fixed image, but a collection of instances, traces related to space not merely by resemblance but also by causality and process. But is such a writing capable of satisfying the criteria of textuality? Projecting such a documentarist attempt into drawing, would the dynamics of the original text remain effectively active within the new field? Is this new condition kinetic as the city-text, or is it a static fixture that has drained its subject from any latent possibility?

Working Drawings

In the essay 'From Work to Text' (1979), literary theorist Roland Barthes makes the distinction between the *literary work* and the *text*. (Barthes 1979) In doing so, Barthes points out the characteristics of the text. According to Barthes, works and texts do not differ materially, but they do intrinsically differ in terms of content and more importantly function. Barthes describes the text as a writing open to, almost awaiting, an interpretative reading. As he writes, the text reaches the limits of enunciation; it is experienced only in an activity of production and it only exists in the dialectic existence of discourse. The text is kinetic while the work is static: the text is re-written through reading and is experienced in reaction to sign, as opposed to the work that itself constitutes a general sign. To sum up, the text is not a product for consumption, it is itself the site of the production of meanings.

Like the city, the text is then only activated through the act of reading. Its potential lies not in its origin, but in a destination that is only achieved through the reader. In this context, it appears that the authority of the writer is highly challenged with respect to the text's value. The writing acquires a power of its own through the return to the sign and its interaction with the reader. The author's intentions become liable not only to the intentions and interpretations of the reader, but also to the autonomy of language and notation.

To think of the architect as author, however, would not traditionally allude to the script of a drawing. The drawing is usually considered a secondary product, a

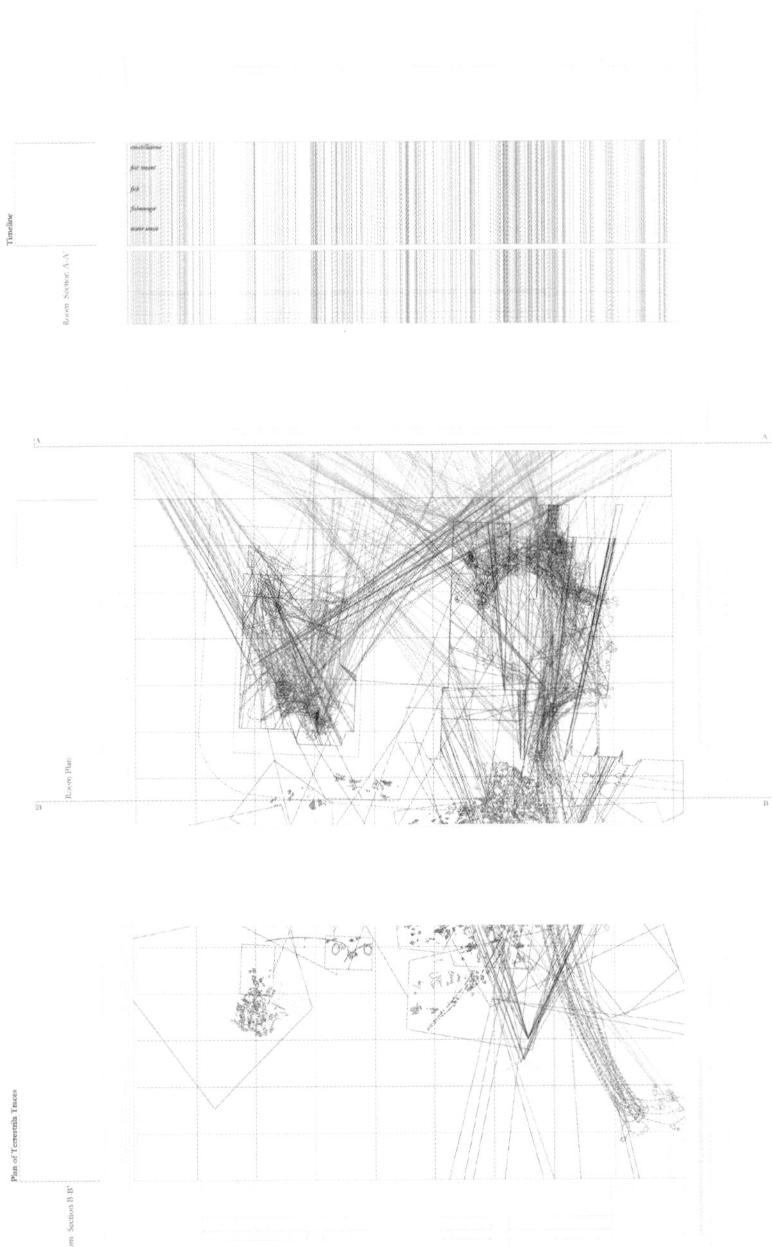

Figure 3. Sophia Banou, WL/LN: Room Key. CAD Drawing. The drawing, presented in a scale 1:2, folded along the walls of a room. Serial perspectival representations mapped against time along the wall were collated to planar traces on the plywood sheets by means of a linear weave.

mere 'allographic' sign: the prescription of a design to be built.[7] (Allen: 45) This kind of drawing is fixed and indisputable. Like the literary work, it is an end: the writing of a universal language of conventions that aims towards a precise, prescriptive communication. On the other hand, it is by means of writing that architects carry out the journey from an existing reality to what can be. This writing is not a fixed but a *working* drawing. It is not an end in itself, but it is only through its operation as a constant rewriting that design is fulfilled. The working drawing is the actual space of labour of the architect and cannot therefore be any less important than the space of a building, or city. This drawing inevitably works as a text, representing and instrumentalizing the very textuality of real space.

Within this working drawing the issues of authority that arise in the context of Barthes's notion of the text can be further understood. The drawing, as design or as documentary, is always a process of transcription. It is not concluded in a one-off process of writing and it therefore involves a series of 'readings'. The particularity of this process of consecutive significations lies in the fact that the architect carries the double role of being both the 'author' and the 'reader'. It is exactly by means of this suspension that occurs between writing and reading that the operative character of the drawing is facilitated. Moreover, in the space of the drawing the architect does not work alone but among a series of agents that originate from both an external pre-existing spatial reality and the meaning and matter of the graphic. In the working drawing there is no privileging of the static or the physical, no privileging of a certain scale or matter. It is a drawing open to all expressions of spatial experience, hence accumulating at once all parts of the process, from experience to sign, and back to experience again.

Looming Narratives

The value of this text is not found in its nature as a writing. It is found in its power of uncovering the latent realities that are manifested in the negotiations between writing and reading, between representation and experience. As the locus of reading is transposed from city to drawing, the text becomes informed by the conventions of a new 'regime of representation',[8] new practices and materialities. (Dorrian 2005: 62) This depth emerges in drawing beyond, or perhaps below, the limitations of figuration. It is not concluded in the formal duplication of a subject, nor in the notational description of a tangible reality. Yet it is always looming, at work upon the weaving of the lines and points that introduce the seemingly disparate elements of reality into drawing convention.

1 The *dérive* was a concept of urban experience based on spontaneous, unplanned movements across the city. Deriving from the practices of the Letterist International in the 1940s, this form of urban 'interpretation' became more prominent through the Situationist theory that emerged in the late 1950s, particularly in the writings of Guy Debord (1956).

2 The correct English word to be used here would be that of *scripture*. However, this word has come to be most commonly associated with a specific type of religious texts. As Susan Sontag writes, what best describes this is the French word *ecriture* (Sontag: xiii-xiv), which through Roland Barthes (Barthes, 1995) she defines as 'personal utterance'. To Barthes, *ecriture* defines not an object but the accumulative function of synergy among the elements of writing (such as language, tone, etcetera) that assigns to it the quality of a text rather than a pure manifestation of language.

3 From Latin *anima*, meaning *soul*, the animate stands here for that which is alive.

4 Before Barthes, this term can be traced back to Jean-Paul Sartre's characterization of *ecriture-blanche*, as it was introduced in Sartre's review of *L'Etranger* (The Strange) by Albert Camus. (Sontag: xvii)

5 Evans points out that the instrumentality of drawing lies not in its likeness to the subject of representation, but to its 'unlikeness' and the agency that its role as a means of abstraction suggests.

6 Although Dalí's experiment primarily constitutes a verbal representation, his attempt included notational drawings.

7 The allographic is used here to suggest a product that does not constitute a final work, but is a mediative reference to an external value, such as architectural drawing or musical notation. This term is used by Stan Allen through Nelson Goodman to point out that the architect's direct engagement is with the drawing rather than the built space itself.

8 Mark Dorrian writes on representation: 'The regimes of representation deployed continually produce alienation-effects as they instantiate the architectural object. Even if we are a master of a technique or we employ the most conventional, technical, and stable representational mode, the result is always to some extent surprising and unanticipated. It is always "other" and is open to being read in ways we did not imagine.' (Dorrian 2005: 62)

Moments and Spaces

Wim Cuyvers

The house is always neat and tidy. It smells of bleach, the floors sparkle – the mother takes care of that. She always seems to be on the go: cleaning. Chairs are stacked on the table, legs in the air, carpets are folded back, greys pools of soapy water gather on the shining red cement-tile floor. The ironing board is always opened out, the red-hot iron always stands menacingly at the corner of the ironing board. The fringes of the rug are combed, the wall-to-wall carpeting in the bedrooms perpetually vacuumed with the whining cleaner. The vacuum cleaner smells like its counterparts worldwide. The gleaming white retractable clothesline is always pulled out; the laundry is white and cold. The dishes are washed as soon as the meal is finished, and stored away in Formica cupboards. The cupboards are emptied twice a week and wiped clean. The shoes are arranged on racks in the boiler room and the laundry room. Every evening the shoes are cleaned: four pairs in a row on an old newspaper. They are brushed off with a hard brush, rubbed with grainy shoe polish – the polish has first to soak in, then the shoes are buffed, after which hands are washed in scalding hot water from the copper tap in the laundry room. The mother kneels beside the bath. She kneads the little one's hair with her knuckles, scalp and skull glow. There's no room for you where cleaning is done. No spot is overlooked. The mother shouts in a loud, shrill voice if someone sits on the edge of a chair. The voice sets one's teeth on edge. She says the little one makes too much noise when he breathes. The little one holds his breath, makes no sound whatsoever, and then when he can no longer hold it, sucks in another deep breath, very deep, and then nothing for two minutes. The mother shrieks when she hears the loud deep breath – almost a sob. The little one doesn't know how he should breathe to stop his mother hearing it. He can see only one possibility: to get away, outside, where no-one hears you breathing, where the wind breathes louder than he does. But the mother says it's not good weather to be outside. The little one would love to go out. Outside, not in the garden: the garden is just like the house, the garden is part of the house. The garden belongs to the house: demarcated with barbed wire, overlooked by the house. The garden is a room belonging to the house, hardly different from the kitchen or the living room. The garden with dry, sandy soil first has to be hoed, not one weed may remain; then the dry sandy soil is raked into patterns – the hands of the person who tends the garden are as dry as the sandy ground itself. The little one is only *outside* when he can rummage on the garbage site. The garbage site is a big sand pit. The little one's grandfather dug it, he used the sand in bricklaying: for hundreds of houses. The grandfather is dead. He looked like Gramsci. The huge hole in the sand has filled with water. The sand is yellowy-white. The water is pitch-black. There's a smell of rotting refuse, it smoulders constantly. The dump teems with life: salamanders, ducks, rats, frogs, herons, sometimes people come there. Fat Corry for one – he sells scrap metal and actually lives on a garbage site dump, he visits this one for the fun of shooting rats with his air gun. Beyond the garbage site there is a forest, the needles of the pine trees are pale blue-grey. The soil is acidic. You walk on an even carpet of pine needles on the sandy ground. The little one often walks in the forest, but he never gets to the end. The forest is a dark, gentle place: rough, scaly trunks of countless, similarly shaped and sized pines: *Pinus sylvestris*. There are hardly any animals in the forest, no warbling birds. Sometimes the little one sees two people meeting at the edge of the forest, they don't go far into it. The little one watches them, but doesn't spy on them. He sees them enter the forest and leaves them alone. All of a sudden the little one knows he must turn round, go home: it's dinner time at the house. The little one must take off his shoes before he goes indoors and get straight into the bath, as if he must be decontaminated. The little one hurries to the house. He hopes the mother won't call him, that her shrill voice will not resound far into the forest and reach the other houses.

The children walk to school; they wear black pinafores made from corded nylon over their pants and vests. They have to walk fast to reach school on time before the bell rings, before the gate is closed irrevocably to whoever is late. The bell is as strident as the mother's voice. The big children shout admonishments at the smaller ones, their shouts are loud, they whirl their arms round, they are strong and harsh. Every day the little one remembers the profound sense of betrayal on his first day of school. A child vomited on the black and white speckled cement tile floor. Using a small metal shovel with a wooden handle, a nun dressed in the blackest of black and a starched white headpiece shovelled orange sawdust from a zinc bucket over the orange vomit. How can someone be so far-sighted as to keep a bucket of sawdust at the ready in the corner of an empty classroom for that one occasion when someone would throw up?

Would you have to view the world through starched white blinkers? The mother wants the little one to be the best in the school. But in the large, rectangular, light-beige classroom the little one sits among the others, dreaming, he dreams of the beat of the lark's wings and he hears the lark's song, time and again, while the nun and the kindergarten teacher and the schoolmaster and the professor will keep on nagging, keep on teaching him what they want to hear, the way they want to hear it: they teach him to play-act. The mother said he had to be the best. The best at play-acting, the little one thinks. In the classroom the little one has to dream about keeping the ever-growing tension inside his too small a body. In school even time is caged. In school those who smell of bleach hate those who smell of grease, and vice versa: they hate the smells that others have brought from their homes. When the little one walks back home from school, alone, surrounded by the others, he stares at the abandoned house. He stands still. The girl from next door, who isn't a girl to him but a kind of schoolmistress, someone who acts as if she is already a schoolmistress, calls him. The little one stands on the threshold of the house that no longer has a door. He sees the crack that slants up from the top left corner of the door. The little one looks into the black space, there is orangey-red rubble and grey crumbling mortar on the floor. Between the fragments grows fluorescent green moss specked with orange. The little one would love to stand there, stock-still, with the sun on his back and the damp, black space ahead. He cringes when he hears the teacher-to-be calling and he returns with the others. At school the little one learns nothing, but on the way to and from school he has understood the house.

There is a wooden shed at the edge of the garbage site. The shed is built from pine planks. The planks are grey and thin and were once used for making formwork. There is fibre-cement sheeting on the roof. For hinges, the shed door has two pieces of thick grey leather. The door closes with a chain and a lock. Because of the chain there is a gap of around ten centimetres between the door and the wall. The little one pushes the door, which gives a little. The little one wriggles into the V-shaped crack. First his legs, then his hips, which almost get stuck. Then his stomach – that's easy – then his chest, the little one breathes out several times to make himself as thin as possible. He lies flat on the ground, that's where there is the most space in the V-shaped opening between the door and the wall. His chest chafes, gets stuck, chafes and slides further. Now his neck is in the opening. Only his head protrudes. The childish body is inside the shed, the little one turns his head, wanting to pull it in, but his temples are jammed between the wood. With his hands the little one pushes as hard as he can to open the door. His head twists and presses agonizingly slowly inside. The opening is too small.

The little one feels the pain, but knows he will manage. The narrow space shouts it out in the little one's ears. He is inside the shed completely. The shed resonates with evidence. It is a space that appears to have been there always. It contains bricklayers' materials. Everything is grey and desolate, dry: spades and trowels, a couple of buckets, three bags of cement, a pile of sand on a wooden board, a rusty drum, a mark indicating where the grey water once reached, a few lengths of string. The little one is protected from everything: rain and wind, but more especially, no-one can see him lying here, no-one can get in; grownups are too fat to squeeze themselves in. There is only the man who has the key to the shed. The little one is constantly aware, the entire time, that the man might come. If he did not have that awareness the shed would be nothing, would have no significance.

The world is simple: the world consists of just a few elements, a few simple materials – the child realized that very early on. The child can easily draw that world. He draws the world like a map, a plan view, with a stick in the wet grey sand. The map is triangular – an isosceles triangle. Yes, isosceles not equilateral. The child does not want to think that a map should always be rectangular. The child draws the map the way other children would draw a treasure map. The child draws a small square, the square represents *the house*, the house where he lives. The child has no idea of bisectors or dividing lines, yet he draws the square perfectly at the intersection of the bisectors. Many people believe that to be the centre of the triangle, but it is not: the centre is the point at which the medians intersect, and the medians are the lines leading from a vertex to the middle of the opposite side. The bisectors on the other hand are the lines through a vertex that divide the interior angle into two equal angles. Perhaps the child does not want the house to be at the centre of the drawing. Then he draws a small triangle, that small triangle represents *the school*. The small triangle is in the smallest corner of the triangular map in the sand, the child does not envisage it as the top of the triangle, nor as the bottom, the child continues to circle around the triangular map. He does not have a preference. The child stirs up the sand in the triangle that represents the school. Between the square and the triangle, at the bisector of the smallest angle in the map, the child again draws a small square, carefully adding diagonals in the square. The small square with diagonal lines is *the abandoned house*. Behind the square that has no diagonals – the house – the child draws a line parallel to the shortest side of the triangle. On the other side of the line he places *the garbage site*. Then he draws one more line, parallel to the last, between the last line and the shortest side of the triangle. On that line and on the bisector of the smallest angle he draws another small square with the diagonals passing through it. The same symbol as for the abandoned house, but this square represents *the shed*. The child makes dotted lines for what he sees as the garbage site. He makes scratches on the other side of the line he has just drawn, like he did in the small triangle. The area between the last line he drew and the shortest side of the map stands for the *endless forest*.

The young man does not wonder how he has ended up here, this Saturday night, against the concrete panel wall of the kindergarten playground. He does not wonder how he managed to remember this place, this place to which he had never returned since he was around five years old and about which, at that time, he could not possibly have known why he would now need it. He must have needed something then, something similar. The young man follows the body to the space and the place that ensure the body does not blow apart. Society and the body have shown him the way here. They will also show him the way to the dark lavatories under the lean-to, with no flush facilities and always reeking of piss. The lean-to roof shelters you from the rain; you can lean against the cement panels and rub your back against them as you can against the old lime trees in the playground. They hide him from the scrutinizing and admonishing looks of neighbours and passers-by. When locked up and dark, the school is a place of ineptitude. Anyone who has been inept remembers as a child the possibilities of the school's lifeless architecture after school hours. 'This is where I could be,' he must have thought then. Clearly he has never forgotten.

The young man cycles, undoubtedly faster than he has ever cycled before. He doesn't tire. When he is no longer moving along fast he has the impression it's the bike's fault, not his, not the fault of his lungs or his leg muscles, but of the bike. He rides at the bike's maximum speed, the same as a motorcycle. He does not get tired. The flashing blue light of the police vehicle approaches fast, the light speeds ahead of the car, he hears the typical sound of the Volkswagen engine, especially when the driver changes to a higher gear. The blue light comes and goes. Each time it comes back, it is closer. Since the moment he first saw the flashing light, he hasn't given it any more thought, just kept on cycling, without faltering. If he had waited for them he would probably have got off with a warning. But he does not want to hear the pedantic tone – he does not want to be checked out. He pedals and pedals, stands upright on the pedals at the transition from the asphalt road just in time to take the sandy track. It is pitch-dark here, but he does not slow down, he knows the sandy path, not every pothole, but he knows how the holes even out and how there is always a slight hump – an almost flat strip – in the middle, with grass on it that is never mown, but never grows higher than a few centimetres. The flashing light does not get any closer, because of the tunnel formed by the bushes growing along the sandy path, meaning that the light cannot shine fully there, but also that the police vehicle has to drive more slowly. He cycles a few hundred metres over the sandy track, two bends. The walls of the abandoned house are slightly lighter against the dark sky; there is no moon. He leaps into the pitch-black hole of the door opening where there is no door, he drags the bike in after him, across rubble and nettles, planks containing nails. He doesn't know the way, but it seems as if he cannot be mistaken, as if he is at one with the space. He crawls into a corner, the bike is lying in another corner, fortunately the wheels are no longer turning, there is no sound other than the hammering of his heart and the rushing of blood in his ears. The police vehicle drives past, stops further on, the light of a torch shines in, shines over the small field of lupins and wild cherries, then the light shines in again. He hears the engine start up, he hears the car drive off. The young man remains seated for a long time, until the car has driven past slowly. Now he knows it's over. He gets the bicycle, trails his hand along the walls of the abandoned house, in the way a person might stroke his own skin or old people can do sometimes: not a caress, but merely a moment of acceptance.

He's left, away from the house; left home; a flaming row. He made a fifty-kilometre detour to get here, taking a whole day, just before midnight, close to home but away from home. He hasn't been searching all day, the need only built up slowly until the need took over his body and showed him the way to the shed. On the exterior little has changed, only the lock is different: the chain with the Yale lock has been replaced by a lock screwed on the inside of the door. That means there is no room to spare between the door and the doorframe. The young man cannot imagine the fact that he has grown will mean he can no longer slip through the opening between the frame and the door. But he does not hesitate for an instant. It is as if everything is happening outside him. He finds the metal handle of an old paint tin. He pushes the metal wire between the ends of two planks, twists it to form an 'L' with a short end of about one-and-half centimetres. He pushes the other end of the wire between the planks, turning it until the tip is almost bent round. The 'key' is ready. He does not wonder if it will fit. He cannot remember ever having been so certain of success. He sticks the twisted wire into the lock, turns. The lock grates. He pushes the flat aluminium latch down and allows the door to open. He is not surprised. The smell is identical to that time, over ten years ago. Smells and fears never change. He immediately lies down, in the same place as before. There's different material underneath. The shed seems to be even less used than in the past. It is colder and damper than before. He curls into a ball, like a dog. For the first and last time in his life, he sleeps for sixteen hours solid.

> The child lies down in the warm grey sand. He looks at the drawing he has just made. Because the child is now lying down, with his head close to the plan drawing, he sees the triangle far more precisely than before. The child holds his breath for too long. The drawing wavers and multiplies in the child's head, there is not one triangular plan drawing, but several, a great many, together all the clearly-defined triangles form a circle: the triangles have become segments of a circle. The small scratched triangles in the smallest corners of the triangles coincide and cluster to form a small circle in the middle of the circle. On the edge of the circle a dark band forms. No, that's wrong: the child does not see an outer edge or a middle – nor a centre in that circle. The child knows there are lots of schools, other schools, where the big children go, the child knows there are masses of houses, and abandoned houses and sheds. He knows that the garbage sites converge to form a ring and that the world is bordered by the endless forest. And of course the child knows that there are factories and shops and offices, but they don't count in the concept of the world, the child knows that for certain.

The man works on houses and schools. He is not usually the one to build them; other people do that, so you could hardly say he makes houses and schools. Nor does he think it's designing. Designing would mean that he dreamed up those houses and those schools, devised them to serve a purpose he wished to achieve. That is not what he does, he looks for the houses and schools he works on, he retrieves them. He retrieves something that already existed for a long time, or at least pieces of what has existed for a long time. He believes that he recycles things rather than inventing them; he deploys them from memory, he can find them within himself. No doubt it is an unimportant occupation, just as life is unimportant. The man knows the houses he envisages are not real houses. The houses he envisages are desolate like the sheds he knows and to which he always has access. He would like the houses he works on to always be ramshackle, as much as is acceptable for the clients: like abandoned houses that crack and creak. Time and again it comes as a shock when people hang up curtains and roll out carpets there, but time will always be his ally. And the schools are conceived as if they were always closed, as if no lessons were held there, as if there were never teachers. The man who sees himself as a child builds canopies and lean-to roofs at schools. He remakes views out of fears. The fears of the child and of the adolescent are incorporated and ritualized in concrete, steel, brick, planks. They are places where a person can sometimes stand still, for a moment. When he sees someone doing that, when he sees someone taking up an orchestrated position, he feels a warm glow: it is a momentary contact, but the built space stands there as a monument to that moment. Through that space the man and the person who stood in the sheltering outdoor space have touched each other. The schools he builds have been conceived recalling the young man's fear and drift.

The man walks across graveyards and garbage sites in the cities he visits, he looks, the way he used to look as a child, it is impossible to cheat on the garbage site. Suddenly he recognizes the heavenly smell of the garbage site, even though it is thousands of kilometres from his own seminal garbage site, even though the garbage site of his youth is long gone. He looks at people wandering over the graves like hooded crows, and he looks at people combing through the rubbish, at those who like rubbish, he sees people but prefers not to talk to them. He prefers an encounter to take place soundlessly, through space. He does not need to shape the spaces in order for the ritual to take place. Like a stray dog in the city, he can find those spaces. Schools ask the man to teach there: the height of perversion: they will *supply* him with the youths. He heads the youths away from the school to garbage sites and graveyards, to cities destroyed by bullets, disintegrated cities, cities full of abandoned houses. The places of the graveyards and garbage sites give them insight into the city, help them to understand the city, but that is just a fallacy, a reason to hang around the graveyards and the garbage sites. The graveyard and the garbage site give them insight into the city's structure, but no insight, no understanding of mortality. On the garbage site tip all you can do is wander around. Very occasionally they touch each other, for a moment: then they weep: the man and the youth.

> The child knows the map of his world which he drew in the grey sand has swelled to become a map of the world, *tout court*, that together the segments form a map of the world. But that isn't all, the child continues to lie there, shuts his eyes. Now it's no longer the segments but the circle itself that wavers and multiplies. The circular map turns around one point, becomes a globe, a sphere. The sphere is transparent for the child, he can look through it. He

sees the outer, thick, scratched skin, he sees the next dotted layer, he sees the globe with the small squares with the diagonal lines and then the globe with all the small squares and no diagonals, and then further inside the sphere he sees the next globe with small squares and diagonal lines, and further in the scratched centre of the sphere like a small globe, almost a dot. But for the child the words 'core' and 'skin' have no meaning or undertone: the diagram the child draws contains no hidden criticism, just as, in the universe, there is no hidden criticism. That is the world: a school globe around which abandoned houses revolve like moons, beyond the abandoned houses circle the abandoned houses bordered by the skin of the garbage site, with at its far end the scattering of sheds, and farther still, like a thick layer of fog, the skin of the endless forest.

The old man is in the endless forest. He walks back and forth in the endless forest. He carts stuff along, like a homeless person, like a stranger: he is not at home, he is a stranger. Everyone thinks it's ridiculous when other people cart stuff around. The businessman does not understand why the vagrant hauls a sack of smelly clothes around, the vagrant cannot imagine why the businessman walks back and forth with a briefcase full of annoying papers. The old man is a child, a young man, a man. He sees at the start of the endless forest, where the forest and the city touch, heaps of rubbish: building rubble, work clothes, old drums, empty paint tins. He sees two cars parked there side by side. He sees two people sitting together in one car. Youths and adults come here, before going to work, to school, home, before they have to go home. The old man recognizes the rituals, he recognizes the clues, he recognizes their desires, he has not forgotten his own. And whenever he sees the clues, whenever he sees them looking furtively, whenever he sees the turning off the road, whenever he sees the path petering out at the tree trunks, whenever he sees the small garbage site beneath the trees, he feels a warm glow. The old man knows that some people make inventories of forests, in order to exploit the forest, they are people who know which trees grow where, they know how many cubic metres of timber there are per hectare and of what quality, they know what diseases affect the trees, what the subsoil is like. They resemble the people who exploit the city, they know how many buildings there are, how well or how badly the buildings are fitted out, they are the ones who know the value of the neighbourhoods. There are two open spaces in the endless forest. On one there is an abandoned house – *une maison abandonée* – the old man sleeps there, but it is not his house. On the other open space there is the shed, hut, shack where the spades, saws and axes are kept. The old man knows that the abandoned house and the shed in the endless forest are necessary to make the endless forest a place, so that in the endlessness there are places: common places. Common places that could lure people out of their houses, like schools can. The old man keeps on longing for no re-proaches, for approaches. Far away a dog barks. In the endless forest you cannot tell where the sound comes from. He does know it will never happen, but still . . . he would really like someone to stand with him and look into the dark, damp space of the abandoned house, frozen, with the sun on his back. In the endless forest everyone is a stranger. A foreigner, someone who is not at home, who sees scope in the abandoned house, in the shed, in the edge of the endless forest. The old man lies on the damp ground in the endless forest. He follows the lines of the tall trunks with his eyes. In the endless forest no-one knows what tree should be where. At the edge there is perhaps recognition, but in the forest the forest is the forest. In the forest nothing happens, nothing is wrong. You go there to die.

The trees often touch, then they make a slow groaning sound devoid of rhythm, rubbing the bark off one another. Sometimes, all of a sudden, a tree snaps: the upper part of the tree that grew upwards towards the light comes crashing down. He imagines himself buried beneath the bulk of the tree, crushed into the mass of limestone like a fossil dating back millions of years. A plane drones past high overhead, undoubtedly on its way to the city, communication and orientation satellites blink even higher up, if you don't look carefully you might think they are stars. An animal passes by, panting. The high-voltage cable crackles in the damp night air, a tick crawls up to his groin. The forest is endless but the city is close by, the world is close by, the universe is close by, like his own body.

Often he is not alone in the endless forest. The endless forest, close to the city is not a place for a hermit. He is often there with a youngster, a youngster that, society has decided, has a problem. It is a young guy that cannot attune his body to society: his body collides with society or vice versa. He admires the way the youngster appears unable to learn – impossible. He is there at the same moment, in the same place with the youngster in the endless forest. The old man and the youngster walk to the abandoned house that shelters them. The old man can only see the black doorway. He feels only the heat of the sun on his back. He can only think about the moment the youngster might dawdle, might stand still and stare into the black hole. But the youngster walks on, at his irregular pace, through the door, to cut himself a slice of bread: he is hungry. The young guy takes a bite, turns the knob of the portable radio. Radio

Energy blares out commercials. Sometimes the old man tells the youngster that the forest is a school, a school where there is nothing to learn, a school for those who do not learn. 'architecture – school' the man mutters. It is not clear whether he wants to say 'architecture school' or possibly 'school architecture'. At all events, he is not talking about forestry classes. The old man and the boy are in the forest or in the abandoned house together; the space is their *common* ground. But the old man is old and the other is young. They take the same path through the forest, but they have a different rhythm. They have nothing to gain from each other – as in 'architecture – school': no diploma, no wages. The old man longs for his body's centre of gravity to coincide with the boy's. He knows it is not possible, he has always known, but that does not mean the longing ceases. Language cannot help them to become close.

There are a few leaves on the trees, not many yet, at this time of the year he can still see a lot of stars. The sky is black, the tree trunks even blacker. He recognizes through the leaves and the treetops a few constellations: the illusion of insight: there are billions of stars and in a few he sees a constellation. The old man takes a branch, draws without thinking a triangle in the wet black decaying soil. He draws an isosceles triangle. At the intersection of the bisectors of the isosceles triangle he draws a small square. In the smallest angle of the isosceles triangle he draws a small triangle. Between the small square and the small triangle, on the bisector of the smallest angle of the plan, the old man draws another small square; in the small square he carefully traces diagonals. Behind the small square without diagonals the old man draws a line parallel to the shortest side of the triangle. Then he draws just one more line, parallel to the other line between that and the shortest side of the triangle. On that line, as well as on the bisector of the smallest angle, he draws another small square intersected by diagonals. He slowly adds dots to the area. He scratches in the area between the triangle's shortest side and the parallel line, and makes dots in the next area. It is freezing. The old man is amazed at how little fear remains, all the lust has gone: the old man is ready to go.

BIBLIOGRAPHY

This bibliography includes the references from the contributions in this volume, as well as a number of titles that we consider crucial for our emerging field of research. In this way, we hope to offer a set of references that allows the reader to further investigate the connections between architecture and literature.

Abbott, H. Porter (2008), *The Cambridge Introduction to Narrative* (Cambridge: Cambridge University Press)

Ackerman, James S. (1991), 'The Geopolitics of Venetian Architecture in the time of Titian', in: *Distance Points: Essays in Theory and Renaissance Art and Architecture* (Cambridge, MA: MIT Press,), 453-494, originally published in 1982

Aksamija, Nadja (2011), 'Architecture and Poetry in the Making of a Christian Cicero: Giovanni Battista Campeggi's Tuscolano and the Literary Culture of the Villa in Counter-Reformation Bologna', *I Tatti Studies in the Renaissance*, no. 13 (2011), 127-191

Allen, Stan (2009), 'Notations+Diagrams: Mapping the Intangible', in: *Practice: Architecture, Technique and Representation* (London: Routledge), 41-69

Alquié, Ferdinand (1939), *Leçons de philosophie: Psychologie* (Toulouse: Didier)

Anderson, J.R. (1980), *Cognitive Psychology and Its Implications* (San Francisco: Freeman)

Aristotle (1929), *Poetics*, translated by S.H. Butcher (London: Macmillan)

Aurenhammer, Hans H. (1994), '*Multa aedium exempla variarum imaginum atque operum*: Das Problem der *imitatio* in der italienischen Architektur des frühen 16. Jahrhunderts', in: *Intertextualität in der Frühen Neuzeit: Studien zu ihren theoretischen und praktischen Perspektiven* (Frankfurt: Peter Lang), 533-605

Austin, Norman (1975), *Archery at the Dark of the Moon: Poetic Problems in Homer's Odyssey* (Berkeley: University of California Press)

Aureli, Pier Vittorio (2011), *The Possibility of an Absolute Architecture* (Writing Architecture) (Cambridge, MA: MIT Press)

Awan, Nishat, Tatjana Schneider and Jeremy Till (2011), *Spatial Agency: Other Ways of Doing Architecture* (London: Routledge)

Bachelard, Gaston (1994), *The Poetics of Space* (Boston: Beacon Press, 1994), originally published as La poétique d'espace (1958)

Bakhtin, Mikhail (1981), *The Dialogic Imagination*, edited by Michael Holmquist (Austin: University of Texas Press), originally published as *Voprosy literalury i estetiki* (1975)

Bakhtin, Mikhail (1984), *Rabelais and His World* (Bloomington, IN: Indiana University Press), originally published as ***Творчество Франсуа Рабле и народная культура средневековья и Ренессанса***, *Tvorčestvo Fransua Rable i narodnaja kul'tura srednevekov'ja i Renessansa* (1965)

Bakhtin, Mikhail (1986), *Speech Genres and Other Late Essays*, edited by Caryl Emerson and Michael Holquist (Austin: University of Texas Press), originally published as *Estetika slovesnogo tvorchestva* (1979)

Bakhtin, Mikhail (1990), *Art and Answerability : Early Philosophical Essays*, edited by Michael Holquist, translated by Vadim Liapunov and Kenneth Brostrom (Austin: University of Texas Press)

Bañón, José Joaquín Parra (2004), *Pensamento arquitectónico na obra de José Saramago: acerca da arquitectura da casa* (Lisbon: Caminho)

Barthes, Roland (1967), 'Death of the Author', Aspen, no. 5-6, available online at www.ubu.com/aspen/aspen5and6/threeEssays.html#barthes (accessed 12 March 2012)

Barthes, Roland (1978), *Image, Music, Text*, edited and translated by Stephen Heath (London: Macmillan)

Barthes, Roland (1979), 'From Work to Text', in: J.V. Harari (ed.), *Textual Strategies: Perspectives in Poststructuralist Criticism* (Ithaca, NY: Cornell University Press), 73-81

Barthes, Roland (1995), *Writing Degree Zero* (New York: Hill and Young), originally published as *Le Degré Zéro de L'Ecriture* (1953)

Bataille, Georges (1962), *Eroticism* (London: Calder)

Bayard, Pierre (2007), *Comment parler des livres que l'on a pas lus?* (Paris: Les Éditions de Minuit)

Beasley-Murray, Tim (2008), *Mikhail Bakhtin and Walter Benjamin: Experience and Form* (New York: Palgrave Macmillan)

Beckett, Samuel (1953), *L'Innommable* (Paris: Les Éditions de Minuit)

Beckett, Samuel (1963), *Watt* (London: Jupiter Books)

Beckett, Samuel (1986), 'Quad', in: *The Complete Dramatic Works* (London: Faber and Faber)

Beckett, Samuel (1991), *Cap au pire* (Paris: Les Éditions de Minuit, 1991), originally published as *Worstward Ho* (1983)

Beckett, Samuel (1994), *Waiting for Godot* (New York: Grove Press, originally published as *En attendant Godot* (1949)

Benjamin, Walter (1969), 'The Task of the Translator', in: Hannah Arendt (ed.), *Illuminations* (New York: Schocken Books), originally published as *Gesammelte Schriften . . .* (1923)

Blondel, Jacques-François (1752), *Architecture Française* (Paris)

Blondel, Jacques-François (1771), *Cours d'Architecture ou Traité de la Decoration, Distribution et Construction des Bâtiments*, 9 vols. (Paris)

Blumenberg, Hans (1999), *Wirklichkeiten, in denem wir leben* (Stuttgart: Reclam)

Blumenberg, Hans (1990), *Work on Myth* (Cambridge, MA: MIT Press), originally published as *Arbeit am Mythos* (1979)

Booth, Wayne (1988), *The Company We Keep: An Ethics of Fiction* (Berkeley: University of California Press)

Borges, Jorge Luis (1941), *El Jardin de senderos que se bifurcan* (Buenos Aires: Editorial Sur)

Borges, Jorge Luis (2000), *Fictions* (London: Penguin Classics), originally published as *Ficciones* (1944)

Borges, Jorge Luis and Adolfo Bioy Casarès (1979), *Chronicles of Bustos Domecq* (London: Penguin Books), originally published as *Crónicas de Bustos Domecq* (1967)

Boullée, Etienne-Louis (1968), *Essai sur l'art* (Paris: Hermann)

Bourdieu, Pierre (1977), *Outline of a Theory of Practice* (Cambridge: Cambridge University Press), originally published as *Esquisse d'une théorie de la pratique* (1972)

Buzzati, Dino (1965), 'Seven Floors' (Milan), originally published as 'Sette Piani', in *La Lettura* (1937)

Cacciari, Massimo (1980), 'Eupalinos or Architecture', *Oppositions* no. 21, 106-116

Calatrava, Juan and Winfried Nerdinger (eds.) (2010), *Arquitectura escrita* (Madrid: Círculo de Bellas Artes)

Calvino, Italo (1956), *The Path to the Nest Spiders* (London: Collins), originally published as *Il sentiero dei nidi di ragno* (1947)

Calvino, Italo (1980), 'Il midollo del leone', in: *Una Pietra sopra* (Turin: Einaudi), 3-18, originally published in 1955

Calvino, Italo (1983a), 'A Plunge into Real Estate', in: *Difficult Loves*, translated by William Weaver (London: Secker & Warburg), originally published as 'La speculazione edilizia' (1957)

Calvino, Italo (1983b), *Marcovaldo or the Seasons in the City* (San Diego: Harcourt Brace Jovanovich), originally published as *Marcovaldo, ovvero le stagioni in città* (1963)

Calvino, Italo (1991), *Adam, One Afternoon* (London: Secker & Warburg), originally published as *Ultimo viene il Corvo* (1949)

Čapek, Karel (2001), R.U.R. (*Rossums' Universal Robots*) (Mineola, NY: Dover Publications), originally published as *Rosumovi Univerzální Roboti* (1920)

Careri, Francesco (2002), *Walkscapes: Walking as an Aesthetic Practice* (Barcelona: Editorial Gustavo Gili)

Carpentier, Alejo (1957), *The Kingdom of this World* (New York: The Noonday Press), originally published as *El reino de este mundo* (1949)

Carpentier, Alejo, (1995a), 'Baroque and the Marvellous Real', in: Parkinson Zamora, Lois and Wendy B. Faris (eds.) *Magical Realism: Theory, History, Community* (Durham, NC: Duke University Press Books), 89-108, originally published in 1975

Carpentier, Alejo (1995b), 'Marvellous Real in America', in: Parkinson Zamora, Lois and Wendy B. Faris (eds.) *Magical Realism: Theory, History, Community* (Durham, NC: Duke University Press Books), 75-88

Cassirer, Ernst (1955), *The Philosophy of Symbolic Forms*, vol. 2: *Mythical Thought* (New Haven, CT: Yale University Press), originally published as *Philosophie der symbolischen Formen*, Band 2: *Das mythische Denken* (1925)

Certeau, Michel de (1984), *The Practice of Everyday Life* (Berkeley: University of California Press), originally published as *L'invention du quotidian*, vol. 1: *Arts de faire* (1980)

Certeau, Michel de (1990), *L'invention du quotidian*, vol. 1: *Arts de faire* (Paris: Éditions Gallimard), originally published in 1980

Clarke, Georgia and Paul Crossley (eds.) (2000), *Architecture and Language: Constructing Identity in European Architecture, c. 1000-1650* (Cambridge and New York: Cambridge University Press)

Clark, Katerina and Michael Holquist (1984), *Mikhail Bakhtin* (Cambridge, MA: The Belknap Press of Harvard University Press)

Clay, Grady (2003), 'Crossing the American Grain with Vesalius, Geddes and Jackson: The Cross Section as a Learning Tool', in: Wilson, Chris and Paul Groth (eds.), *Everyday America: Cultural Landscape Studies after J.B. Jackson* (Berkeley/Los Angeles/London: University of California Press) 109-129

Coates, Nigel (2012), *Narrative Architecture: Architectural Design Primers series* (Wiley)

Coleridge, Samuel Taylor (1960), *Coleridge's Shakespeare Criticism*, vol. 1, edited by Thomas Middleton Rayson (London: Constable)

Cook, Peter and John Hejduk (1991), *House of the Book (Black Dog Series)* (New York: Rizzolli)

Currie, Gregory (1990), *The Nature of Fiction* (Cambridge: Cambridge University Press)

Dalí, Salvador (1998a), 'Documentary – Paris 1929 – I', in: *Oui: The Paranoid-Critical Revolution*, edited by Robert Descharnes (Boston: Exact Change),93-95, originally published as *Oui: la révolution paranoïaque-critique* (1971)

Dalí, Salvador (1998b), 'Documentary – Paris 1929 – VI', in: *Oui: The Paranoid-Critical Revolution*, edited by Robert Descharnes (Boston: Exact Change),106-107, originally published as *Oui: la révolution paranoïaque-critique* (1971)

Danielewski, Mark Z. (2001), *House of Leaves* (London: Doubleday/Transworld Publishers)

Debord, Guy (1956), 'Theory of the Dérive', *Les Lèvres Nues*, no. 9. Collaboratory for Digital Discourse and Culture - Virginia Tech., available online at www.cddc.vt.edu/sionline/si/theory.html, accessed on 15 June 2015

Deleuze, Gilles (1992), *L'Épuisé* (Paris: Les Éditions de Minuit)

Derrida, Jacques (2001), 'What Is a Relevant Translation', *Critical Inquiry*, vol. 27, no. 2, 174-200

Diderot, Denis (2004), *Lettre sur les aveugles à l´usage de ceux qui voient* (Paris: Éditions Gallimard, Collection Folio)

Dorrian, Mark (2005), 'Architecture's "Cartographic Turn"', in: Pousin, Frédéric (ed.), *Figures de la Ville et Construction des Savoirs* (Paris: CNRS Editions), 61-72

Doshi, B.V. and Christopher Alexander (1963-1964), 'A Role for the Individual in City Planning: Main Structure Concept', *Landscape*, vol. 13, no. 2, 17-20

Doussan, Jenny (2013), *Time, Language and Visuality in Agamben's Philosophy* (London: Palgrave McMillan)

Durand, Jean-Nicolas-Louis (1802-1805), *Précis des leçons d'architecture*, 2 vols. (Paris)

Eck, Caroline van (2007), *Classical Rhetoric and the Visual Arts in Early Modern Europe* (Cambridge and New York: Cambridge University Press)

Edwards, Sarah and Jonathan Charley (2012), *Writing the Modern City: Literature, Architecture, Modernity* (London: Routledge)

Efland, Arthur (2003), 'Imagination in Cognition: The Purpose of the Arts', *JAE*, vol. 1, no. 1, 26-50, available online at http://ed.arte.gov.tw/uploadfile/Periodical/428_26_66.pdf

Elam, Caroline (2005), '"Tuscan Dispositions": Michelangelo's Florentine Architectural Vocabulary and Its Reception', *Renaissance Studies*, vol. 19, no. 1, 46-82

Ende, Michael (1986), *Mirror in Mirror* (New York: Viking), originally published as *Der Spiegel im Spiegel* (1983)

Eriksen, Roy (2001), *The Building in the Text: Alberti to Shakespeare and Milton* (University Park: The Penn State University Press)

Escola, Marc and Sophie Rabau (2012), 'Inventer la pratique: pour une théorie des textes possibles', *La Lecture litteraire*, no. 8 (Reims: Université de Reims Champagne-Ardenne)

Evans, Robin (1997), 'Translations from Drawing to Building', in: *Translations from Drawing to Building and Other Essays* (London: Architectural Association), 153-193

FAT (2011), 'A Field Guide to Radical Post-Modernism', *Architectural Design*, vol. 81, no. 5, editors: Charles Jencks, Sean Griffiths, Charles Holland, Sam Jacob, 46-61

Fez-Barringten, Barie (2012), *Architecture: The Making of Metaphors*, edited by Edward Hart (Newcastle: Cambridge Scholars Publishing)

Folch-Serra, Mireya (1990), 'Place, Voice, Space: Mikhail Bakhtin's Dialogical Landscape', *Environment and Planning*, D: Society and Space 8, 255-274

Forster, E.M. (1927), *Aspects of the Novel* (New York: Harcourt, Brace & World, Inc)

Foucault, Michel (1994), 'Des espaces autres', in: *Dits et écrits IV* (Paris: Éditions Gallimard), 752-762

Frank, Ellen Eve (1979), *Literary Architecture: Essays Toward a Tradition: Walter Pater, Gerard Manley Hopkins, Marcel Proust, Henry James* (Berkeley: University of California Press)

Gadanho, Pedro and Susana Oliveira (eds.) (2013), *Once Upon a Place: Architecture and Fiction* (Lisbon: FAUL/Caleidoscópio)

Gardiner, Michael (2004), 'Wild Publics and Grotesque Symposiums', in: Nick Crossley and Jonn M. Roberts (eds.), *After Habermas: New Perspectives on the Public Sphere* (Oxford: Blackwell Publishing), 28-48

Gendler, Tamar (2011), 'Imagination', in: *Stanford Encyclopedia of Philosophy, available online at* http://plato.stanford.edu/entries/imagination/

Genette, Gérard (1983), *Nouveau discours du récit* (Paris: Seuil)

Goethe, *Johann Wolfgang von (1970), Faust,* translated by Jane K. Brown (Ithaca, NY: Cornell University Press), originally published in 1806

Grafe, Christoph, Klaske Havik and Madeleine Maaskant (eds.) (2006), *OASE 70 Architecture & Literature, Reflections / Imaginations* (Rotterdam: NAi Publishers)

Grillner, Katja (ed.) (1998), 'Narratives of Cities and Landscapes – Poetic Representations', *Nordic Journal of Architectural Research*, no. 1-2 (Göteburg)

Grillner, Katja (2000), *Ramble, Linger and Gaze: Dialogues from the Landscape Garden* (Stockholm: KTH)

Grillner, Katja (2005), 'Writing Architecture', in: 01.AKAD *Beginnings: Experimental Research in Architecture and Design* (Stockholm: AKAD), 64-67

Guarini, Guarino (1737), *Architettura Civile,* 2 vols (Turin)

Hamon, Philippe (1992), *Expositions: Literature and Architecture in Nineteenth-Century France* (Berkeley/Los Angeles/Oxford: University of California Press)

Handa, Rumiko and James Potter (2011), *Conjuring the Real: The Role of Architecture in Eighteenth- and Nineteenth-Century Fiction* (Lincoln: University of Nebraska Press)

Havik, Klaske (2014), *Urban Literacy: Reading and Writing Architecture* (Rotterdam: nai010 publishers)

Hays, Michael K. (ed.) (1998), *Oppositions Reader* (Cambridge, MA: MIT Press)

Hejduk, John (1988), 'Evening in Llano', in: Elizabeth Diller, Diane Lewis and Kim Shkapich (eds.), *Education of an Architect* (New York: Rizzoli International), 340-341

Hejduk, John (1991), 'Conversation: John Hejduk or The Architect Who Drew Angels', with David Shapiro, *Architecture and Urbanism*, no 1 (244), 3-134

Hemsoll, David (2001), 'A Question of Language: Raphael, Michelangelo and the Art of Architectural Imitation', in: Lauren Golden and Martin Kemp (eds.), *Raising the Eyebrow: John Onians and World Art Studies: An Album Amicorum in His Honour* (Oxford: Archaeopress)

Hemsoll, David (2009), 'Raphael's New Architectural Agenda', in: Roy Eriksen and Magne Malmanger (eds.), *Imitation, Representation and Printing in the Italian Renaissance* (Pisa and Rome: Fabrizio Serra Editore)

Herman, David (2002), *Story Logic: Problems and Possibilities of Narrative* (Lincoln: University of Nebraska Press)

Herman, *David (2003a), 'How Stories Make Us Smarter: Narrative Theory and Cognitive Semiotics', Recherches en communication*, no. 19, 133-153. Available online at http://sites.uclouvain.be/rec/index.php/rec/article/viewFile/5231/4961

Herman, David (2003b), 'Stories as a Tool for Thinking', in: David Herman (ed.), *Narrative Theory and the Cognitive Sciences* (Stanford: CSLI Publications), 163-192

Herman, David (2005), 'Conflict', in: David Herman, Manfred Jahn, and Marie-Laure Ryan (eds.), *The Routledge Encyclopedia of Narrative Theory (London: Routledge)*

Herman, *David (2009), Basic Elements of Narrative* (Oxford: Wiley-Blackwell)

Herman, David (2013), *Storytelling and the Sciences of Mind (Cambridge, MA: MIT Press)*

Heynen, Hilde (1999), *Architecture and Modernity (Cambridge, MA: MIT Press)*

Hirschkop, Ken (2004), 'Justice and Drama: On Bakhtin as a Complement to Habermas', in: Nick Crossley and John M. Roberts (eds.), After Habermas: *New Perspectives on the Public Sphere* (Oxford: Blackwell Publishing), 49-66

Hollis, Edward (2010), *The Secret Lives of Buildings: From the Ruins of the Parthenon to the Vegas Strip in Thirteen Stories* (New York: Picador)

Holloway, Julian and James Kneale (2000), 'Mikhail Bakhtin: Dialogics of Space', in: Nigel J. Thrift and Mike Crang (eds.), *Thinking Space (London: Routledge), 71-88*

Hyvärinen, Matti (2006), 'Towards a Conceptual History of Narrative', in: Matti Hyvärinen, Anu Korhonen and Juri Mykkänen (eds.), *The Travelling Concept of Narrative* (Helsinki: Helsinki Collegium for Advanced Studies), 20-41, available online at http://www.uta.fi/yky/yhteystiedot/henkilokunta/mattikhyvarinen/index/TCH-hyvarinen.pdf

Jackson, John Brinckerhoff (1951), 'The Need of Being Versed in Country Things', *Landscape, vol. 1, no. 1, 1-5*

Jackson, John Brinckerhoff (1953), 'The Westward-Moving House: Three American Houses and the People Who Lived in Them', *Landscape,* vol. 2, no. 3, 8-21

Jackson, John Brinckerhoff (1957), 'The Stranger's Path', *Landscape,* vol. 7, no. 1, 11-15

Jackson, John Brinckerhoff (1967-1968), 'Pretensions and Delusions', *Landscape,* vol. 16, no. 2, 1-3

Jackson, John Brinckerhoff (1969), '1951-1968: Postscript', *Landscape,* vol. 18, no. 1, 1

Johnson, Mark (1987), *The Body in the Mind: The Body Basis of Meaning, Imagination and Reason* (Chicago: Chicago University Press)

Jones, Lindsay (2000), *The Hermeneutics of Sacred Architecture,* vols. 1 and 2 (Cambridge, MA: Harvard University Press)

Kaplan, Rachel, Stephen Kaplan and Robert L. Ryan (1998), *With People in Mind: Design and Management of Everyday Nature* (Washington, DC: Island Press)

Kearney, Richard (1988), *The Wake of Imagination* (Minneapolis: University of Minnesota Press)

Kearney, Richard (2001), *On Stories (Thinking in Action)* (London: Routledge)

Kenniff, Thomas-Bernard and Ben Sweeting (2014), 'There Is No Alibi in Designing: Responsibility and Dialogue in the Design Process', *Opticon,* 1826 16, 1-8

Keunen, Bart (2011), *Time and Imagination: Chronotopes in Western Narrative Culture* (Evanston, IL: Northwestern University Press)

Keunen, Bart and Sofie Verraest (2012), 'Landscapes and Mythical Chronotopes in Urban Designs for Twenty-first Century Paris', Sofie Verraest, Bart Keunen and Katrien Bollen (eds.), *Thematic Issue New Work on Landscape and its Narration*, CLCWeb: Comparative Literature and Culture, 14.3

Keunen, Bart, Pieter Uytenhove and Laurence van Nuijs (2014), 'Espace, temps et récit: imagination narrative et urbanisme', in: Pierre Hyppolite, Antoine Leygonie and Agnès Verlet (eds.), *Architecture et littérature: une interaction en question XXème-XXIème siècles* (Aix-en-Provence: Presses universitaires de Provence), 105-115

Lakoff, George and Mark Johnson (2003), *Metaphors We Live By* (Chicago: The University of Chicago Press)

Lamontagne, André (1998), 'Métatextualité postmoderne: de la fiction à la critique', *Études littéraires,* vol. 30, no. 3 (Montréal: Université du Québec à Montréal et Université de Montréal), 61-76

Latour, Bruno and Emilie Hermant (2006), *Paris ville invisible* (Paris: La Découverte-Les Empêcheurs de penser en rond), first published in 1998, available online at www.bruno-latour.fr/sites/default/files/downloads/viii_paris-city-gb.pdf, accessed 7 December 2011

Leatherbarrow, David (2004), *Topographical Stories: Studies in Landscape and Architecture* (Philadelphia: University of Pennsylvania Press)

Ledoux, Claude-Nicolas (1804), *L'architecture considérée sous le rapport de l'art, de moeurs et se la législation* (Paris)

Lefkowitz Horowitz, Helen (1997), 'J.B. Jackson and the Discovery of the American Landscape', in: Helen Lefkowitz Horowitz (ed.), *Landscape in Sight: Looking at America / John Brinckerhoff Jackson* (New Haven: Yale University Press), ix-xxxi

Levé, Edouard (2002), *Œuvres* (Paris: P.O.L.)

Lévesque, Carole (2013), 'Welcome to Bachoura, or the Found City as Interstice', in: Patrick Barron and Manuela Mariani, *Terrain Vague: The Interstitial as Site, Concept, Intervention* (New York: Routledge), 33-47

Lévesque, Luc (2002), 'The Terrain Vague as Material – Some Observations', in: *House Boat / Occupations Symbiotiques* (Hull/Gatineau: AXNEO 7), 6-7

Lévi-Strauss, Claude (1966), *The Savage Mind (Chicago: University of Chicago Press), originally published as La Pensée Sauvage* (1962)

Levinas, Emmanuel (1986), 'The Trace of the Other', in: Mark C. Taylor (ed.), *Deconstruction in Context* (Chicago: University of Chicago Press), 348-349, originally published as 'La Trace de L'Autre' (1963)

Lewis, Peirce (2003), 'The Monument and the Bungalow', in: Chris Wilson and Paul Groth (eds.), *Everyday America: Cultural Landscape Studies after J.B. Jackson* (Berkeley/Los Angeles/London: University of California Press), 85-108

Limerick, Jeffrey W. (2003), 'Basic "Brinckmanship": Impressions Left in a Youthful Mind', in: Chris Wilson and Paul Groth (eds.), *Everyday America: Cultural Landscape Studies after J.B. Jackson* (Berkeley/Los Angeles/London: University of California Press), 130-141

Littlewood, A.R. (1987), 'Ancient Literary Evidence for the Pleasure Gardens of Roman Country Villas', in: Elisabeth Blair Macdougall (ed.), *Ancient Roman Villa Gardens: The Tenth Dumbarton Oaks*

Colloquium on the History of Landscape Architecture, 1987 (Washington, DC: Dumbarton Oaks)

Livholts, Mona (ed.) (2012), *Emergent Writing Methodologies in Feminist Studies* (London: Routledge)

Lotman, Jurij M. (1977), *The Structure of the Artistic Text (Ann Arbor: University of Michigan Press), originally published as Struktura khudozhestvennogo tekst* (1971)

Lynch, Kevin and Malcolm Rivkin (1959), 'A Walk Around the Block', *Landscape,* vol. 9, no .1, 24-34

Malpas, Jeff (2007), *Place and Experience* (Cambridge: Cambridge University Press)

Mamber, Stephen (2003), 'Narrative Mapping', in: *New Media: Theories and Practices of Digitextuality* (New York: Routledge), 145-158

Manguel, Alberto (1996), *A History of Reading* (London: Penguin Books)

Manguel, Alberto and Gianni Guadalupi (1980), *The Dictionary of Imaginary Places* (New York: Macmillan)

Martin, Louis (1990), 'Transpositions: On the Intellectual Origins of Tschumi's Architectural Theory', *Assemblage*, no. 11, 22-35

Massey, Doreen (2005), *For Space* (London: SAGE)

McDonough, Tom (2002), 'The Crimes of the Flâneur', *October*, no. 102, 101-122

Merleau-Ponty, Maurice (1964), *Signs* (Evanston, IL: Northwestern University Press), originally published as Signes (1960*)*

Merleau-Ponty, Maurice (1991), *The Prose of the World* (Evanston, IL: Northwestern University Press), originally published as La Prose du Monde (1969*)*

Mezières, Nicolas Le Camus de (1780), *Le génie de l'architecture* (Paris)

Miller, Arthur (2000), *Death of a Salesman* (New York: Penguin), first published in 1949

Montale, Eugenio (1970), *Provisional Conclusions: A Selection of the Poetry of Eugenio Montale*, translated by Edith Farnsworth (Chicago: Henry Regnery Company)

Mouffe, Chantal (2000), *The Democratic Paradox* (London: Verso)

Muf (Katherine Shonfield and Adrian Dannat) (2001), *This Is What We Do: A Muf Manual*, edited by Rosa Ainley (London: Ellipsis*)*

Mulholland, Terri and Nicole Sierra (eds.) (2015), *Spatial Perspectives: Essays on Literature and Architecture (Cultural Interactions: Studies in the Relationship between the Arts)*, book 37 (Bern: Peter Lang AG, Internationaler Verlag der Wissenschaften)

Nerdinger, Winfried (ed.) (2007), *Architektur wie sie im Buche steht, Fiktive Bauten und Städte in der Literatur* (Munich: Architekturmuseum der Technische Universität München, Verlag Anton Pustet)

Norberg-Schulz, Christian (1971), *Existence, Space and Architecture* (London: Praeger Publishers)

Pallasmaa, Juhani (2006), 'Existential Space in Architecture and Cinema', in: B. Uluoğlu, A. Ensici and A. Vatansever (eds.), *Design and Cinema: Form Follows Film* (Newcastle: Cambridge Scholar Press), 11-20

Pavel, Thomas (1986), *Fictional Worlds* (Cambridge, MA: Harvard University Press)

Pavese, Cesare (1946), 'Del mito, del simbolo e d'altro', in: *Feria d'Agosto* (Turin: Einaudi), 209-218

Perec, George (1999), *Species of Spaces and Other Pieces*, edited by John Sturrock (London: Penguin Books), originally published as *Espèces d'Espaces* (1974)

Pérez-Gómez, Alberto (1983), *Architecture and the Crisis of Modern Science (Cambridge, MA: MIT Press)*

Pérez-Gómez, Alberto (1992), *Polyphilo or the Dark Forest Revisited, an Erotic Epiphany of Architecture* (Cambridge, MA: MIT Press)

Pérez-Gómez, Alberto and Pelletier, Louise (1997), *Architectural Representation and the Perspective Hinge* (Cambridge, MA: MIT Press)

Pérez-Gómez, Alberto (2006), *Built upon Love: Architectural Longing after Ethics and Aesthetics* (Cambridge, MA and London: MIT Press)

Pérez-Gómez, Alberto (2007), 'Byen er ikke et postkort: Problemet med Genius Loci', *Arkitektur N, The Norwegian Review of Architecture* (April)

Pérez-Gómez, Alberto (2016), *Attunement: Architectural Meaning after the Crisis of Modern Science* (Cambridge, MA: MIT Press)

Perrault, *Claude (1683), Ordonnance des cinq espèces de colonnes selon la méthode des anciens* (Paris)

Psarra, Sophia (2003), 'The Book and the Labyrinth Were One and the Same': Narrative and Architecture in Borges' Fictions', *The Journal of Architecture*, vol. 8, no. 3, 369-391

Psarra, Sophia (2009), *Architecture and Narrative: The Formation of Space and Cultural Meaning* (London: Routledge)

Rendell, Jane (2006a), *Art and Architecture: A Place Between* (London: IB Tauris)

Rendell, Jane (2006b), *Site-Writing: The Architecture of Art Criticism* (London: IB Tauris)

Reynolds, Nicole (2010), *Building Romanticism: Literature and Architecture in Nineteenth-Century Britain* (Ann Arbor: University of Michigan Press)

Ricoeur, Paul (1978), *The Rule of Metaphor (London: RKP), originally published as La métaphore vive* (1975)

Ricoeur, Paul (1979), 'The Function of Fiction in Shaping Reality', *Man and World*, vol. 12, no. 2, 123-141

Ricoeur, Paul (1983), *Temps et récit I: L'intrigue et le récit historique* (Paris: Éditions du Seuil)

Ricoeur, Paul (1984), *Temps et récit II: La configuration du temps dans le récit de fiction* (Paris: Seuil)

Ricoeur, Paul (1987-1990), *Time and Narrative,* 3 vols. (Chicago: Chicago University Press), originally published as *Temps et Récit* (1983-1985)

Ricoeur, Paul (1988), *Time and Narrative III* (Chicago: University of Chicago Press), originally published as *Temps et Récit III (1978)*

Ricoeur, Paul (1990), *Time and Narrative I* (Chicago/London: University of Chicago Press)

Ricoeur, Paul (1998), 'Architecture et narrativité', *Urbanisme* (November-December), 44-51

Ricoeur, Paul (2006), 'Archives, Documents, Traces', in: Charles Merewether (ed.), *The Archive* (London: Whitechapel; Cambridge, MA: MIT Press)

Rodrigues dos Santos, Cecilía (1998), 'SESC – Pompéia: An American Citadel', in: *SESC - Pompeia Factory* (Lisbon: Editorial Blau)

Ronen, Ruth (1988), 'Completing the Incompleteness of Fictional Entities', *Poetics Today*, vol. 9, no. 3, 497-514

Rosa, Alberto Asor (2013), *Storia della letteratura italiana* (Turin: Einaudi)

Ryan, Marie-Laure (1991), *Possible Worlds, Artificial Intelligence, and Narrative Theory* (Bloomington: Indiana University Press)

Ryan, Marie-Laure (2001), *Narrative as Virtual Reality: Immersion and Interactivity in Literature and Electronic Media* (Baltimore: Johns Hopkins University Press)

Rykwert, Joseph (1998), 'Translation and/or Representation', *RES: Anthropology and Aesthetics*, no. 34

Rykwert, Joseph (2008), *The Judicious Eye: Architecture Against the Other Arts* (Chicago: University of Chicago Press)

Ryle, Gilbert (1990), *The Concept of Mind (Harmondsworth: Penguin),* first published in 1968

Saint-Maux, Jean-Louis Viel de (1787), *Lettres sur l'architecture des anciens et celles des modernes* (Paris)

Sartre, Jean Paul (1943), *L'Etre et le Néant* (Paris: Gallimard)

Savidis, George (ed.) (1992), *Constantine Cavafy: Collected Poems* (Princeton: Princeton University Press)

Scarry, Elaine (2001), *Dreaming by the Book* (Princeton: Princeton University Press)

Schaeffer, Jean-Marie (1999), *Pourquoi la fiction?* (Paris: Seuil)

Schank, Roger (1995), *Tell Me a Story: Narrative and Intelligence* (Evanston, IL: Northwestern University Press)

Scheerbart, Paul (2001), *The Gray Cloth: Paul Scheerbart's Novel on Glass Architecture*, introduced, translated and with drawings by John A. Stuart (Cambridge, MA: MIT Press)

Schütz, Alfred (1962), 'Common-sense and the Scientific Interpretation of Human Action', in: *Collected Papers*, vol. 1, edited by M. Natanson (The Hague: Martinus Nijhoff)

Scott-Brown, Denise (1968), 'Mapping The City: Symbols and Systems', *Landscape*, vol. 17, no. 3, 22-25

Scott-Brown, Denise (2003), 'Learning from Brinck', in: Chris Wilson and Paul Groth (eds.), *Everyday America: Cultural Landscape Studies after J.B. Jackson* (Berkeley/Los Angeles/London: University of California Press), 49-61

Shaftoe, Henry (2008), *Convivial Urban Spaces: Creating Effective Public Spaces* (London: Earthscan)

Soja, Edward (1999), *Thirdspace, Journeys to Los Angeles and Other Real-and-Imagined Places* (Oxford: Blackwell), first published in 1996

Solà-Morales, Ignasi de (1995), 'Terrain Vague', in: Cynthia C. Davidson (ed.), *Anyplace* (Cambridge, MA: MIT Press), 118-123

Sontag, Susan (1995), 'Preface', in: Roland Barthes, *Writing Degree Zero* (New York: Hill and Young), vii-xxi

Spurr, David (2012), *Architecture and Modern Literature* (Ann Arbor: University of Michigan Press)

Steiner, George (1989), *After Babel* (Chicago: University of Chicago Press)

Stephenson, Susan (2000), 'Narrative, in: Gary Browning, Abigail Halcli and Frank Webster (eds.), *Understanding Contemporary Society: Theories of the Present* (London: Sage), 112-135

Tafuri, Manfredo (2006), *Interpreting the Renaissance: Princes, Cities, Architects*, translated by Daniel Sherer (New Haven and London: Yale University Press)

Tappan, Mark B. (1991), 'Narrative, Authorship, and the Development of Moral Authority', *New Directions for Child and Adolescent Development,* no. 54, 5-25

Taylor, George H. (2006), 'Ricoeur's Philosophy of the Imagination', *Journal of French Philosophy*, vol. 16, nos. 1 and 2, 93-104

Thompson, Evan (2010), *Mind in Life, Biology, Phenomenology and the Science of the Mind* (Cambridge, MA: Harvard University Press)

Todorov, Tzvetan (1984), *Mikhail Bakhtin: The Dialogical Principle* (Manchester: Manchester University Press), originally published as *Mikhaïl Bakhtine, le principe dialogique* (1981)

Treib, Marc (2005), 'The Measure of Wisdom: John Brinckerhoff Jackson', in: Marc Treib (ed.), *Settings and Stray Paths: Writings on Landscapes and Gardens* (London: Routledge), 184-193

Tschumi, Bernard (1976), 'Architecture and Transgression', *Oppositions*, no. 7, 55-63

Tschumi, Bernard (1978), *Architectural Manifestoes* (New York: Artists Space)

Tschumi, Bernard (1979), *Architectural Manifestoes II* (London: Architectural Association Publications)

Tschumi, Bernard (1980), 'Architecture and Limits', *Artforum*, vol. 19, no. 4, 36

Tschumi, Bernard (1981a), 'Architecture and Limits II', *Artforum*, vol. 19, no. 7, 45

Tschumi, Bernard (1981b), 'Architecture and Limits III', *Artforum*, vol. 20, no. 1, 40

Tschumi, Bernard (1981c), *The Manhattan Transcripts* (London: Academy Editions, St Martin's Press)

Tschumi, Bernard (1983a), 'Sequences', *Princeton Journal*, no. 1, 29-36

Tschumi, Bernard (1983b), 'Illustrated Index: Themes from the Manhattan Transcripts', *AA Files*, no. 4, 65-74

Tschumi, Bernard (1990), *Questions of Space: Lectures on Architecture* (London: Architectural Association Publications)

Tschumi, Bernard (1993), 'Modes of Inscription', *ANY*, no. 0, 50-53

Tschumi, Bernard (1996), *Architecture and Disjunction* (Cambridge, MA: MIT Press)

Tschumi, Bernard and Enrique Walker (eds.) (2006), *Tschumi on Architecture: Conversations with Enrique Walker* (New York: Monacelli)

Tuan, Yi-Fu (1977), *Space and Place: The Perspective of Experience* (Minneapolis: University of Minnesota Press)

Varela, Francisco, Evan Thompson and Eleanor Rosch (1991), *The Embodied Mind* (Cambridge, MA: MIT Press)

Varro, Marcus Terentius (1993), *On Agriculture (De re rustica)*, translated by William Davis Hooper, revised by Harrison Boyd Ash (Cambridge, MA and London: Harvard University Press)

Vesely, Dalibor (2004), *Architecture in the Age of Divided Representation* (Cambridge, MA: MIT Press)

Vidler, Anthony (1987), *The Writing on the Walls: Architectural Theory in the Late Enlightenment* (Princeton: Princeton Architectural Press)

Vidler, Anthony (1994), *The Architectural Uncanny: Essays in the Modern Unhomely* (Cambridge, MA: MIT Press)

Vidler, Anthony (2011), *The Scenes of the Street and Other Essays* (New York: The Monacelli Press)

Vitruvius, M.P. (1931), *De Architectura*, bilingual edition by Frank Granger (Cambridge MA: Harvard University Press)

Walton, Kendall (1990), *Mimesis as Make-Believe* (Cambridge, MA: Harvard University Press)

Wilde, Oscar (1905), *Intentions* (New York: Brentano's)

Williams, John (2012), *Stoner* (London: Vintage Books), first published in 1965

Wilson, Chris and Paul Groth (2003), 'The Polyphony of Landscape Study: An Introduction', in: Chris Wilson and Paul Groth (eds.), *Everyday America: Cultural Landscape Studies after J.B. Jackson* (Berkeley/Los Angeles/London: University of California Press), 5-14

Zancan, Marina (1996), *'Le città invisibili di Italo Calvino', in: Letteratura italiana Le Opere, IV/2. Il Novecento: La ricerca letteraria* (Turin: Einaudi)

Zumthor, Peter (1998), 'A Way of Looking at Things', in: Nobuyuki Yoshida (ed.), *A+U Extra Edition: Peter Zumthor* (Tokyo: A+U publishing)

Zumthor, Peter (2006), *Atmospheres: Architectural Environments, Surrounding Objects* (Basel: Birkhauser)

BIOGRAPHIES

Editors

Klaske Havik is associate professor of Architecture, Methods & Analysis at Delft University of Technology. She studied architecture in Delft and Helsinki, and literary writing in Amsterdam. Her book *Urban Literacy. Reading and Writing Architecture* (NAi010, 2014), based on her PhD research, developed a literary approach to architecture and urban regeneration, proposing the three notions description, transcription and prescription. She initiated and organized the 2nd international conference on architecture and fiction: *Writingplace. Literary Methods in Architectural Research and Design* (2013). Havik is editor of the Dutch-Belgian peer-reviewed architecture journal *OASE*, she recently co-edited *OASE*#91 *Building Atmosphere with Juhani Pallasmaa and Peter Zumthor* (2013), *OASE* #89 Medium. The Mid-Size City as a European Urban Condition and Strategy (2012) and *OASE*#85, Productive Uncertainty (2011). With Hans Teerds and Tom Avermaete, she co-edited the anthology *Architectural Positions: Architecture, Modernity and the Public Sphere* (2009). Havik's literary work has been published in Dutch poetry collections and literary magazines.

Jorge Mejía Hernández studied Architecture at the Universidad del Valle (Cali, Colombia) where he graduated in 1996. He holds a Master in History and Theory of Art and Architecture (2002) as well as a Master in Architecture (2008), both from the Universidad Nacional de Colombia. His teaching includes Architectural Theory, History of Architecture and Design Studio at the Universidad Nacional de Colombia since February 2005, where he became Profesor Catedratico Asociado in 2007. He started his PhD research on architectural methodology in 2010 at Delft University of Technology (under professors Barbieri and Avermaete), where he has been tutoring students from the Design Studios and Theory Seminars at a Master's level during the past four years. Aside from receiving an Honorary Mention from the Colombian National Natural Park System – Ministry of the Environment in 1998, and a Colfuturo Scholarship in 2009, he is the author of *Enrique Triana: Obras y Proyectos* (Bogotá: Planeta, 2006) and co-author of *Vivienda Moderna en Colombia* (Bogotá: Universidad Nacional de Colombia, 2004) and *XX Bienal Colombiana de Arquitectura* (Bogotá: Sociedad Colombiana de Arquitectos, 2006). His built projects include the San Jose de Castilla High School (2009) and the Casa de Justicia de Bosa (2004), both in Bogotá.

Susana Oliveira teaches Drawing and Visual Communication at the Faculty of Architecture in Lisbon. She was one of the initiators and organizers, with

Arch. Pedro Gadanho, of the first conference on architecture and fiction: *Once Upon a Place: Haunted Houses and Imaginary Cities* in Lisbon, 2010 (http://www.onceuponaplace.fa.utl.pt/). She edited the *Once Upon a Place* proceedings book (Lisbon: Caleidoscópio, 2013) as well as a book series where literary works are transcribed to architectural drawings and models. The first book, now in print, is a eighteenth-century novel by Bastide, *La Petite Maison*, with drawings by Siza Vieira (Abysmo). She was a Visiting Scholar at GSAPP-Columbia University early 2014 and is currently developing her postdoctoral research on Architectural Imagination in Literature, funded by the Portuguese Science Foundation. She also works as a freelance illustrator, having plublished over 20 children's books.

Mark Proosten graduated as an architect in 2011 from Eindhoven University of Technology. After graduating he started working as an independent architect in the region of Maastricht, the Netherlands. Mark is an assistant for Prof. ir. Wim van den Bergh, within the chair of Wohnbau at the RWTH in Aachen. He is a guest teacher at the interior Master of ArtEZ in Zwolle and lectures at the Maastricht Academy of Architecture. He is one of the contributors of WRITINGPLACE, laboratory for architecture and literature. Mark co-organized the symposium 'Against the Grain, on the narrative characteristic of architecture' and participated in conferences and symposia such as 'The Story of the Netherlands' and 'Writingplace, Literary Methods in Architectural research and Design'. His research, teaching and writing is devoted to narratives in general and the relationship between architecture and literature in particular.

Mike Schäfer is an architect based in 's-Hertogenbosch. He graduated from Delft University of Technology in 2010 with a project that explored the senses through literary design methods, and is one of the initiators of and contributors to Writingplace. With Writingplace, he participated and spoke at several symposia and conferences, and he co-organized the international conference *Writingplace. Literary Methods in Architectural Research and Design.* He was also involved as a research and project assistant at Delft University of Technology for the Venice Biennale 2014. At the moment he is working on his PhD research, which investigates the influence of empathy on the architecture of Bruno Taut, Josef Frank and Lars Spuybroek.

Bart Keunen, PhD, is professor of Comparative Literature at Ghent University, Belgium. He teaches graduate and postgraduate courses in European Literary History, Sociology of Literature and Comparative Literature. He is co-director of the interdisciplinary Ghent Urban Studies Team (GUST; since January 2002). He has published articles on topics concerning urban studies, genre criticism, literary historiography and literary sociology in international journals and books. Book publications include: *Verhaal en Verbeelding. Chronotopen in de westerse verhaalcultuur* (Ghent: Academia Press, 2007), *Tijd voor een verhaal. Mens- en Wereldbeelden in de populaire verhaalcultuur* (Ghent: Academia Press, 2005); (with GUST) *Post-ex-sub-dis: Fragmentations of the City* (Rotterdam: 010 Publishers, 2002); (with Bart Eeckhout) *Literature and Society. The Function of Literary Sociology in Comparative Literature* (Brussels/Bern: Peter Lang/PIE, 2001); *De verbeelding van de grootstad. Stads- en wereldbeelden in het proza van de moderniteit* (Brussels: VUBpress, 2000); (with GUST) *The Urban Condition: Space, Community, and Self in the Contemporary Metropolis* (Rotterdam: 010 Publishers, 1999).

Daria Ricchi is currently working on her PhD in History and Theory of Architecture at Princeton University. Her dissertation 'From *Storia* to History back to stories: Literature and Fiction in Italian Architectural Writing, 1937-1957' challenges the boundaries of historical genres and narratives. She holds a Master's degree in architecture from the University of Florence, and she works as a writer and critic for several architecture magazines (*A10*, *Area*, *Il Giornale dell'Architettura*) and newspapers (*Casamica*, *il Corriere della Sera*). She is the author of *Modern Times* (2005), on Dutch neo-modernism; and *DS+R The Ciliary Function* (2007), on the work of the New York-based office.

Deborah Levy studied architecture at ISACF La Cambre in Brussels. She is a practicing architect and maintains space for research activities in diverse fields. Her interests range from interdisciplinary exchanges between architecture and fiction to Belgian architecture. In 2011, she created *orthodoxe* with five other architects. The collective's aim is to explore architecture as a cultural practice rooted in history, theory and criticism. The members dedicate time collectively or individually to the practice of architecture through design, teaching or cultural mediation.

2 MEMORY
Narrative and Poetics in Architectural History

Alberto Pérez-Gómez was born in Mexico City in 1949, where he studied and practiced architecture. He did postgraduate work at Cornell University, and was awarded an MA and a PhD by the University of Essex (England). He has taught at universities in Mexico, Houston, Syracuse, Toronto and at London's Architectural Association. In 1983 he became the Director of Carleton University's School of Architecture. Since January 1987 he has occupied the Bronfman Chair of Architectural History at McGill University, where he founded the History and Theory Post-Professional (Master's and Doctoral) Programmes.

Pérez-Gómez has lectured extensively around the world and is the author of numerous articles published in major periodicals and books. His book *Architecture and the Crisis of Modern Science* (MIT Press, 1983) won the Hitchcock Award in 1984. Later books include the erotic narrative theory *Polyphilo or The Dark Forest Revisited* (1992), *Architectural Representation and the Perspective Hinge* (co-authored with Louise Pelletier, 1997), which traces the history and theory of modern European architectural representation, and most recently, *Built upon Love: Architectural Longing after Ethics and Aesthetics* (2006). This last book examines points of convergence between ethics and poetics in architecture history and philosophy, drawing important conclusions for contemporary practice. Perez-Gomez is also co-editor (with Stephen Parcell) of a well-known series of books entitled *Chora: Intervals in the Philosophy of Architecture*. The seventh volume in this series was published in February 2106. His most recent work, titled *Attunement, Architectural Meaning after the Crisis of Modern Science* (MIT Press, March 2016), examines connections between phenomenology, recent cognitive science and emerging language, seeking attunement in architecture and the urban environment.

Yvonne Elet is a historian of early modern Italian art and architecture and assistant professor at Vassar College. She previously taught in NYU's Architecture and Urban Studies Program. She holds an MA and PhD from the Institute of Fine Arts, New York University, and a BS in computer science from Yale. Her articles appear in the *Journal of the Society of Architectural Historians* and *I Tatti Studies*, and she has received fellowships from the Metropolitan Museum, the Center for Advanced Study in the Visual Arts, Washington, DC, the Mellon Foundation at the Frick Collection, the Getty Research Institute, the Max-Planck-Institut, Berlin, and the American Council of Learned Societies (ACLS).
The current article presents material she expands in the book *Architectural Invention in Renaissance Rome: Artists, Humanists, and the Planning of Raphael's Villa Madama*, which will be published by Cambridge University Press in 2016. She is

currently working on a monograph about Villa Madama, considered as an integrated ensemble of architecture, decoration, landscape and waterworks; and on a book about stucco in the architecture and decoration of early modern Europe. Other research interests include early modern gardens, and their reception and recreation in the twentieth century.

Nora Wendl is assistant professor of Architecture at the University of New Mexico. Her compositions upon architecture and its histories have resulted in numerous exhibitions, performances and publications. She is co-editor of *Contemporary Art About Architecture* (Ashgate, 2013), with Isabelle Loring Wallace. She has two collections of poetry forthcoming, the concrete poetry collection *Glass Document* (Ugly Duckling Presse, 2016) and *Ave Maria* (A-B Editions, 2016), in collaboration with photographer Rylan Steele – which in 2015 was recognized as a finalist for the Lange-Taylor Prize by the Duke University Center for Documentary Studies.

She is widely published in numerous journals, including *306090*, *Architecture and Culture: Journal of the Architectural Humanities Research Association*, *Flyway*, *Forty-Five*, *Journal of Architectural Education*, *Offramp*, *On Site: Review*, *Studies in the History of Gardens and Designed Landscapes* and *Thresholds*. Over the past decade, she has presented, performed and exhibited her poems and artifacts at numerous national and international venues including, most recently, the Biennale Sessions at La Biennale di Venezia, Association of Collegiate Schools of Architecture, The Universities Art Association of Canada, Seattle Art Museum, Blue Sky Center for Photographic Arts (Portland, Oregon), Seattle Public Library, Center for Architecture (Portland), Westbrook Artist's Site (Madison County, Iowa) and Wordstock.

Nadia Sels is a lecturer of Cultural History at the Faculty of Design Sciences of Antwerp University and lecturer of Art History at PXL-MAD, School of Arts in Hasselt, where she is also a member of the research group FRAME. She obtained her PhD at Ghent University, where as a guest professor she gave courses in Classical Mythology, Reception of Antiquity and Greek and Latin Literature. She publishes on art, architecture, literature and mythology.

3 OPENNESS

Narrative Experiments in Architecture

Ioanna Angelidou is an architect and PhD candidate at Yale University, where she also teaches. She studied at Columbia University in New York and Aristotle University in Greece, and has worked as an architect in Europe and Japan, most notably with Kengo Kuma and Associates in Tokyo. Her publications include contributions to the journals *Log, Arch+, GAM, San Rocco* and *GA Document*, among others, as well as the book *Small Tokyo* (Keio University Press, 2012). She has been awarded a Visual Arts Grant from the Japan Foundation as well as fellowships from the A.W. Mellon Foundation and the Society of Architectural Historians.

Wim van den Bergh is an architect and writer, and full professor of Housing and Design at RWTH Aachen. A graduate of Eindhoven University of Technology, he has taught at the Architectural Association School of Architecture in London, the Cooper Union in New York, and in Denmark, Finland, Germany and Switzerland. He was the head of the Academy of Architecture in Maastricht, and has held professorships at Delft University of Technology and Eindhoven University of Technology. His extensive published work includes studies of Russian avant-garde architecture, the houses of Curzio Malaparte and Constantin Melnikov, the penthouse of Charles De Beistegui, and the work of such architects as F.P.J. Peutz, John Hejduk, Dom Hans van der Laan and Luis Barragán.

Esteban Restrepo Restrepo moves between Literature and Architecture . . . between Paris (FR) and Medellín (CO). Restrepo Restrepo's work is a permanent crossing between these two disciplines and these two hemispheres. After finishing his education on Architecture and Urbanism at the UPB and on Aesthetics at the Universidad Nacional in Medellin, he finished a Master in *Lettres, Arts et Pensée contemporaine* (Paris 7- Diderot), and a Master in *Littérature, Textes, Langues et Théories* (Paris 8- Vincennes /Saint Denis). He is a current PhD student in Comparative Literature at the Université Paris 8 with a co-direction in Architecture. His thesis *The Writer as an Architect* is about the processes of architectural conception within literary texts.

Esteban is cofounder of architecture studio ESCAMPA, he teaches at the École Nationale Supérieure d´Architecture de Paris-La Villette as a member of the interdisciplinary group on *Architecture, Art et Cinéma* and he is an invited professor in the Master's programme *Arquitectura, Crítica y Proyecto* at the UPB. He has published two books: *(anti) Chambres. Les architectures fragiles dans l´œuvre de Samuel Beckett* (Les Presses du réel, 2014) and *Cosmética. Por un espesor de la banalidad* (Ediciones UPB, 2008) and he is currently working on his first novel.

4 COMPLEXITY
Writing as a Mode of Architectural Investigation

Katja Grillner is Dean of Faculty at KTH Royal Institute of Technology and professor of Critical Studies in Architecture. Grillner's research on architecture and landscape combines theoretical, historical and literary strategies for spatial exploration. Among her book publications are her PhD dissertation *Ramble, Linger and Gaze – Philosophical Dialogues in the Landscape Garden* (Stockholm: KTH, 2000), as main-editor *01-AKAD – Experimental Research in Architecture and Design* (Stockholm: AxlBooks, 2005), and, as co-editor, *Architecture and Authorship* (London: Black Dog, 2007). Grillner is the director of Architecture in Effect, a national initiative for a strong research environment funded by Formas 2011-2016, and co-founded the feminist architecture teaching and research group FATALE in 2007.

Thomas-Bernard Kenniff is a professor of Environmental Design at the Université du Québec à Montréal (UQAM) School of Design. He holds a PhD in Architectural History and Theory from the UCL Bartlett School of Architecture and a professional Master of Architecture from the University of Waterloo. His work addresses the relationship between critical and interdisciplinary design practices, dialogue and public space.

Carole Lévesque holds a technical degree in Architecture, an undergraduate degree in *Design de l'Environnement*, a Masters of Architecture from the University of British-Columbia as well as a PhD in the History and Theory of Architecture from the University of Montreal. Concerned with temporary architecture as a means to articulate exploratory and alternative discourses on the city and as a tool with which to engage architectural education, she published *A propos de l'inutile en Architecture*. Her current work revolves around the architectural representation of derelict and vague spaces within the city.

She has spoken at several international events, exhibited her drawings and photography at the *Maison de l'architecture du Québec* and has received the jury prize in the national competition *Paysages Éphémères* in Montreal, the Young Scholar grant from the Canadian Center for Architecture, among others. She taught at the University of Montreal and at the American University of Beirut. She is now professor at the School of Design at UQAM.

5 INCLUSIVITY
Towards an 'Architextural' Praxis

Wim Cuyvers is a Belgian architect living in the French Jura. He lectured at the Academy for Architecture of Tilburg, Design Academy Eindhoven, Sint-Lucas Ghent, Ecole d'Architecture Paris Malaquais, Vakgroep Architectuur en Stedenbouw, Ghent and Labo, Sociale en Culturele Pedagogiek Leuven and was affiliated to the Jan van Eyck Academy of Maastricht as advising researcher. More often than not, controversy encircles his work, which he nevertheless does not seek, yet when asking fundamental questions, these easily show themselves as problematic questions. He does not make a distinction between his architecture, texts or art. As an architect Wim Cuyvers is looking for existential spaces – space that questions, that nurtures a degree of confrontation or concentration, that can only be negatively defined: not privatized, not economical, not claimed and not controlled.

Sophia Banou studied architecture at the National Technical University of Athens (Diploma in Architectural Engineering, 2008), and the University of Edinburgh (MSc in Advanced Architectural Design, 2009). She currently teaches Architectural Design and Theory at the University of Edinburgh and Newcastle University (UK), while she is an editor for the architectural design research journal *Drawing On*. Sophia recently completed a PhD in Architecture by Design at the University of Edinburgh. Her doctoral research, funded by the Bodossaki Foundation (Greece), focused on the concept of space as a temporal and ephemeral condition and the understanding of drawing as situated experience. In this context Sophia is interested in issues of architectural convention and the use of installation as an expanded form of drawing 'in space'.

Bruno Notteboom is an engineer-architect, urban planner and holds a PhD in Urbanism and Spatial Planning. Since 2015 he is an associate professor at the Faculty of Design Sciences at the University of Antwerp. His research focuses on the relationship between landscape and urban planning from the perspective of history, policy and design. He is an editor of *OASE Journal for Architecture* and the *Journal of Landscape Architecture*.

CREDITS

Editors: Klaske Havik, Jorge Mejía Hernández, Susana Oliveira, Mark Proosten and Mike Schäfer
Texts: Bart Keunen, Daria Ricchi, Deborah Levy, Alberto Pérez-Gómez, Yvonne Elet, Nora Wendl, Nadia Sels, Wim van den Bergh, Ioanna Angelidou, Esteban Restrepo Restrepo, Katja Grillner, Thomas-Bernard Kenniff, Carole Lévesque, Bruno Notteboom, Sophia Banou and Wim Cuyvers
Copy editing: D'Laine Camp
Design: Studio Sanne Dijkstra with Femmy Kloos
Lithography and Printing: Epos Press
Publisher: Marcel Witvoet, nai010 publishers

This publication was made possible by financial support from Creative Industries Fund NL, ArtEZ University of the Arts Arnhem, Aachen, Gent, the Faculty of Architecture - UTLisboa and Delft University of Technology, Chair of Methods and Analysis

254

nai010 publishers is an internationally orientated publisher specialized in developing, producing and distributing books in the fields of architecture, urbanism, art and design. www.nai010.com

nai010 books are available internationally at selected bookstores and from the following distribution partners:

North, Central and South America - Artbook | D.A.P., New York, USA, dap@dapinc.com

Rest of the world – Idea Books, Amsterdam, the Netherlands, idea@ideabooks.nl

For general questions, please contact nai010 publishers directly at sales@nai010.com or visit our website www.nai010.com for further information.

Printed and bound in the Netherlands

ISBN 978-94-6208-281-6 (paperback)

Writingplace: Investigations in Architecture and Literature is also available as e-book:
ISBN 978-94-6208-282-3 (e-book)

Chair of Methods and Analysis

TU Delft

creative industries fund NL

WOHNBAU
Lehrstuhl und Institut für Wohnbau
Univ.-Prof. ir. Wim van den Bergh

FCT
Fundação para a Ciência e a Tecnologia
MINISTÉRIO DA CIÊNCIA, TECNOLOGIA E ENSINO SUPERIOR

CiAUD
FACULDADE DE ARQUITETURA
UNIVERSIDADE DE LISBOA

ArtEZ

UNIVERSITEIT GENT